Nathaniel William Wraxall

The History of France Under the Kings of the Race of Valois

From the accession of Charles the 5th, in 1364, to the death of Charles the 9th, in 1574. Vol. II

Nathaniel William Wraxall

The History of France Under the Kings of the Race of Valois
From the accession of Charles the 5th, in 1364, to the death of Charles the 9th, in 1574. Vol. II

ISBN/EAN: 9783744743129

Printed in Europe, USA, Canada, Australia, Japan

Cover: Foto ©ninafisch / pixelio.de

More available books at **www.hansebooks.com**

THE HISTORY OF FRANCE,

UNDER THE KINGS OF

THE RACE OF VALOIS,

FROM
THE ACCESSION OF CHARLES THE FIFTH,
IN 1364,
TO THE DEATH OF CHARLES THE NINTH,
IN 1574.

THE SECOND EDITION,
WITH VERY CONSIDERABLE AUGMENTATIONS.

BY
NATH^L WILLIAM WRAXALL, Esq.

IN TWO VOLUMES.

VOL. II.

LONDON:
PRINTED FOR C. DILLY, IN THE POULTRY.
M.DCC.LXXXV.

OF THE

SECOND VOLUME.

CHAPTER THE EIGHTH.

Character of Henry the second.—Changes in the state.—Diana de Poitiers—her character.—Romantic attachment of the king to her.—Disgrace of the duchess d'Estampes.—Duel of Jarnac and la Chataigneraie.—Insurrections in Guyenne.—Persecution of the Protestants.—Death of Margaret of Valois, queen of Navarre—her character. —Renewal of war between Henry and the Emperor.—Catherine of Medecis left regent.—Siege of Metz.—Continuation of the war.—Abdication of the Emperor.—Power of Diana de Poitiers,

CONTENTS.

duchess of Valentinois.—Expedition under the duke of Guise against Naples.—Battle of St. Quentin—Capture of Calais.—Marriage of Francis the Dauphin to Mary queen of Scotland.—Conclusion of the peace of Cateau-en-Cambresis.—Carousals of the court.—The king's death.—Enumeration of the circumstances which attended it.—Character of Henry the second.—His Mistresses.—Reflections. Page 1

CHAPTER THE NINTH.

State of the kingdom at the death of Henry the second.—Character of the duke of Guise—of the cardinal of Lorrain—of the king of Navarre.—of the prince of Condé.—Catherine of Medecis.—Her character, person, and political conduct.—Disgrace of the duchess of Valentinois.—Accession of Francis the second.—Power of the Guises.—The king's weak state of health.—Assassination of Minard.—Conspiracy of Amboise, and its defeat.—Executions.—Suspicions against the prince of Condé.—Convocation of Fontainbleau.—Arrival of the king of Navarre and the prince of Condé at court.—They are arrested.—Trial of the latter prince.—Francis's illness.—Condemnation of the prince of Condé.—Intrigues and cabals of Catherine of Medecis.—Death of Francis the second.—Circumstances of it.—His Character.—Funeral.—Arrival of Montmorenci.—Release of Condé. 54

CHAPTER

CONTENTS.

CHAPTER THE TENTH.

Reflections on the situation of affairs at the accession of Charles the ninth.—Catherine of Medecis secures to herself the regency.—Formation of the " triumvirate."— Pernicious policy of the regent.—Assembly of the states.—Massacre of Vassy.—Duplicity of Catherine.—The young king carried to Paris by Anthony king of Navarre.—Commencement of the civil wars.—Prince of Condé is declared chief of the Hugonots.—Unsuccessful attempts to effect an accommodation.—Siege of Rouen.—Death of the king of Navarre.—Battle of Dreux.—Consequences of that action.—Siege of Orleans.—Assassination of the duke of Guise.—Account of the circumstances attending it.—His funeral, and character.—Conclusion of Peace.—Death of La Cipierre.—Character of the Marechal de Retz.—The prince of Conde's amours, and second marriage.—Charles the ninth attains to majority.—Administration of Catherine.—Interview of Bayonne.—Commencement of the second civil war.—Ineffectual enterprize of Meaux.—Battle of St. Denis.—Death of the Constable de Montmorenci.—Circumstances of that event.—Character of the young king.— Second pacification.

CONTENTS.

CHAPTER THE ELEVENTH.

Attempt to seize on the prince of Condé.—Third civil war.—Battle of Jarnac.—Death of Condé.—Character of the admiral Coligni, and of Jane, queen of Navarre.—Siege of Poitiers.—Battle of Moncontour.—Arrival of the king in the camp before St. John d'Angeli.—March of Coligni.—Conclusion of peace.—Duplicity of the court.—Marriage of the king to the archduchess Elizabeth.—Her character.—Festivities at court.—Policy of Catherine of Medecis.—Reflections.—Dissimulation of Charles and of the queen-mother.—Arrival of Coligni at court.—Commencement of disunion between the king and Henry duke of Anjou.—Contrast of their characters.—Betrothal of Henry, prince of Navarre to Margaret of Valois.—Death of Jane, queen of Navarre.—Circumstances attending it.—Determination of Coligni to remain at Paris.—Margaret of Valois.—Her nuptials, and character.—Attempt to assassinate Coligni.—Treachery of Charles.—Resolution taken to exterminate the Hugonots.—Terrors and irresolution of the king previous to the massacre.—Death of Coligni.—Deaths of the Hugonot chiefs.—Detail of the principal circumstances attending the massacre of Paris.—Conduct of Charles, consequent to that event.—Fourth civil war.—Siege of Rochelle.—Character of Francis duke of Alençon.

Alençon.—*Remorse of the king.—Election of the duke of Anjou to the crown of Poland.—Carousals at court.—Charles's impatience for his brother's departure.—Mary of Cleves.—Her character and amour with the duke of Anjou.—Quarrels between the king and his mother.—Henry duke of Anjou begins his journey.—Illness of Charles.—Suspicions on that event.—Arrival of the king of Poland at Cracow.—His subsequent conduct.—New commotions in France.—Change in the king.—Conspiracy of the duke of Alençon, discovered.—Progress of Charles's indisposition.—Intrigues of the queen-mother to secure the regency.—Execution of La Mole and of Coconas.—Circumstances of the king's last illness.—Death of Charles the ninth.—Enquiry into the causes of it.—His character, issue, and funeral.—Conclusion.*   173

HISTORY

HISTORY
OF
FRANCE,
UNDER THE KINGS OF
THE RACE OF VALOIS.

CHAPTER THE EIGHTH.

Character of Henry the second.—Changes in the state.—Diana de Poitiers—her character.—Romantic attachment of the king to her.—Disgrace of the duchess d'Estampes.—Duel of Jarnac and la Chataigneraie.—Insurrections in Guyenne.—Persecution of the Protestants.—Death of Margaret of Valois, queen of Navarre—her character.—Renewal of war between Henry and the Emperor.—Catherine of Medecis left regent.—Siege of Metz.—Continuation of the war.—Abdication of the Emperor.—Power of Diana de Poitiers, duchefs of Valentinois.—Expedition under the duke of Guife againft Naples.—Battle of St. Quentin —Capture of Calais.—Marriage of Francis the Dauphin to Mary queen of Scotland.—Conclufion of the peace of Cateau-en-Cambrefis.—Caroufals of the court.—The king's death.—Enumeration of the circumftances which attended it.—Character of Henry the fecond.—His Miftreffes.— Reflections.

1547.
31ft
March.

THOUGH the death of fo able and experienced a prince as Francis the firft, at a period of life when his character promifed happinefs and tranquillity to his people, was an event deeply to be lamented by thofe to whom the interefts of the ftate were dear; yet as his fucceffor had attained to years of manhood, and did not appear to be deficient in the qualities requifite for government, his lofs might be deemed not irreparable.

Henry the fecond, who afcended the throne, was the handfomeft prince of his age, and one of the moft accomplifhed cavaliers in his dominions. He excelled in all the martial exercifes where vigour and addrefs are neceffary; and bore away the prize in tournaments with diftinguifhed grace. His heart was beneficent and humane; his temper courteous, open, and liberal; his intentions ever honourable, and directed to the public good: but he neither poffeffed the capacity or difcernment which Francis difcovered;
and,

and, naturally tractable, and yielding to others, he was formed to be under the guidance of favourites.

His father's dying exhortations made no impression on his heart, nor produced any effect upon his conduct; and scarce were the late king's funeral rites performed, when Henry violated them in every point. Montmorenci, who had been during several years in disgrace, was recalled to court, and loaded with honours: the admiral d'Annebaut was dismissed, and the Cardinal de Tournon only retained a shadow of authority. In their place, Francis duke of Guise, so celebrated in the subsequent reigns, and the Marechal de St. André, were substituted. That pernicious profusion, which had characterised the commencement of the late king's reign, was carried to a more unjustifiable length; and the treasures amassed during his concluding years, were dissipated with a wanton extravagance.

Diana de Poitiers, duchess de Valentinois, who may be said to have almost divided the crown with her lover, and who carried her influence, personal and political, to a height which the duchess d'Estampes never could attain under his predecessor, was the directing principle of Henry's councils, the object of his tenderest attachment, and unlimited homage. This extraordinary woman, unparalleled in the

1547. annals of history, retained her beauty undiminished even in the autumn of life, and preserved her powers of captivating, in defiance of time and natural decay. She was already forty-eight, while Henry had scarce attained his twenty-ninth year. Her father, John de Poitiers, Seigneur de St. Vallier, had been condemned to die, in 1523, as an accomplice in the revolt of the Constable, Charles of Bourbon; and though he escaped with his life, yet he was degraded from the rank of nobility, and all his estates were confiscated *. She was married, in the last year of Louis the twelfth's reign, to Louis de Brezé, Count de Maulevrier, and grand Senechal of Normandy, by whom she had two daughters then alive. It is not certain when her

* Diana de Poitiers was born on the 5th of September 1499. Mezerai, the president Henault, and many other writers have asserted, that she preserved her father's life, by the sacrifice of her chastity to Francis the first, from whose embraces she passed into those of his son; but this story is very doubtful, and most probably false. She had been married near ten years to Louis, Count de Maulevrier, at that time, and consequently had not, as those authors seem to imagine, her *virgin honour* to bestow. Besides, though her father's life was not taken away, his punishment was changed for another rather worse than death; that of being immured perpetually between four walls, in which there should be only one little window, through which his provisions might be given him. St. Vallier died of a fever, occasioned by his terror, in a very short time afterwards.

connections

connections with the Dauphin Henry first commenced; but it appears, that before he had completed his eighteenth year, her afcendancy over him was well eftablished. All the cotemporary authors agree, that her charms were of the moft captivating kind, and worthy of a monarch's love: to thefe perfonal endowments, fhe united a cultivated and juft underftanding, wit, and an animated converfation. Warmly devoted to her friends and partizans, fhe was likewife a dangerous and implacable enemy: of high and unfubmitting fpirit, fhe transfufed thofe fentiments into the royal bofom, and impelled him to actions of vigour and firmnefs. Fond of power, fhe was yet more fo of flattery and fubmiffion. The nobles crouded to exprefs their dutiful attentions to this idol; and even the Conftable Montmorenci, rude, haughty, and more accuftomed to infult than to flatter, bent beneath her, and condefcended to ingratiate himfelf by the moft fervile adulation.

The tyes which chiefly bound Henry to Diana de Poitiers, were probably firft thofe of pleafure, and afterwards of tafte and habit. In vain did the duchefs d'Eftampes exert every art of female rivality and hatred, to difunite them; in vain did fhe publifh, that Diana was married in the fame year, which gave herfelf birth.—Thefe efforts only encreafed the paffion which they were defigned to extinguifh. The

1547. king carried it to an incredible heighth, and gave her every public, as well as private proof of her afcendancy over him. The furniture of his palaces, his armour, the public edifices of the kingdom, were all diftinguifhed with her device and emblems; a " moon, bow, and ar-
" rows." Every favour or preferment was obtained thro' her intereft; and Briffac, the moft amiable and gallant nobleman of the court, who was fuppofed to be peculiarly acceptable to her, was created grand mafter of the artillery, at her particular requeft *. The Count de Boffu, who had been intimately connected with the late king's miftrefs, and who was accufed of treafonable practices with the emperor, could only fhelter him-

felf

---

* Charles de Coffé, Marechal de Briffac, was brought up with Francis Dauphin of France, and eldeft fon to Francis the firft, whofe premature and lamented death in 1536, deeply affected Briffac, and induced him to dedicate himfelf entirely to the profeffion of arms. He eminently diftinguifhed his courage at the fiege of Perpignan in 1541, where he was wounded, after having refcued, at the imminent hazard of his life, the artillery, which had fallen into the hands of the Spaniards. He was flender, and of a very delicate figure; but his face was fo uncommonly handfome, that the ladies of the court named him always " Le beau Briffac." In all the campaigns towards the conclufion of Francis the firft's reign, but peculiarly at the fiege of Landrecy in 1543, he gained immortal reputation.—Under Henry the fecond he commanded the armies of France in Piedmont, where he fuccefsfully oppofed the

greateft

self from punishment by a resignation of his palace at Marchez to the Cardinal of Lorrain. The duchess d'Estampes, unsupported by the croud of flatterers who had attended on her in Francis's reign, was compelled to quit the court; but Diana, whether from motives of prudence or magnanimity, did not attempt to deprive her of the possessions which she had acquired from that monarch's generosity. Disgraced, and forsaken, she retired to one of her country houses, where she lived many years in perfect obscurity*.

Henry, on his return from a visit which he had made soon after his accession, to the fron-

---

greatest imperial generals, Ferdinand de Gonzague, and the duke of Alva.—After the death of Henry in 1559, he returned into his own country, and was made governor of Picardy: he expired of the gout, at Paris, on the 31st December 1563, being only fifty-seven years of age.—It cannot be doubted, that he was beloved by the duchess de Valentinois; and jealousy was believed to have been the motive which induced Henry the second to confer on him the command in Italy, as it necessarily compelled Brissac to quit his mistress.

* It is somewhat extraordinary, that the year of the duchess d'Estampes's death is not mentioned by any cotemporary author. All we know is, that she was alive in 1575, as she did homage at that time for one of her estates. She became a protectress of the Lutherans or Hugonots, for whom she had always entertain'd a concealed affection; and this is the only circumstance with which we are acquainted relative to her retreat.

1547. tier of Picardy, not only permitted, but was publicly prefent with all his court, at the celebrated duel between Guy de Chabot-Jarnac, and François de Vivonne-La Chataigneraie, which was fought in all the forms of chivalry, at St. Germain-en-Laye. The quarrel had originated from an accufation of La Chataigneraie refpecting the duchefs d'Eftampes's infidelity to the late king; and was increafed by a fecond imputation thrown on Jarnac, more difhonourable; that of his having been criminally intimate with his father's fecond wife. La Chataigneraie was one of the moft accomplifhed cavaliers in France, and the moft perfonally acceptable to the king: fkilled in the practice of arms, vain of his acknowledged addrefs, and relying on the royal favour, he defpifed his antagonift; while Jarnac, more cautious, and neither fupported by fuperior force, or any hope of Henry's partial protection, endeavoured to fupply thefe defects by artifice. A fever had diminifhed even his ufual ftrength and activity; but the prefumptuous negligence of La Chataigneraie decided the duel in his honour. By a thruft totally unexpected, Jarnac wounded him in the ham, and threw him to the ground, Henry inftantly flung down his baton, to put an end to the engagement, and Jarnac, as the law of arms required, defifted; but his competitor, ftung with difappointment, covered with fhame, and incapable of furviving thefe accumulated mortifications,

mortifications, would not accept of a life which he deemed ignominious; and having torn off the bandages applied to his wounds, soon after expired. The king was so deeply affected with this combat, and its event, so opposite to his wishes and expectations, that he made a solemn vow, never during his reign to permit of a second, on any pretext whatsoever.

1547.

The causes of future wars, which were not extinguished by the death of Francis the first, began to display themselves between the emperor and Henry; though as yet many circumstances conduced to retard any open rupture. This latter prince made a progress through part of his dominions, accompanied with splendid entries into the principal cities; and on his return he celebrated the nuptials of Anthony duke of Vendome with Jane d'Albret, heiress of the kingdom of Navarre, at the city of Moulins *.

1548 and 1549.

18th October.

A dan-

---

* The young princess had been espoused several years before to the duke of Cleves; and Francis the first was present at that ceremony, which was performed with great splendor at Chatelleraud in Poictou; but the marriage was not consummated, on account of her extreme youth, she being at that time little more than twelve years old. The day was rendered remarkable by the dismission and disgrace of the Constable Montmorenci; which was preceded by a very singular circumstance, supposed to foretel his approaching fall. The young bride, according to the manners of the age, was dressed in robes so weighty, and loaded with so many pearls and jewels, that not being able to move,

Francis

1549. A dangerous infurrection, which broke out at this time in Guienne, rendering it neceffary to fend into that province fome general of rank and experience, the duke of Guife and the Conftable were both charged with the commiffion. The former, courteous, humane, and

Francis commanded the Conftable to take her in his arms, and carry her to the church. Though this cuftom was ufual at the nuptials of great perfons, yet Montmorenci was deeply hurt by being felected for fuch an office; and regarding it as an inconteftible proof of his ruin, hefitated not to declare to his friends, that his favour was at an end. The event juftified his fufpicion; for immediately after the banquet, the king difmiffed him from his fervice, and he quitted the court directly. Margaret of Valois, queen of Navarre, and mother to Jane d'Albret, was fuppofed, by her intereft with her brother, to have accelerated his difgrace. The Conftable had not fcrupled to accufe her to Francis, of being attached to, and of protecting the Hugonots. By this imputation againft his beloved fifter, he offended the king, and raifed up an implacable and powerful enemy in Margaret herfelf.

The marriage of Jane with the duke of Cleves, which had been chiefly made in compliance with the wifhes of Francis the firft, was afterwards diffolved from motives of policy, the duke having fubmitted to, and reconciled himfelf with the emperor. But Brantome fays, that Anthony duke of Vendome had great fcruples of delicacy relative to efpoufing the princefs; and that he had recourfe to the Senechale of Poictou, who was a lady of honour to the young queen of Navarre at the time of her firft nuptials, to clear up his fufpicions. She did fo; and gave him the moft folemn and fatisfactory proofs, that Jane's firft marriage had been merely a ceremony, and was never confummated.

warmly

HENRY THE SECOND.

warmly defirous to conciliate the popular favour, entered Saintonge and Angoumois, difpenfing pardon, or only punifhing with lenity and gentlenefs; but Montmorenci, inexorable, and with a feverity of temper which approached to cruelty, marked his courfe along the river Garonne with blood; and, deaf to the fupplications of the inhabitants, who had recourfe to fubmiffions and entreaties, put to death above a hundred of the principal citizens of Bourdeaux, and deprived the city of all its municipal rights and privileges. A conduct fo oppofite, produced among the people fentiments equally diffimilar with refpect to the two commanders; and from this æra the family of Guife began to date that popularity, which in the fequel they carried to fo prodigious and dangerous a length againft the crown and monarchy itfelf.

1549.

October.

The court meanwhile was wholly engaged in caroufals and feftivities. A gallant and warlike prince of the character of Henry the fecond, who delighted in exercifes of prowefs and dexterity, was naturally followed in his paffion for thofe diverfions, by his nobility. Diana de Poitiers, created duchefs of Valentinois, prefided at thefe entertainments, given in her honour; and the queen, Catherine of Medecis, though young, beautiful, and of uncommon capacity, though endowed with diffimulation and manners the moft temporifing, yet acted only an inferior and

fubfervient

1549.
10th June.

subservient part. She had however the honour of being solemnly crowned at St. Denis, and of making afterwards a triumphal entry with her husband into the capital; but these were only pageantries of state, and Henry, who never admitted her to a real participation of his authority, seems to have been aware, that her character and genius were more calculated to embroil, than to assist the affairs of government.

By a transition wonderful and inexplicable, if any thing in human nature can be so esteemed, these tournaments and entertainments were immediately succeeded by exhibitions of a very different nature, which mistaken piety and the intemperate zeal of the age substituted by turns in the place of gallantry and pleasure. A number of proselytes to the doctrines of Luther and Calvin were publickly and solemnly burnt, as an example to their companions; while the king and his whole court were present at these inhuman sacrifices, which were performed with a refinement of mercilefs cruelty, and varied in different modes of punishment.

21st December.

Margaret of Valois, queen of Navarre, died about this time, at the castle of Odos in the province of Bigorre. She had never recovered the afflicting news of her beloved brother's death. If Francis the first was the greatest monarch of his age, Margaret was indisputably the most accomplished princess. Devoted to the

love

love of letters, she encouraged and patronized men of genius and learning, from whom she received the flattering epithets of, "the Tenth Muse," and "the Fourth Grace." Herself an author, she has left us inconteſtible proofs of her elegant genius, her wit, and graceful style, which though negligent, is full of beauty. Suspected of a partiality towards Hugonotism, she was likewise suspected of gallantry; and perhaps might have been equally sensible in turn to those grand movements of elevated minds, devotion and love. Her Tales, which are scarce inferior to those of Boccacio, seem to confirm this sentiment; and though they ever inculcate and commend the virtues of chastity and female fidelity, yet contain in certain parts an animation and warmth of colouring, that give room to suppose the writer of them was fully sensible to the delights of the passion which she censured and condemned *.

Boulogne,

---

* Margaret was born on the 11th of April 1492. Bonnivet, presuming on his personal accomplishments, concealed himself under her bed, and attempted to violate her honour; but she repulsed him, tore off the skin from his face with her nails, and afterwards complained to the king her brother of this daring attempt, at which he only laughed. She has related this adventure, though somewhat enigmatically, among her Tales.—Though Margaret was sometimes so devout as to compose hymns, yet she was certainly an "Esprit fort," and had even great doubts concerning the

1550.
March. Boulogne, after a long siege, was at length surrendered to France, from the weakness and dissentions incident to a minority; Edward the sixth, king of England, being very young, and the

the immortality of the soul. Brantome has preserved a very curious story relative to the death of one of her maids of honour, at which she was present. The queen was much attached to her, and could not be induced by any entreaties to quit her bed-side, when expiring: on the contrary, she continued to fix her eyes on the dying person with uncommon eagerness and perseverance, till she had breathed her last. The ladies of her court expressed to her majesty their astonishment and surprise at this conduct; and requested to know, what satisfaction she could derive from so close an inspection of the agonies of death? Her answer marked a most daring and inquisitive mind. She said, "that having often heard the most learned doctors and "ecclesiastics assert, that on the extinction of the body, the "immortal part was unloosed and set at liberty, she could "not restrain her anxious curiosity to observe if any indi- "cations of such a separation were discernible: that none "such she had been able in any degree to discover; and "that, if she was not happily very firm in her faith and "adherence to the catholic religion, she should not know "what to think of this departure of the soul."

Francis the first took a pleasure in publicly declaring, that to her tenderness, care, and attentions, he was indebted for his life, during the severe illness which he suffered in his confinement at Madrid. She had the boldness and spirit to reproach the emperor and his council, in the most animated terms, for their unmanly and cruel treatment of the king her brother. It is said that Charles the fifth was so much irritated by these reprehensions, which he was conscious he merited, that he had intended to seize on her person,

HENRY THE SECOND.

the authority of his uncle the lord protector 1550. ill established.—The house of Guise, firmly united with Diana duchess of Valentinois, continued to aggrandize itself, and acquired every year some new establishment. The genius and great qualities of the duke and the cardinal of Lorrain, different from each other, but equally pre-eminent and distinguished, eclipsed all other merit: even the Constable Montmorenci, though superior to any rival in the king's favour, and possessing an unlimited influence over him, yet could not see unmoved the rapid progress which the Guises made in universal admiration; and

son, and detain her prisoner, if she had outstayed the time granted her to remain in the Spanish dominions. Margaret received intimation of this design; and, without being in the least afraid, she mounted on horseback, crossed all the provinces between Madrid and Bayonne, and arrived on the frontier of France a very few hours before the expiration of her safe conduct.

She was seized, says Brantome, with a catarrh of which she died, while she was intently gazing on a comet, supposed to predict the death of pope Paul the third: her illness lasted eight days. She seems to have had the same constitutional dread and terror of death, which characterised her mother Louisa. The ladies who attended about her bed announcing to her when in extremity, that she must prepare herself for her end, and fix her thoughts on the joys of a celestial state; "Tout cela est vrai," replied the expiring queen; "mais nous demeurons si long temps en terre " avant que venir la."—She was above two years older than Francis the first; and fifty-eight years of age at the time of her decease.

beheld

KINGS OF FRANCE.

1550. beheld with jealousy these new competitors for fame and glory.

1551. Italy, destined during more than half a century to be the principal scene of war, was again menaced with indications of approaching hostilities. The grandsons of the late pontiff Paul the third, against whom Julius the third, newly elected pope had taken up arms, with intent to dispossess them of the duchy of Parma, claimed the protection of Henry, who gladly afforded it to them *. He was pleased to find an occasion again to interfere in the affairs beyond the

---

* Alexander Farnese, who ascended the pontifical throne under the name of Paul the third, had been raised to the purple by Alexander the sixth, in 1493, and was about sixty-seven years of age at the time of his election, after the death of pope Clement the seventh. He was a prince of some ability, and taste in the arts; but his reign was sullied by the excessive fondness which he shewed for his son, Peter Louis Farnese, to whom he sacrificed the dearest interests and possessions of the holy see. To this son, whom he had by a lady to whom he was married before he embraced the ecclesiastical profession, he gave the duchy of Parma in sovereignty; but the ingratitude of his grandson Octavio Farnese, who had menaced the pope to join the Imperial general Ferdinand de Gonzague against his own grandfather, affected him so deeply, as to occasion his death. On receiving this news, he fainted, and remained in a sort of lethargy for near four hours, without betraying any sign of life; at the end of which time he was seized with a violent fever, which terminated his existence on the tenth of November, 1549, at his palace on the Quirinal Hill, in Rome, after a pontificate of fifteen years.

Alps, and of confequence to renew his attempts on the Milanese, so long and so unfortunately contended for by the French. Briffac was sent into Piedmont, and directed to assist the duke of Parma, though without any open declaration of war against the emperor. Julius, after an ineffectual attempt to induce the king to renounce his allies, made an equally unsuccessful effort upon the capital of the duke of Parma, of which his general was obliged to raise the siege.

Charles the fifth, though he had scarce passed his fiftieth year, was already oppressed with all the maladies and infirmities of a premature old age. Solyman, sultan of the Turks, his great and constant antagonist, threatened his Hungarian dominions; while the emperor himself, on the other hand, had alarmed all the princes of the empire, by the arbitrary deposition of John Frederic, elector of Saxony, by his imprisonment of the Landgrave of Hesse, and his open infringement of the Germanic rights and liberties. Even his brother Ferdinand, king of the Romans, was justly irritated by Charles's endeavours to compel him to resign the succession of the Imperial crown in favour of Philip prince of Spain, his only son.—These united considerations induced Henry no longer to dissemble his intentions, or to delay a rupture with the emperor. Briffac began the campaign in Piedmont, while Anthony duke of Vendome

1551. Vendome entered the provinces of Artois and Hainault. The king strengthened himself still further by a secret alliance with Maurice, the new duke of Saxony, head of the protestant league; whom he promised to assist with troops and money against Charles, who evidently aimed at despotism.

October.

1552. The effects of this confederacy were soon visible, in the extraordinary and rapid march of Maurice, who had nearly taken the emperor prisoner in the city of Inspruck, while he amused him with proposals of peace. Charles, terrified, amazed, and on the brink of a shameful captivity, fled in a litter by torch-light over the mountains of the Alps, with a few attendants; and scarce imagined himself in security at Villach in Carinthia, upon the frontier of the Venetian territories. Henry, improving this favourable juncture, marched in person into Lorrain; and having first possessed himself of the person of the young duke Charles, nephew to the emperor, seized on the cities of Metz, Toul, and Verdun, which, being dependants of the empire, did not expect, and were unprepared for such an attack. These important acquisitions have since remained to France, without any interruption.

March. Previous to his departure, Henry vested the regency in the queen, though he at the same time associated with her Bertrandi, who was keeper of
the

the seals, and implicitly devoted to the duchess de Valentinois. Catherine of Medicis, during the short time in which she was entrusted with the administration, was not guilty of any public act injurious to her own character, or to the interests of state. That complicated and intriguing genius, that perplexed and pernicious policy, those flattering but ruinous artifices, which afterwards so eminently marked her government under the reigns of her three successive children, were as yet unexerted, or unobserved. Accommodating in her manners, and mistress of all her passions, she bent beneath the duchess de Valentinois's superior power; and, so far from making any efforts to diminish or oppose it, Catherine professed for her the most strict and disinterested friendship.

Maurice's success and masterly conduct soon reduced the emperor to a necessity of complying with his offers of peace; and a treaty was signed between them, at Passau, which for ever secured the independence of the German princes, ecclesiastical and civil. Charles hastened, and gladly accepted these overtures, from the desire of being in a condition to revenge himself on the king of France. The insult and indignity which had been offered to him, as supreme head of the empire, in the height of his prosperity, by the capture of three great cities under the Imperial protection, stung him sharply; and full of resentment, he levied

1552.	levied a prodigious army, with the refolution of immediately laying fiege to the city of Metz.
18th October. The feafon was already far advanced when he began his attack; but as the place was of a large extent, and only furrounded with weak and ruinous fortifications, he would probably have rendered himfelf mafter of it, if the duke of Guife had not fruftrated all his efforts. This great prince, endowed with every talent of a courtier and a warrior, had thrown himfelf into Metz, and withftood the emperor's affaults with unfhaken intrepidity and perfeverance. The feverity of the winter and the froft affifted his valour, and contributed to the deftruction of
1553. 1ft Jan. the Imperial forces. Charles at length raifed the fiege, after having loft thirty thoufand foldiers before the place, and began his retreat back into Germany. His flight acrofs the Alps, after the unfortunate campaign of Provence in 1536, was infinitely lefs difaftrous than the prefent retreat; and the duke of Guife's humanity and attention towards the numbers of unhappy wretches who fell into his hands, and who were unable to accompany their commander in his flight, fhone as confpicuoufly as his courage had done during the fiege, and rendered his fame immortal.

In Piedmont the war was feebly fupported between Briffac and Ferdinand de Gonzague. Solyman, the firm ally of Henry the fecond, as he had

been

been of Francis the first, aided the king of France 1553. with his fleets, while he gained possession of the city of Sienna by intrigue; a place which, had it been preserved, would have facilitated in the greatest degree, any attempts on the Milanese, or the kingdom of Naples.

In the spring the emperor was again in the field, and anxious to repair his past defeats, he re-entered France, where Terouenne, which resisted his attacks, first felt the weight of his vengeance. He took and utterly demolished it; Francis de Montmorenci, the Constable's eldest son, who had gallantly defended it, being made prisoner in the place. Emanuel Philibert, the young duke of Savoy, had the supreme command of Charles's forces during this campaign, and began already to display that heroism and capacity for war, by which he was afterwards so eminently distinguished. He besieged Hesdin, which capitulated; but while the articles were under agitation, a grenade thrown by a priest into the town, set fire to a mine, under the ruins of which, Horace Farnese, duke of Castro, grandson to Pope Paul the third, and who had married Diana of France, the king's natural daughter, was destroyed with fifty others *,—On the other hand, the Constable,

* Diana was one of the most amiable, accomplished, and beautiful princesses who have appeared in France; her mother's

1553. ble, to whom Henry had given the command of his whole army, performed scarce any exploits worthy of remembrance; and his illness, which followed soon after, put an end to the campaign; and permitted the troops to return into winter quarters.

21st June. The death of young Edward the sixth, king of England, interrupted the harmony between the two crowns, as Mary his sister who succeeded, in opposition equally to the wishes of her people and of Henry, soon after espoused Philip

1554. July. prince of Spain, the emperor's son. This union, as it encreased the influence and power of the house of Austria, was little calculated to diminish the jealousy of the king of France, or to produce a peace: on the contrary, both sides prepared anew for war. The emperor, though disabled by the gout, which had contracted the sinews of one of his legs, and had deprived him of the use of one of his arms, appeared for the last time, in the field in person. Henry, who had ever studiously sought the occasion of combating his great antagonist, endeavoured to pro-

---

mother's name was Philippa Duc, of Montcaillier in Piedmont. She was infinitely dear to Henry her father, and not less so to the three succeeding kings her brothers. When left a widow by the duke of Castro's death, she was only fourteen years old: she afterwards married Francis, duke of Montmorenci. Her name occurs frequently in the history of Henry the third's life and reign.

voke

voke him to a general engagement. He ra- 1554.
vaged Hainault, Brabant, and the Cambresis;
demolished Mariemont, a palace of pleasure belonging to Mary queen of Hungary, who was
governess of the Low Countries; and razed the
magnificent castle of Bins, which she had lately
constructed *. Charles marched to the relief of
Renty, besieged by the French; and a considerable skirmish ensued, in which the Imperial 13th
forces were obliged to retreat, after a considera- August.
ble loss of men and artillery. The place itself,
notwithstanding, continued to hold out; and the
king,

---

* Mary, sister to the emperor Charles the fifth, and widow of Louis the second king of Hungary, who perished
in the battle of Mohatz gained by the Turks in 1521, was
a princess of virtue and capacity. She was made governess of the Low Countries in 1531; and, during an administration of twenty-four years, rendered herself exceedingly beloved by the Flemings. She conducted the war in
which the emperor her brother was engaged against Henry
the second of France, with equal vigour and ability. In
1555, she laid down the government of the Netherlands,
and retired into Spain, where she remained till the death
of Charles the fifth in 1558, whom she followed to the
grave within a very few days, at a time when she had intended to return into the Low Countries. The French
writers have accused her of a propensity to gallantry,
and have named Barbançon, a Flemish nobleman, distinguished by the beauty of his person, as her lover; but
this imputation is contradicted by the whole tenor of the
queen's life and character. Calumny even has ventured to
go further, and to name Mary as the mother of Don John

1554. king, leaving part of his army under the command of the duke of Vendome, difmiffed the remainder, and returned to Paris. After fome few inconfiderable conquefts, Charles the fifth clofed for ever his military exploits, and put an end to all his campaigns.

April. In Italy, Sienna was loft, after a long and obftinate defence; but Briffac maintained the national honour in Piedmont, though he was ill fupported at court, and oppofed by the duke of Alva, who infolently threatened, that he would drive him over the mountains. This gallant commander would even have relieved Sienna, and forced the enemy to raife the fiege, if the oppofition of Montmorenci and the Guifes, who were jealous of his glory, had not defeated his

1555. meafures. Mary, queen of England, attempted to bring about an accommodation between the

May. contending princes, and a congrefs was held in a fplendid tent near Calais for that purpofe; but it produced no beneficial confequences.

of Auftria, by her own brother, the emperor Charles; but as fhe was born in 1503, and Don John in 1547, the queen muft have been forty-four at the time when it is pretended fhe brought this fon into the world. It was however generally believed by the cotemporaries, that the mother of Don John was a princefs of the higheft rank; and that to cover and conceal the difhonour of her family, Barbe Blomberg, a lady of Ratifbon, was afferted to have been the mother of that prince.

The

HENRY THE SECOND.

The death of Henry d'Albret, king of Navarre, who expired about this time at Hagetmau in Bearn, left his crown and dominions exposed to the enterprizes and attacks of the king of France, who had intended to incorporate this small kingdom with the French monarchy; but the diligence of Anthony duke of Vendome, who had married Jane, heirefs to the kingdom, preserved the independance of Navarre *. The king, who was desirous of making a compensation to Anthony by the exchange of other lands, was highly offended at his conduct; and refusing to grant the government of Picardy to his brother Louis prince of Condé, he instantly conferred it on Coligny.

1555.
25th May.

The emperor, chagrined and mortified at the decline of his military glory, and at the succeffes of Henry; broken by difeafes, and perhaps partaking in fome degree of his mother, the arch-duchefs Joanna's † more deplorable

and

---

* Henry d'Albret, king of Navarre, was an amiable prince, but not distinguished by any extraordinary endowments of mind. He was born in 1503, and in 1520 he recovered from Charles the fifth his kingdom of Navarre, but lost it again with equal rapidity. He married, in 1527, Margaret, duchefs of Alençon, and fifter to Francis the firft, by whom he had only one daughter, who furvived him, named Jane, mother of Henry the fourth, who, at length, united in his perfon the kingdoms of France and Navarre.

† The princefs Joanna terminated her wretched life only

fix

1555.

and remedilefs diforder of mind, determined to refign all his vaft poffeffions to his fon Philip. He executed this extraordinary renunciation foon after at Bruffels, referving only to himfelf the imperial dignity, which he retained a year longer.

The profufion and magnificence of the court, added to the unavoidable expence attendant on wars to be maintained againft fuch powerful enemies, rendered it neceffary to encreafe the revenues, by additional taxes, oppreffive to the people. The duchefs de Valentinois was chiefly accufed as the caufe of thefe exactions; and fo far was her influence over the king from fuffering any diminution, that it appeared to be every year confirmed and extended. Henry, flexible and eafily led by thofe whom he loved, only acted according to the fuggeftions or impulfe of his miftrefs.—She built the fuperb palace of Anet, to which the two lovers frequently retired, and which

---

fix months before her fon the emperor's abdication: fhe furvived her hufband the archduke Philip, forty-nine years, and was above feventy at her own deceafe, which happened on the 12th April 1555. Her attachment to him, and his untimely death, chiefly contributed to deprive her of her intellects. She was fhut up in the caftle of Tordefillas, almoft abandoned, and fleeping upon ftraw, which fhe fometimes wanted; her only recreation being to fight with cats, and to crawl up the tapeftry with which her apartments were hung. Such was the lamentable deftiny of Ferdinand and Ifabella's daughter; of the mother of two emperors, and four queens!

was

HENRY THE SECOND.

was the chief scene of their amorous pleasures*; while the nation, unable to account for an attachment so unusual between persons of such unequal ages, attributed it to sorcery, and supernatural causes. It was reported that the duchess wore magical rings, which equally prevented the decay of her own beauty, and of the monarch's passion. Catherine of Medicis supported and confirmed this absurd opinion, which soothed her own vanity, by accounting for her rival's triumph †.

The

---

* Anet, which is situated near Dreux, in the isle of France, upon the river Eure, yet exhibits the remains of splendor and elegance. Philibert de Lorme was the architect employ'd by Henry the second in its construction, and the emblems and devices of the duchess of Valentinois are visible in every part of the edifice. Voltaire has immortalised it, in these beautiful lines of the ninth canto of his "Henriade," where Love is described as on his flight to the plain of Ivry.

" Il voit les murs d'Anet batis aux bords de l'Eure,
" Lui-meme en ordonna la superbe structure;
" Par ses adroites Mains, avec art enlacés,
" Les Chiffres de Diane y sont encore tracés;
" Sur sa tombe, en passant, les plaisirs et les graces
" Repandirent les fleurs qui naissoient sur leurs traces."

† Monsieur de Thou, though so judicious and able an historian, was not superior to this weakness, characteristic of the age in which he lived; and very gravely mentions as a fact, the magic powers of which Diana availed herself, to continue, and support her ascendancy over Henry.—— Brantome knew her personally, and has given a minute description of her beauty in its most advanced period,

which

1555.
March.

The death of pope Julius the third, and the election of Cardinal Caraffa to the chair of St. Peter, who assumed the name of Paul the fourth, gave another face to the affairs of Italy *. The new pontiff, though more than eighty years

* John Marie del Monté, who ascended the pontifical throne by the name of Julius the third, was of a very low extraction, and had been raised to the purple by Paul the third in 1536. On the death of that Pope, Julius was elected his successor on the 8th of February 1550, after long deliberations and intrigues in the conclave.

Tho' a prince of intrepidity, and, previous to his election to the tiara, even a prelate of austere manners, he abandoned himself when Pope, to every species of voluptuousness and immorality. The first act of his reign was to confer his own cardinal's

which is too curious and extraordinary to be passed over.

"I saw that lady," says he, "only six months before she "died; and at that time she was so lovely, that the most "insensible person could not have looked on her without "emotion. She was then on her recovery from a very se- "vere indisposition, occasioned by a fracture of her leg, "which she had broke by a fall from her horse, in riding "through the streets of Orleans. Yet neither the accident, "nor the intense pain which she underwent from it, had in "any degree diminished her charms."

Though Brantome does not absolutely account for this extraordinary beauty by any magic influence, yet he endeavours to explain the cause of it, by means somewhat similar.—" Mais, on dit bien," adds he, " que tous les ma- "tins elle usoit de quelques bouillons composez d'or "potable, et autres drogues que je ne sçai pas."—At the period of life when he speaks of the duchess in these terms, she was full sixty-five years old.

years of age, and of manners the moſt auſtere, 1555.
no ſooner attained to his new dignity, than pur-
ſuing a line of conduct the reverſe of that
which he had hitherto held, he united an unexampled pomp and luxury to projects of the
moſt irregular ambition. Irritated by his nephews againſt the emperor for ſome pretended
miſbehaviour of the Imperial generals, he demanded the protection of France, offered the
inveſtiture of Naples to the king, and endeavoured to negotiate a ſtrict alliance with him

cardinal's hat on a young man of the name of Innocent, who was a ſervant in his family, and had the care of an ape; from which circumſtance he was called in deriſion the " Cardinal " Simia." The ſacred college having even complained to his holineſs of the degradation which they ſuffered by the introduction of ſo improper a perſon into their body, Julius replied, " You have choſen to elect me Pope; what merit " have you ever diſcovered in me, to raiſe me to ſo high a " dignity?"——Julius the third, like almoſt all his pre-
deceſſors in the chair of St. Peter, abandoned himſelf to the government of his two nephews, John Baptiſt, and Fabien del Monté; but the firſt of theſe having been killed before the city Mirandola, and the latter being of a more tranquil character, the Pope purſued, unreſtrain'd, his paſſion for pleaſures, and immerſed himſelf in debaucheries, equally unbecoming his ſtation, and unfit for his age. His palaces were a ſcene of intemperance, and of elegance, where magnificent entertainments, heightened by all that genius and refinement could furniſh, continually ſucceeded each other. Julius haſtened his death by theſe pleaſures, which carried him off on the 24th March 1555, after a ſhort pontificate of five years.

for

1555. for their mutual advantage.—The wiſeſt and the moſt diſintereſted part of the French council were averſe to theſe dangerous and chimerical propoſitions. They foreſaw only diſgrace and ruin, in the renewal of the antiquated pretenſions on the crown of Naples; they knew that no confidence ought to be placed in the honour or good faith of Italian politicians; and leaſt of all, in the promiſes of an old man ſinking under the weight of infirmities, impotent in mind, iraſcible, and actuated by two perfidious and violent men, his nephews. They conſidered the ſtate of the kingdom, already exhauſted by the long and continual wars with the emperor, and they beheld future ones in proſpect againſt Philip his ſon and ſucceſſor. They remembered the numerous and unfortunate attempts under Louis the twelfth, and Francis the firſt, to gain poſſeſſion of the Neapolitan crown. Theſe conſiderations ſo truly weighty, ought to have prevented any political union or connection with the court of Rome; but the ſubſerviency of all the cabinet to the duke of Guiſe, and his brother the cardinal of Lorrain, did not permit Henry to follow this ſalutary advice. The cardinal, impetuous and vain, embraced the papal overtures with his accuſtomed enthuſiaſm, with the intention of placing the duke of Guiſe at the head of the army deſtined againſt Italy: he was immediately diſpatched in perſon to Rome,

Rome, to ratify and conclude the treaty; but 1555.
during his abſence, by the intervention of Mary
queen of England, a truce was agreed upon for
five years between the emperor and France. 1556.

With a view of reſcinding the agreement for this February.
ſuſpenſion of hoſtilities, the Cardinal Caraffa was
ſent to Paris as embaſſador on the part of his uncle
the pope, with a ſuperb train. He waited on the
king at Fontainbleau, preſented his majeſty with
a hat and ſword bleſſed by the ſovereign pontiff,
and made a magnificent entry into the capital.
Intriguing and artful, he moved every ſpring,
and availed himſelf of every means to obtain the
purpoſe of his embaſſy. Catherine of Medicis
and Diana de Poitiers were both rendered ſubſervient to his views; while flattery, preſents, and
ſacrifices to their vanity, or ambition, were by
turns employed to gain their ſuffrages. Henry,
wavering and irreſolute, after long heſitation,
and in contradiction to the dictates of his own
judgment, ſuffered himſelf to be borne away by
the ſtream, and conſented to the league.

Francis duke of Guiſe, nominated to the ſu- 1557.
preme command of the army, paſſed the moun- January.
tains, carrying with him the flower of the French
nobility, whom the ſplendor of his character,
and his reputation for courteſy, courage, and liberality, allured to follow his ſtandard. Not
one of the Italian powers could however be induced to afford him aſſiſtance; and though the
pope

1557.
March.
pope received him with every external mark of satisfaction, and celebrated his arrival by public festivities and honours, yet neither the pecuniary or military aids were ready, which by treaty he had promised and stipulated. The duke of Alva, Philip's general, with an army, ravaged the territories of the Church; and the French commander, after an unsuccesful attempt upon the frontier of Naples, was obliged to return to Rome for the protection of his allies.—No progress was made in the plan proposed; and every thing seemed to portend an inglorious termination to the campaign, when an event equally unexpected and disastrous to France, recalled the duke of Guise, and extricated him from so critical and dangerous a situation.

Charles the fifth, who for near half a century had spread terror throughout Europe, no longer acted upon the great political theatre; and having retired to the monastery of St. Justus in Estremadoura, was already forgotten while yet alive. —Philip the second, his son, not less ambitious than Charles, assisted by his wife, Mary queen of England, and desirous on his accession to impress the European princes with the idea of his extensive power, assembled a prodigious army; but not possessing himself either the bravery or conduct necessary to command it, he entrusted that important commission to Emanuel Philibert, the young duke of Savoy. That general, after a

number of feints, attacked the town of St. Quen- 1557.
tin in Picardy, into which Coligny had thrown 3d Au-
himself, and which by his determin'd valour he guft.
preserved for a considerable time, though the
place was otherwise ill calculated for defence.
The Constable Montmorenci, his uncle, meanwhile advanced at the head of the French army,
with intent to give him all the assistance possible;
but it was with infinite difficulty that d'Andelot,
brother to Coligny, found means to enter the
town with five hundred soldiers. This service
being effected, Montmorenci would have retired
at noon-day, and in sight of the enemy, who 10th Au-
were greatly superior in numbers, and particu- guft.
larly in cavalry. The duke of Savoy, soon perceiving the rashness of the attempt, and seizing
instantly the occasion which presented itself,
charged the Constable furiously before he had
time to issue the necessary orders, or to draw up
his forces in a proper manner to receive the attack. The French horse were routed, and thrown
into confusion; but the infantry stood firm, and
were almost all cut to pieces; Montmorenci himself, and the Marechal de St. André, with a number of inferior officers, being taken prisoners.—
Philip, who had not contributed in any degree
in his own person to this important victory, prevented the decisive effects which it might have
produced, by his jealousy of the duke of Savoy.
Instead of marching directly to the capital, which

1557. was already in the utmoſt conſternation, and ready to have been deſerted at his approach, he compelled his general to continue the ſiege of St. Quentin, which Coligny yet defended ſome days, and in which he was at length taken priſoner *.

Henry

* The duke of Savoy, by a very able and maſterly manœuvre, after having appeared to menace the town of Guiſe by a forced march inveſted St. Quentin, into which Coligny immediately threw himſelf, with about ſeven hundred ſoldiers. Montmorenci, who had taken the command of the French army, advanced up to the ſuburbs of St. Quentin, and attacked the Spaniſh forces who formed the ſiege with ſo much vigour, that the whole camp wa thrown into diſorder, the duke of Savoy's tent was over turned by the artillery, and he himſelf had ſcarcely time to put on his cuiraſs, and to retire to the quarters of Coun Egmont. A little rivulet, and ſome marſhes, which inter ſected the ground, unfortunately prevented Montmorenc from profiting in its fulleſt extent of the confuſion in th enemy's camp; and it was with difficulty that d'Andelo found means to enter the city, with a ſmall number of fol lowers. The Conſtable then endeavoured to retreat; bu Count Egmont, at the head of two thouſand cavalry, takin him on one flank, while the duke of Brunſwic, Count Horn and Erneſt of Mansfeldt attacked him on the other, hi troops began to give way. The rout commenced amon the ſutlers and followers of the army, and ſpread from then to the ſoldiery, the action having laſted four hours befor the French were totally defeated. Only two pieces of canno were ſaved, all the others falling into the hands of th enemy, who loſt only about eighty men, while two thouſan five hundred of Montmorenci's troops remained dead upo th

Henry meanwhile, in this great emergency, neglected no measures requisite for the safety of his dominions. Levies of Swifs and Germans were 1557.

the field. John of Bourbon, brother to the king of Navarre and the prince of Condé, who had several times rallied the troops, and renewed the engagement, was unfortunately shot with a ball from a harquebusse, while he was still displaying the most undaunted courage, and endeavouring to retrieve the fortune of the day : he was carried into the Spanish camp, and expired in a very few moments. The Constable himself was wounded in the hip, and taken prisoner, as was the marechal de St. André, the duke de Longueville, and many others of the first nobility. Louis, prince of Condé, and the duke of Nevers, retreated to La Fere in Picardy. Philip the second was not personally present in this action, so glorious to the duke of Savoy : he contented himself with offering up vows to St. Laurence for his general's success, without having the courage to expose himself to danger; nor did he join his victorious troops till sixteen days after, on the 27th of August, when he arrived in the camp before St. Quentin, with ten thousand English, and as many Flemish soldiers.—Coligny merited immortal honour for his obstinate defence of St. Quentin against this numerous army; and the assault being made at noon-day, he was abandoned by his troops, only a page and four followers remaining with him, when he was taken prisoner.— D'Andelot, his brother, still continued to defend himself against the Spaniards, till, covered with wounds, and overwhelmed with numbers, he was obliged to surrender. On the following night, he found means to escape.—Had Philip pushed forward instantly towards Paris, after the victory at St. Quentin, the monarchy of France had probably been shaken to it's foundation; but his jealousy of the duke of Savoy rescued Henry the second and his kingdom from this imminent and alarming danger.

1557. made with all possible expedition; Paris was fortified towards the side of Picardy; the duke of Guise was recalled to the defence of France; and even the most pressing solicitations were made to Sultan Solyman for assistance against the Spanish monarch. These vigorous efforts were attended with a proportionable success. Animated by their prince's firmness and intrepidity, and recovering from the first impressions of terror, the Parisians gave the most distinguished proofs of their loyalty and liberality.

1558. The duke of Guise's arrival, the lustre of his name, and the reliance upon his great abilities, completed the general tranquillity. — Philip, during the remainder of the campaign, made no conquests or acquisitions proportionate to the importance of the battle which he had gained: the capture of the three towns of Ham, Catelet, and Noyon were comparatively slight advantages, and were not attended with any decisive consequences.

On the contrary, the duke of Guise, though impeded by the rigour of winter, and the severity of the season, lost not a moment in endeavouring to raise the drooping genius of his country. After having been declared lieutenant-general within and without the kingdom, he undertook the siege of Calais, which was deemed almost impregnable;

8th January. and made himself master in eight days of that city, so long held by the English, though it had cost

cost Edward the third above a year's blockade. This signal success was followed by the capture of Thionville, in the duchy of Luxembourg; but the Marechal de Termes, although an able and experienced commander, was completely routed near Gravelines by the young Count Egmont; and he himself fell into the hands of the enemy *.

1558.
June.

So

---

* The Marechal de Termes, having taken Dunkirk, laid siege to Gravelines; but being subject to the gout, and at that time attacked by a violent fit of the disorder, he left the command of his forces to Estouteville, who relaxing the discipline, permitted the soldiers to quit the camp in great numbers, and to occupy themselves with plundering the peasants. Count Egmont, governor of Flanders, profiting of this error, hastily assembled the garrisons of Aire, St. Omer, and Bethune; to which being added a reinforcement which he received from the duke of Savoy, they formed a body of twelve thousand infantry, and three thousand cavalry, with which he instantly marched to attack the French. Termes no sooner received the news of the enemy's approach, than he mounted on horseback notwithstanding his indisposition, and prepared to receive the attack. He took a strong position, his right flank being covered by the sea, his left by the carts of his baggage, and his front protected by eight pieces of artillery. Count Egmont, on the other side, was totally destitute of any cannon, and only following the dictates of his courage, he led on his troops, exclaiming, " We are " conquerors. Let those who love glory and their country, " follow me!"—He was, however, repulsed at the first onset, his ranks were thinned by the French artillery, and his own horse killed under him.—The advantage was nearly equal on both sides, and the victory more than doubtful on the part of the Count, when ten English vessels, whom the

1558. So astonishing and so favourable a reverse of fortune served to heighten, and add new splendor to the reputation of the defender of Metz and conqueror of Calais. As he only, amid the calamities of the state, seemed able to command the events of war, and uniformly to attach victory to his party, upon him alone the public confidence rested, as the guardian and protector of France. By a combination of events, all contributing to the elevation of the house of Guise, their power was still farther confirmed and

the noise of the firing had brought to the coast, decided the fortune of the battle. Having brought their cannon to play on the right wing of the French army, which lay exposed to the fire from the ships, the cavalry, unable to withstand this unexpected and severe attack, fled in confusion, and were followed by the infantry. The defeat was entire, fifteen hundred of the French remaining on the field of battle, and a much greater number being massacred by the peasants, in revenge for the calamities which they had experienced from the depredations of the soldiery. Termes, with several other generals, was made prisoner. It may not be improper to remark, that Count Egmont, who had been so instrumental in the defeat of the French at St. Quentin, and to whom alone the glory of the victory at Gravelines was due, terminated his life on a scaffold at Brussels, only ten years afterwards, in 1568, by order of the tyrant Philip the second. His execution is one of the many atrocious deeds of blood which the duke of Alva committed in the Netherlands, and which stain the annals of Philip's sanguinary reign.—The emancipation of seven provinces from the yoke of Spain, in some degree revenged and expiated the death of this gallant commander.

extended

HENRY THE SECOND.

extended by an alliance with the heir to the crown, which took place about this time.—Francis the Dauphin, being enamoured of their niece, the young queen of Scotland, who had been sent, after the death of her father James the fifth, to the court of Henry for an asylum, obtained the king's consent to his marriage. Mary, so renowned for her beauty, her talents, and her misfortunes, was at this time in her sixteenth year; and her charms, though not yet fully expanded, are yet described by all the French historians as so touching and irresistible, that a young prince, however destitute of sensibility, could not fail to pay them homage.—The nuptials were solemnised with unusual splendor at the church of "Notre Dame;" and consummated the same day, at the "Palais," amidst the greatest festivities, which were succeeded by a triumphal entry into the capital, where the Dauphin appeared on horseback, and the young bride in a magnificent litter. They assumed the titles of king and queen of England and Scotland, after the death of Mary, queen of England, which happened the same year. The court of France was engaged in all the entertainments and diversions usual at such a time; and the duke of Guise, together with the Cardinal of Lorrain, found themselves at the zenith of their glory and authority.

Two great armies, commanded by their respective sovereigns in person, threatened each

1558.

24th April.

1558. other on the approach of summer: Henry and Philip seemed to be on the eve of a decisive engagement, but mutual fear restrained them from coming to a general action; and towards the autumn, by the intervention of the papal nuncio and of the duchess of Lorrain, a negotiation was October. opened for the conclusion of peace at the abbey of Cercamp, near Hesdin, in Picardy. The treaty was facilitated and accelerated by the Constable Montmorenci, and the Marechal de St. André, who, weary of their imprisonment, and jealous of being supplanted in the royal favour by the Guises during their absence from court, made use of the duke of Savoy to incline Philip to listen to terms of pacification. The Constable had previously requested and obtained permission to go to Henry in person at Amiens, with the design of effecting a general peace; and he was received with testimonies of the warmest affection by his master on that occasion, who (according to the manners of the age, which knew none of the delicacies of the present century) carried his condescension and attachment so far, as even to make him sleep in his own bed. It was determined to put an end to the war, at whatever price, or by whatever means; and the death of Mary, queen of England, which took place during the course of the negotiation, removed the principal obstacle to peace, as Philip, after her decease, no longer maintained with the same ardour

HENRY THE SECOND.

ardour the interests of her successor Elizabeth, or insisted, as he had previously done, on the absolute restitution of Calais. After several conferences at Cercamp, the preliminaries were finally adjusted, and signed at Cateau in Cambresis.—All the conquests made during the late or present reign, in Piedmont, Tuscany and Corsica, were ceded to Spain, to procure the restitution of Ham, Catelet, and Noyon, three inconsiderable towns in Picardy; but, in recompence, Calais, Metz, Toul, and Verdun remained to France.—The princess Margaret, sister to the king, was affianced to the duke of Savoy*; and Elizabeth, his eldest daughter, transferred

1558.
1559. January.

---

* Margaret, daughter of Francis the first, was born in 1523. Her person was beautiful, and she possessed many of the most engaging and amiable qualities of the king her father, as well as all the elegance of mind by which he was peculiarly characterised. After his death, she continued that protection and liberality to men of genius which had acquired Francis so high a reputation over all Europe. Her marriage with Emanuel Philibert, duke of Savoy, was consummated in the last moments of the life and reign of her brother, Henry the second, the princess being then thirty-six years of age. She was infinitely beloved, and revered by her subjects, who called her the mother of her people. On the return of her nephew, Henry the third, from Poland into France, in 1574, she received him at Turin, and is said to have given him some excellent counsels for his conduct, of which Henry availed himself little. The anxiety and earnestness which she felt to entertain the king and his train during their stay in her capital, added to the exertions which she made

1559. transferred from Don Carlos, Philip's only son, for whom she was first designed, and given to Philip himself, recently become a widower by the death of the queen of England *.

These made to render his residence in Turin agreeable, threw her into a pleurisy, of which she died on the 14th of September, 1574, during the absence of the duke her husband, who had attended the king of France to Lyons, on his entering his own dominions. She was infinitely regretted by her subjects, and her memory was immortalized by the poets, to whom she had extended her patronage and generosity.

* Elizabeth of France, daughter of Henry the second and Catherine of Medici, was born at Fontainbleau, in April, 1545, and had been originally intended for Edward the sixth of England; a marriage which w prevented by the premature death of that prince. She was then destined for Don Carlos, son of Philip the second, and heir to the Spanish monarchy; but the decease of Mary queen of England, during the negotiations which preceded the treaty of Cambresis, leaving Philip free, he demanded the young princess in marriage for himself, and the nuptials were solemnized by proxy at the church of " Notre Dame," only a few days before the catastrophe of Henry the second's death. She was named " Elizabeth de la Paix," because she formed the cement of the great pacification between France and Spain.—Almost all the cotemporary historians agree in asserting, that Don Carlos never forgave his father for having thus deprived him of his intended bride; and they either insinuate or declare, that the young queen was tenderly attached to the prince during her whole life, though they expressly deny her having ever been capable, or guilty of any criminal weakness. In 565, Elizabeth was brought by the duke of Alva to Bayonne, where an interview took place between the queen of Spain and her brother, Charles the ninth, who was accompanied by Catherine

HENRY THE SECOND.

These terms, humiliating and disgraceful to 1559. France, were principally attributed to the Constable, who from self-interested motives, and the desire of obtaining his freedom, was believed to have advised the king to accept of such inadequate conditions. The Guises openly arraigned the treaty, as unbecoming the national honour, and depriving the kingdom in a moment of the conquests of near thirty years; but Henry, not-

rine of Medicis.—The history and lamentable fate of Don Carlos is too well known, to need recital: that unhappy prince expired, though whether by a natural or a violent death is more matter of conjecture and suspicion than of certainty, on the 24th of July, 1568. It is commonly believed that Philip the second caused him to be privately executed, or poisoned; and it was imagined that jealousy of his son's attachment to the queen, hasten'd, if it did not produce this unnatural order. It is certain that Elizabeth was much affected by the misfortunes and death of Don Carlos, whom she only surviv'd about ten weeks: she died in child-bed at Madrid, on the 3d of October, 1568, not without strong suspicions of poison, and infinitely regretted by all her subjects. Brantome says, "On parle fort sinistrément de sa mort." De Thou, and the Abbé de St. Real, likewise insinuate that her death was accelerated by unnatural means; and the unrelenting, gloomy character of Philip too much strengthens the suspicion. Elizabeth was beautiful in her person, and amiable in her manners to the highest degree. By her husband she left two daughters, of whom the eldest was the celebrated infanta Clara-Eugenia, married to the archduke Albert, and who was governess of the Low Countries for a number of years: she was the favourite and beloved child of Philip the second. The second daughter, Catherine, was married to Charles Emanuel, duke of Savoy.

withstanding

1559. withstanding every remonstrance, adhered immoveably to his resolution.

During the reign of Francis the first, and more peculiarly so since his decease, the reformed religion had made a most alarming and universal progress. All ranks of people had imbibed the new doctrines; and persecution unhappily hastened and promoted their influence. D'Andelot, nephew to the Constable, and brother to Coligny, was justly suspected, and even accused of being a proselyte to these opinions. Henry, desirous to be satisfied of the truth or falshood of the imputation, questioned him personally on his sentiments respecting the Mass; and d'Andelot, with an imprudent zeal, made him so bold and undisguised a reply, that the king being exceedingly irritated, was about to have put him to death with his own hand.—It required all his uncle's interest, to procure his pardon and restitution to his post of general of the French infantry *. The severest penalties were denounced against

---

* The king ordered the cardinal de Chatillon, brother of d'Andelot, (and who afterwards openly renounced himself the Catholic religion, though he retain'd his ecclesiastical dignity and the purple) to bring d'Andelot into his presence, that he might question him in person relative to his religious opinions. The culprit having presented himself at the king's dinner, while the court was at Monceaux, Henry interrogated him on the subject of the Eucharist; and d'Andelot not

HENRY THE SECOND.

against the professors of Lutheranism, or Calvinism; and several members of the parliament of Paris having presumed to declare against the rigour of the punishments to which by law the Protestants were made liable, and which were put into execution against them, the king himself went in person, and ordered five of the most refractory members, at the head of whom was Anne du Bourg, to be arrested and carried to the Bastile immediately, who had avowed that sentiment in his presence. Orders were issued for their immediate and rigorous prosecution.

With the return of peace, every species of luxury and dissipation revived. Henry's court, the most refined and polished in Europe, was rendered unusually splendid by the different entertainments exhibited on occasion of the mar-

1559.

10th June.

---

not only avowing his belief in the doctrines of Calvin, but peremptorily refusing to retract his opinion, Henry was inflamed to such a degree of resentment, that taking up a plate with intent to dash it against the ground, he wounded the Dauphin, who sat by him at table. He instantly ordered the sieur de la Bourdasiere to take d'Andelot into arrest, and to conduct him to Meaux, from whence, after some time, he was transferred to the castle of Melun. Blaise de Montluc, to whom his office was tender'd, refused to accept it, from apprehension of the indignation of the family of Montmorenci, to whom d'Andelot was very nearly allied by blood. The Constable's intercession, joined to d'Andelot's submission, procured him, however, a restoration to his military rank and charge.

riage

1559.
27th
June.

riage of the princefs Elizabeth to Philip the fecond, which was celebrated by proxy at Paris. Tournaments and caroufals added a martial magnificence to the other amufements of a gentler nature. The young duke of Savoy, Emanuel Philibert, arriving about the fame time at Paris, accompanied by the duke of Brunfwic, the prince of Orange, and a hundred gentlemen, was received with every demonftration of refpect and attention by Henry, who met and embraced him at the foot of the great ftair-cafe of the Louvre. This incident redoubled the feftivals, which were interrupted only three days after by the tragical cataftrophe of the king's death.

The lifts extended from the palace of the Tournelles to the Baftile, acrofs the ftreet St. Antoine, and Henry himfelf had broken feveral lances with different lords of the court, in all which he had fhewn unufual vigour and addrefs.

30th
June.

On that day, which was the third of the tournaments, he wore the colours of his miftrefs the duchefs of Valentinois, in token of his love, and in compliance with the laws of chivalry, of which gallantry always formed fo diftinguifhing a feature. Thofe colours were black and white, in allufion to her ftate of widowhood.—Towards the clofe of the evening, and before the conclufion of the tournament, Henry had a great inclination to try his prowefs againft the Count de Montgomeri, captain in his life guards. He was fon to that Seigneur

Seigneur de Lorges, who-had formerly wounded Francis the firſt ſo dangerouſly on the head at Romorentin in Berri, and was diſtinguiſhed for his ſuperior addreſs in theſe combats above any nobleman of the kingdom *. Catherine of Medicis,

1569.

---

* Gabriel de Lorges, Count de Montgomeri, was captain of the Scotch guards to Henry the ſecond. He was brave and active in the higheſt degree, and had been ſent by Francis the firſt, in 1545, into Scotland, to command the troops which were then diſpatched to the aſſiſtance of the queen regent, Mary of Guiſe. The death of Henry the ſecond cannot certainly be imputed as a crime to Montgomeri, he having urgently entreated of the king, tho' in vain, to excuſe him from giving the fatal proof of his dexterity which took place: it has even been pretended, tho' probably without reaſon, that Henry, before he breathed his laſt, expreſsly enjoin'd that Montgomeri ſhould not be proſecuted or moleſted for having been innocently and unintentionally the author of his death. The beſt French authors agree in aſſerting, that the king, though he continued to breathe for eleven days after the accident, never recover'd either his ſpeech or intellects. It is plain that Montgomeri conceived himſelf to be in danger; for he immediately retired into England, and having embraced the doctrines of the reformation, returned into France at the commencement of the civil wars, under Charles the ninth. Brantome deſcribes him, as addicted to gaming and pleaſures in the moſt immoderate degree, but equally intrepid and active whenever occaſion called. His own words are vaſtly characteriſtic and amuſing, from their plainneſs and ſimplicity: " C'etoit," ſays Brantome, " le plus noncha-
" lant en ſa charge, et auſſi peu ſoucieux qu'il etoit poſſi-
" ble; car il aimoit fort ſes aiſes, et le jeu; mais, lorſque
" il

1559. dicis, as if by a secret presage of the event, besought the king not to re-enter the lists, but he resisted her solicitations; adding, that he would break one more lance in her honour. Montgomeri himself accepted the challenge with extreme reluctance, and endeavoured by every argument and entreaty to prevail on his sovereign to excuse him; but without effect. Henry commanded him to obey, and even fought with his vizor raised. The shock was rude on both sides; but the count's lance breaking against the king's helmet, he attacked Henry with the stump, which remained in his hand. It entered under the eyebrow of his right eye, and the blow was so violent, as to throw him to the ground, and to deprive him instantly both of his speech and understanding, which he never more recovered, though he survived the accident near eleven days.—The queen ordered him to be carried immediately to the palace of the Tournelles;

"il avoit une fois le cul sur la selle, c'etoit le plus vaillant et soigneux capitaine qu'on eut seu voir; au reste, si brave et vaillant, qu'il assailloit tout, foible ou fort, qui se presentat devant lui." His defence of Rouen, in 1562, against the royal army, and his escape, after having exhausted all the resources of the most desperate bravery, in a boat, with which he broke thro' the chains stretched across the river Seine at Caudebec, raised his reputation to the highest point. His death, and the circumstances of it, will be mentioned hereafter.

every

HENRY THE SECOND.

every affiftance was procured for him, and the divine mercy implored by proceffions and public prayers; but the wound was beyond a cure, and he at length expired, having only paffed his fortieth year, about four months *.

1559.

10th July.

* Authors are not agreed whether the king fought with his vizor raifed, or whether it flew open with the blow received from Montgomeri's lance.—Luc Gauric, a famous aftrologer of the time, is pretended by de Thou to have foretold the manner and circumftances of the king's death; but unfortunately, Gauric's prediction is found in Gaffendi, and exprefsly afferts, that "if Henry could fur-" mount the dangers with which he was menaced in his " fixty-third and fixty-fourth year, he would furvive, and " enjoy great happinefs till the age of fixty-nine years and " ten months."—Mezerai, likewife, relates that Charles duke of Lorrain, fon-in-law to Henry the fecond, was accuftomed publickly and folemnly to declare, that, "while " he was at Paris during the feftivities and tournaments " which preceded the king's death, on the night before that " melancholy event, a lady who was lodged in his own " palace near the Baftile, faw in a dream the king thrown " to the ground by a blow from a lance in his eye; a fplinter " of which ftruck the Dauphin by rebound in the ear, and " extended him breathlefs near the dead body of his fa-" ther."—Thefe dreams and predictions carry with them either fo much folly or fo much falfity, as to become matters of contempt and ridicule in an enlightened age.—As foon as Philip the fecond received intelligence of the king's accident and defperate fituation, he difpatched André Vefal, his own furgeon, from Bruffels to Paris, to attend, and exert his fkill for the recovery of the expiring monarch: but all his efforts were fruitlefs; an incurable abfcefs having formed itfelf in the king's brain, of which he died on the tenth of July, 1559.

1559. Consternation and affright, mingled with intrigue and artifice, divided the court; and the contending factions, headed by chiefs of the greatest capacity, whom the late king's vigour had kept in subjection, now declared their various pretensions without disguise.—The duke of Savoy, finding the king's recovery desperate, solicited so pressingly the completion of his marriage with the princess Margaret, that it was ce-
9th July. lebrated at "Notre-Dame," without any pomp, and in the greatest privacy.—The duchess de Valentinois received an order from the queen to retire to her own house, and not to presume to enter the chamber of the dying king, which command she obeyed.—This mandate was followed by a second from Catherine, enjoining her to deliver up the jewels of the crown, and other rich effects then in her possession. She asked if Henry was dead; the messenger replied, that he yet breathed, but could not possibly remain long alive. "Know," said Diana, with undaunted intrepidity, "that so long as
" he shall retain the least appearance of life, I
" neither fear my enemies, however powerful, nor
" will shew any deference to their menaces or
" commands. Carry this answer to the queen."

If Henry was not a great, he was an amiable and accomplished prince. Generous to his domestics, bounteous to his followers, he was beloved by his courtiers and attendants. His
conversation

conversation was entertaining, and lively; his 1559. manner of expression flowing, and graceful. An affectionate father, a polite and decent husband, a warm and animated friend, he was, in all the walks of private life, peculiarly an object of respect and attachment. Neither destitute of capacity or firmness, though governed by his mistress, and subservient to his favourites, he could exert himself on important occasions, and enforce obedience. Fond of polite literature, as from hereditary right, he encouraged it in his court, where it made a rapid progress. In the prime of life, and with such qualities, his death must at any time have been considered as a loss to his kingdom; but in the critical juncture when he expired, it was a calamity of the most fatal nature, immediately followed by massacres, crimes, and civil discord. He only could repress the enthusiastic spirit and intemperate zeal of the followers of the reformed religion; or restrain the intriguing genius of Catherine of Medicis, and set bounds to the wild ambition of the princes of the house of Lorrain. His untimely end, and the succeeding circumstances which took place under the reigns of his three sons, opened the avenues to every source of public evil and distress.

By the queen he left four sons and three daughters, all of whom will be frequently mentioned hereafter. He never had any children by the duchess de Valentinois; but, besides

1559. Diana, married to the Duke of Caſtro, of whom I have already ſpoken, he left a natural ſon by a Scotch lady, named Henry d'Angouleſme, who was grand prior of France, governor of Provence, and admiral of the Levant ſeas *.

We are now about to enter on a melancholy period of the French hiſtory. Wars of religion, more

* The name of this miſtreſs of Henry the ſecond is ſaid to have been Fleming: ſhe was in the ſervice of Mary queen of Scotland, whom ſhe had accompanied from her own country into France; yet others of the cotemporary writers call her "Mademoiſelle de Lewiſton," and pretend that ſhe was related to Mary by blood. They add, that motives of policy and court intrigue originally produced the connection between this lady and the king. The Guiſes, jealous of the aſcendant which Diana de Poitiers had obtained and preſerved over him, determined to detach him from her, as they found ſhe no longer treated them with her accuſtomed confidence, and that Montmorenci had ſupplanted them in her affections. To this end, they artfully praiſed "Ma-"demoiſelle de Lewiſton," and extolled her greatly to Henry, who ſoon after ſaw, and became enamoured of her. She did not ſcruple to gratify his paſſion; but their intimacy was concealed, even after ſhe had brought him a ſon, with the extremeſt care, to prevent its being known to the ducheſs de Valentinois.—Henry d'Angouleſme, her ſon, was a generous, brave, and accompliſhed prince, though unhappily led, by the prejudices and madneſs of the times, to be particularly active in the dreadful night of St. Bartholomew.—His death was tragical and ſingular; it happened at Aix in Provence, on the ſecond of June, 1588. Philip Altoviti, baron de Caſtelane, was his mortal enemy: Henry having entered his houſe, and having reproached the baron

with

more sanguinary, cruel, and ruinous than even 1559.
those of Henry the fifth and Edward the third,
rise in succession under the three last princes of
the race of Valois. The bright days of Francis
and Henry, the noble and animating contests
for glory with Charles the fifth and Philip the
second, are succeeded by intestine confusion, by
rebellion and revolt. The kingdom, over-run
by foreign auxiliaries, torn by her own subjects,
and bleeding at every vein, becomes a field of
contention and desolation. Catherine of Medicis, like its evil genius, mingles and embroils
all ranks and parties. The spirit of civil discord and religious frenzy seems almost to extinguish every sentiment of humanity, patriotism, and virtue—till at length a stranger prince,
descended from the blood of their ancient kings,
appears; and, as if sent from Heaven to heal the
wounds of his expiring country, restores peace,
and diffuses universal serenity.

with many acts of malignant hatred towards him, at length proceeded to such lengths of violence as to pass his sword through Castelane's body. Altoviti expiring, had yet sufficient force to snatch a poniard from the head of the bed on which he fell, with which he stabbed Henry in the belly. The prince did not apprehend his wound to be mortal; but the friar who confessed him, informing him of his danger, he replied, without emotion, "Il ne faut plus penser à vivre?" "Eh bien, pensons donc à mourir!"—He died twenty-four hours afterwards.

E 3 CHAP-

CHAPTER THE NINTH.

State of the kingdom at the death of Henry the second.—Character of the duke of Guise—of the cardinal of Lorrain—of the king of Navarre—of the prince of Condé.—Catherine of Medicis.—Her character, person, and political conduct.—Disgrace of the duchess of Valentinois.—Accession of Francis the second.—Power of the Guises.—The king's ill health.—Assassination of Minard.—Conspiracy of Amboise, and its defeat.—Executions.—The prince of Condé suspected.—Convocation of Fontainebleau.—Arrival of the king of Navarre and prince of Condé at court.—They are arrested.—Trial of the latter prince.—Francis's illness.—Condemnation of the prince of Condé.—Intrigues and cabals of Catherine of Medicis.—Death of Francis the second.—Circumstances.—Character.—Funeral.—Arrival of Montmorenci.—Release of Condé.

1559. PREVIOUS to entering upon this short, but unhappy reign, which first gave birth to the wars of religion in France, it is requisite to take a view of the great personages who will appear upon the scene, and behold the elements of future calamities yet latent and concealed, 1559. or only faintly unfolding the fatal principles of deftruction with which they were impregnated. The unforefeen and fad cataftrophe of Henry the fecond's death called out thefe principles into action, which might otherwife have remained in tranquillity. That fuperior and coercive power being removed, that had hitherto over-ruled the many jarring and difcordant fpirits with which the court was filled, a tumultuous adminiftration fucceeded, precarious in its bafis, uncertain in its duration, and only fupported by an extraordinary exertion of feverity, circumfpection, and authority.

Amidft the confufion confequent upon the July. deceafe of the late king, the Guifes had gained poffeffion of the perfon of Francis the fecond, the young fovereign. Their alliance by blood to the queen, Mary of Scotland, afforded them a plaufible pretext to juftify their conduct; and the great endowments of the two brothers, Francis duke of Guife and the Cardinal of Lorrain, feemed to render them intitled to the firft employments of the ftate.

The duke poffeffed in an eminent degree all thofe dazzling qualities which are formed to procure an unlimited afcendancy over mankind. Liberal even to munificence, courteous to condefcenfion in his manners and addrefs, he captivated the people; while his renown in arms

E 4   procured

1559. procured him the adherence of the foldiery, and the attachment of the braveft captains, who deemed themfelves certain of fuccefs under his command. Naturally moderate, and averfe to cruelty, he yet zealoufly maintained the ancient religion, and 'oppofed every innovation. Intrepid in the article of danger, either perfonal or political, he furveyed it without trouble or difmay, and applied to it the moft inftant and efficacious remedies; but confcious of his own capacity for government, favoured by the peculiar circumftances of the times, and hurried away by his ambition, he fet no limits to his thirft of power *.

Talents of an oppofite nature, but, perhaps, not lefs calculated to feduce and impofe upon the

---

* Francis, duke of Guife, was, unqueftionably, one of the moft elevated and extraordinary charaƈters, which appeared in the fixteenth century. He was born at the caftle of Bar in Lorrain, on the feventeenth of February, 1519. In 1545 he was wounded by a lance near the eye at the fiege of Boulogne, which, from the fcar that it left, procured him the furname of "Balafré." His defence of Metz in 1553, againft Charles the fifth, and ftill more, his clemency and humanity towards the Imperial foldiers who fell into his hands on the emperor's retreat from before the place, acquired him an immortal reputation. Viƈtory appeared to accompany him wherever he moved; and the recovery of Calais from the Englifh endeared him defervedly to all France. It is to be lamented that the death of Henry the fecond, the relation in which he ftood to the fucceffor by
the

the human mind, characterised his brother the Cardinal. Endowed with eloquence, and animated with an unbounded zeal in the cause of the catholic religion, he was venerated by the clergy as the guardian of the ecclesiastical immunities and privileges. Inferior to the duke in clemency and manly courage, he yet was more enterprizing, presumptuous, and vain; but as he was elated even to arrogance by success, so he sunk into pusillanimity when oppressed by adverse fortune. Violent and vindictive, he could neither restrain nor dissemble his feelings; yet dissolute, and fond of pleasure, he gave offence by the libertinism of his conduct. Greedy of power, rapacious of wealth, and sacrificing every consideration of private tenderness or affection to the dictates of a stern and an unrelenting policy, he knew no motives, and pursued no objects, except those which tended to the elevation of himself and his family.

1559.

Anthony of Bourbon, king of Navarre, and first prince of the blood, was ill calculated to oppose these aspiring and turbulent spirits. Of

the marriage of Mary of Scotland, his niece, to that prince, and the feeble character of Francis the second himself, opened to the duke of Guise a career for his ambition, too alluring to be resisted by a man who felt his capacity. Yet even prejudice must confess that he possessed qualities worthy of government; and such as, if the circumstances of the times had permitted, might have been as beneficial to his country as they were glorious to himself.

1559.
a temper gentle, humane, and flexible, nature seemed to have designed him for times of harmony and tranquillity. Equal to the duke of Guise only in personal bravery, he was far beneath him in every other point of competition. Politically timid and irresolute, he was destitute of that firmness so indispensable in great emergencies; and fluctuating in a continual uncertainty between the two religions, he neither could be deemed a Catholic or a Hugonot; yet voluptuous and fond of women, he was easily induced to break the tyes of policy, from the weakness of private attachment.

Far different was his brother Louis, prince of Condé. His person, which was little and ungraceful, inclosed a soul the most heroic: amorous from complexion, and of an address the most persuasive, he was beloved by women, and received from them the most unbounded and flattering proofs of their affection. Of high and determined courage, he was formed to shine in camps as much as in courts. Though indigent in his fortunes, which were extremely circumscribed, he yet possess'd the liberality becoming his high birth and situation. Professing with zeal the doctrines of Calvin, but little inclined to the rigorous manners of the Reformation, he made religion the pretext for his engaging in those wars, which ambition and his hatred to the Guises really produced. Not inferior to

the

FRANCIS THE SECOND.

the celebrated Charles of Bourbon in the arts 1559.
of retaining a licentious soldiery in subjection,
nature had intended him for war, and vested
him with all the endowments necessary for the
attainment of military glory. With qualities
such as these, he formed no unequal antagonist
to the duke of Guise; whom he ever considered
as his mortal enemy, and boldly opposed on
all occasions.*

The Constable Montmorenci, far advanced
in years, long accustomed to occupy the first
post of state, and too haughty to condescend to
fill an inferior one, did not at once declare for

* Louis of Bourbon, prince of Condé, was the seventh
son of Charles, duke of Vendome, and was born on the
7th of May, 1530. He early distinguished himself in the
field under the reign of Henry the second, and made his
first campaign with that monarch, when he laid siege to
Boulogne: in 1552, he threw himself into Metz, and contributed to the glory which the duke of Guise acquired by
his repulse of the emperor from before that city. At the
fatal battle of St. Quentin, where Montmorenci was taken
prisoner, and the French army was totally defeated, the
prince of Condé, then only twenty-seven years of age, distinguished his courage during the action, and rallied the
flying troops at La Fere, in Picardy.

He imbibed the religious opinions of the reformers before the death of Henry the second; and the tumultuous
times which followed under Francis the second and Charles
the ninth, rendered the prince of Condé too illustrious;
and eventually involved him in rebellion, which was terminated only by a premature and tragical end. He will
be much mentioned in the present and succeeding reign.

either

1559. either faction; but the preſſing inſtances of Henry d'Amville his ſecond ſon, and his averſion to the reformed religion, induced him at length, reluctantly, to join the princes of the houſe of Lorrain.

The Marechal de St. André, one of the moſt accompliſhed noblemen of the court, brave, polite, and elegant, but immoderately addicted to pleaſures, and of a ruined fortune, ranged himſelf under the ſame banner, and devoted himſelf implicitly to the duke of Guiſe's ſervice*.

* Jacques d'Albon, commonly known in hiſtory by the name of the Marechal de St. André, was one of the moſt diſtinguiſhed favourites of Henry the ſecond, who loaded him with dignities and preferments: his bravery, his magnificence of diſpoſition, and the inſinuation of his manners and addreſs, rendered him peculiarly calculated to ſucceed in courts. As early as the battle of Cerizoles under Francis the firſt, in 1544, he had acquired a high reputation for intrepidity; and he had been preſent in every action of danger during the war which took place between Charles the fifth and Henry the ſecond. He received the garter from the young king of England Edward the ſixth, to whom he had been ſent with the order of St. Michael. At St. Quentin he was made priſoner, together with the Conſtable Montmorenci.—Under the reign of Francis the ſecond, and in the firſt years of Charles the ninth, he acted a diſtinguiſhed part in the unhappy ſcenes which deſolated and laid waſte the kingdom. Voltaire ſeems to have conceived more meanly of his talents than perhaps they merited: he calls St. André the " Lepidus of the Triumvirate," which was formed under Charles the ninth, between the duke of Guiſe, Montmorenci, and that nobleman.

On

On the contrary, Coligni, and d'Andelot his brother, both of them avowed proselytes to Calvinism, embraced the party of the princes of the blood, and adhered to it invariably.

1559.

Catherine of Medicis, whom we have so long seen obscured by the superior influence of the two successive mistresses to Francis and Henry, now first came forward, and rose into importance. Her rank, as mother to the young king, made her friendship eagerly sought after by every party; while her talents and capacity rendered her equal to, and capable of the most arduous offices of government. A character too complicated, and containing movements too numerous and intricate for a common description: it is scarce possible accurately to delineate the various and contradictory features of her mind.

Endowed by nature with a thousand great and shining qualities, she only wanted virtue to direct them to honourable and salutary purposes. Fond of pleasure, of letters, of magnificence, these were yet only inferior affections; ambition predominated, and swallowed up all other passions in her bosom. Born with a force of mind, and a calmness which might have done honour to the boldest man, she seemed to look down as from an eminence on human occurrences; while never alarmed even in circumstances the most unexpected and distressful, she

knew

1559. knew either how to oppose them, or, if necessary, how to bend and accommodate herself to them. Mistress of consummate dissimulation, her manners, where she wished to succeed in any attempt, were ingratiating beyond the common powers of female seduction. Sprung from the blood of Cosmo de Medicis, and emulous of the fame which Francis the first had acquired by his protection of learning, she cultivated poetry and all the gentler arts amid the horrors of civil war; and extended her generosity to men of genius, even in the most exhausted state of the finances.—Expensive even to prodigality in the entertainments and diversions which she exhibited, and covering her designs under the mask of dissipation, she planned a massacre amid the festivity of a banquet, and caressed with the most winning blandishments the victim which she had previously destined to destruction. Cruel from policy, not from temper, avaricious from necessity, profuse from taste; she united in herself qualities the most discordant and contradictory *.

Her

* Catherine of Medicis, so celebrated in the annals of France and of all Europe, was the daughter of Lorenzo de Medicis, duke of Urbino, and of Magdelaine de la Tour d'Auvergne: she was born at Florence, on the 13th of April 1519; and during her childhood was exposed to the utmost hazards from the animosity of the Florentines to the house of Medicis, who had been expelled from that city

Her person was noble, and corresponded
with her dignity; the beauty of her countenance being blended with majesty. She knew
how to improve her natural charms by all
the magic of dress, and carried her magnificence on this article to a prodigious length;

city by the opposite faction. Not content with depriving
the young princess of all the possessions of her family, they
confined her at nine years of age in a monastery; and
during the famous siege of Florence in 1530, Baptista
Cei, one of the most violent opponents of the Medicis,
carried his detestation and barbarity to such a length, as to
propose to place Catherine upon the walls of the city between two battlements, where she would have been exposed
to the whole fire of the Imperial artillery. Bernard Castiglioné even advised in the council a more brutal and horrible
vengeance, that of submitting her to the prostitution and
lust of the soldiery; but these cruel propositions were received with horror, and immediately rejected. Philibert,
prince of Orange, who commanded at that time the army of
Charles the fifth before Florence, aspired to Catherine's
hand; and, although the match was displeasing to Pope
Clement the seventh her uncle, who had already entertained
higher views for his niece, the prince of Orange must have
succeeded in his demand of the princess, if the death of that
illustrious commander, which took place previous to the
surrender of the city, had not liberated the Pontiff, and
left Catherine at liberty to give her hand to another.—
John Stuart, duke of Albany, who had married Anne de
la Tour, sister to the duchess of Urbino, negotiated the
alliance between the young princess and Henry duke of
Orleans, which was consummated at Marseilles with so
much magnificence, in October, 1533.

nor

1559. nor were her attractions fugitive and frail, but accompanied her even into age, and hardly quitted her in the moſt advanced period of life *.

Theſe are only faint and imperfect outlines of a character, which cannot be known by deſcription, but by an attentive conſideration of the hiſtory of her life, and of the part which

* Her complexion was unuſually fine, her eyes large, full of vivacity and fire. She had, when young, a faultleſs ſhape; but grew afterwards large and corpulent. Her head was diſproportionately big; nor could ſhe walk any conſiderable diſtance, without being ſubject to a dizzineſs and ſwimming. The extream ſymmetry and admirable ſhape of her legs, made her take a particular pleaſure in wearing ſilk ſtockings drawn very tight, the uſe of which were firſt introduced in her time; and the deſire of ſhewing them more conſpicuouſly, induced her to change the mode of riding on-horſeback, which was by reſting the feet on a ſmall board, to that of placing one leg upon the pommel of the ſaddle.—Catherine piqued herſelf on the addreſs with which ſhe rode; and tho' by her boldneſs in hunting ſhe once broke her leg, and at another time received ſo ſevere a blow on the head, as to be obliged to undergo the trepan, ſhe continued this exerciſe to her ſixtieth year. Her hands and arms excelled thoſe of any lady of the court, both as to form and whiteneſs.—All habits became her, from the exquiſite taſte with which ſhe adjuſted every ornament to her figure; and her wardrobe was equally varied and ſplendid. Her neck and breaſt were of the moſt matchleſs and dazzling whiteneſs; Brantome ſpeaks of them with enthuſiaſtic praiſe and pleaſure.

ſhe

she took in the interesting events of the three succeeding reigns.

1559. July.

While Henry, mortally wounded, lay expiring, Catherine, though in appearance agitated with the deepest sorrow, yet foreseeing the natural consequence of her son's accession, and reflecting on her present situation, was wholly intent on the consideration of what measures it would be proper for her to embrace in so critical an emergency. Though she dreaded the capacity, the ambition, and the influence of the Guises, yet the Constable Montmorenci was more personally and immediately obnoxious to her. He had lately united himself closely with the duchess de Valentinois; and had likewise started suspicions the most injurious to her honour and nuptial fidelity, by asserting, that of all the children which she had brought the late king her husband, not one resembled him [*].

On

---

[*] Davila, with his usual accuracy, assigns several reasons for Catherine's dislike to the Constable: he had originally endeavoured to induce Henry the second to repudiate her for sterility; and when that cause had ceased by her having children, Montmorenci threw indirect, if not open, reflections on her fidelity to her husband, by declaring, that "of all his children, only Diana, his natural daughter, resembled Henry." Besides these personal and wounding insults, the Constable had uniformly persecuted all the Florentines, who from connexions of blood, or of country, had followed Catherine into France, or who had endeavoured

1559. On the contrary, the princes of Lorrain courted her friendship, and promised her the sacrifice of the late king's mistress, as the cement of their common union. This tempting condition, so grateful to a woman's vengeance, determined the conduct of the queen. Diana, abandoned by the croud of parasites and courtiers who had surrounded her in Henry's reign, underwent in her turn the humiliation of the duchess d'Estampes, and retired immediately from a situation where her presence was grown hateful, and her power become extinct. She passed the remainder of her days at the palace of Anet; and Catherine, satisfied with a political victory, and repressing, from regard to her husband's memory any personal pursuit, permitted her to retain all the splendid presents which she had received from the bounty of her lover, without diminution *.

The

endeavoured to gain promotion in her court. All these mortifications, says Davila, the queen bore in silence during her husband's life, being a most skilful and profound dissembler; but, when released from that subjection, her remembrance and resentment of Montmorenci's treatment, induced her to lend a ready assent to the suggestions and requests of the princes of Lorrain.

* It cannot be denied that the queen acted with the highest magnanimity and clemency on this occasion, as she might have taken a bloody and exemplary revenge on her rival. The Marechal de Tavannes offered to cut off

the

FRANCIS THE SECOND.

The young king, Francis the fecond, who afcended the throne, was only fixteen years and fix months old; and a weaknefs both of body and mind, approaching to debility, incapacitated him even more than his youth, for the conduct of ftate affairs. Governed abfolutely by his mother, and by the two princes of Lorrain, uncles to the queen confort Mary of Scotland, he had neither judgment to direct himfelf, or ability to withftand their advice and fuggeftions.—When therefore the deputies of the parliament waited on him to exprefs their duty and allegiance to his perfon, he informed them that he had thought proper to inveft the duke of Guife and Cardinal of Lorrain with the fupreme

1559.

the duchefs's nofe; but Catherine would not permit it to be done: even the Guifes, though intimately connected with her by marriage, and though principally indebted to her for their elevation and favour, yet were fo bafe as to become her open enemies on Henry the fecond's death.—The Cardinal of Lorrain would have been her bittereft perfecutor, if his brother, the duke of Aumale, who had married Diana's daughter, had not reftrained and reminded him, " That it would render himfelf infa-
" mous, to become the executioner of his own mother-in-
" law."—The Conftable would not defert her, from refpect to the memory of his benefactor Henry the fecond, though folicited to that purpofe.—Diana expreffed her gratitude to the queen, by a prefent of the fuperb palace of Chaumont-fur-Loire, fituated in the midft of thofe lands affigned to Catherine for dowry; and received from her in return the caftle of Chenonceaux, in Touraine.

1559. administration of affairs, assigning to the former the military department, and the finances to the latter *.

The Constable, who early saw this inevitable triumph of his enemies, had announced it to the king

* The instant that the late king Henry the second had breathed his last, the Guises without delay carried the young sovereign, Francis, to the Louvre; and Catherine of Medicis, quitting her husband's body, (contrary to the antient invariable custom of the queens dowager of France, which did not allow them to leave their chamber during forty days, or even to see the sun or moon till the royal obsequies were performed,) followed them immediately.—By this means the duke and Cardinal gained the exclusive possession of the new king's person, and effectually prevented Montmorenci from having any access to him; because, by his office of Constable, he was under a necessity of remaining with the corpse of the deceased sovereign, and superintending his funeral, the ceremony of which lasted three-and-thirty days. When, therefore, after these solemnities were performed, Montmorenci came to express his duty to the young king, Francis, instructed by his uncles the Guises, received the Constable with every demonstration of respect and affection; but, under pretence of sparing his age, permitted him to retire to Chantilli, as a retreat becoming his time of life and infirmities. The Constable yielded to a necessity which he was not able to resist, and quitted the court.—Anthony, king of Navarre had retired from thence, previous to the death of Henry the second; in disgust that by the late treaty of peace, signed with Spain at Cateau en Cambresis, no attention had been paid to his interests, nor any endeavours used to compel Philip the second to restore to him the kingdom of Navarre.—On the very day when

king of Navarre, beseeching him to repair 1559.
immediately to court, and claim the authority to which his rank entitled him as firſt prince of the blood; but Anthony, incapable of any bold and deciſive reſolution, and diſtruſtful of Montmorenci's attachment to him, advanced by ſhort journies, and ſtopt at Vendome. This ill-judged and tardy conduct gave the Guiſes time to confirm their acquiſition, and to ſtrengthen their power. Montmorenci was ordered to retire to his own palace in the country: the Cardinal de Tournon was recalled, and admitted to an oſtenſible aſſociation in the government: Bertrandi, to whom Diana de Poitiers had cauſed the ſeals to be entruſted, was diſmiſſed; and Francis Olivier, a man of probity and honour, was created chancellor.

Meanwhile Anthony, by the inſtigation of his brother the prince of Condé, at length arrived at court. His reception was cold even to indignity: the lodging aſſigned him was unworthy his quality, and he would not have had any, if the Marechal de St. André had

when Henry the ſecond received his wound from Montgomeri's lance, the Conſtable, apprehenſive that it would prove mortal, and conſcious of the neceſſity of Anthony's perſonal appearance, diſpatched a courier to preſs his inſtant departure and arrival at court; but the king of Navarre, who imputed to Montmorenci the dereliction of his rights, ſacrificed by the late peace, refuſed to follow the advice given him, or to profit of it with due celerity.

F 3

1559. not lent him that which he himself occupied. When he was presented to the new king, Francis made the same declaration to him which he had already done to his parliament. Anthony's friends still exhorted him to continue firm, and wait the opportunity of regaining his interest and credit; but the Guises acting on his fears by indirect menaces of the king of Spain's resentment, if he presumed to controvert the queen mother's or her son's choice of ministers; and Catherine, on the other hand, alluring him with a promise of procuring for him the restitution of his ancient kingdom of Navarre, he submitted. After the 21st Sept. ceremony of the coronation of Francis the second, he was sent to conduct the young queen of Spain, Elizabeth, to her husband, Philip the second *.

The new ministers, conscious of the precarious foundation on which their authority rested, and

* The prince of Condé, Coligni, and many others of the Calvinist lords having met Anthony at Vendome, a council was held, to deliberate on the steps requisite to be taken for sharing at least the power of the state with the house of Guise. The prince of Condé and d'Andelot were for the most vigorous and violent measures; but the king of Navarre and the admiral Coligni advised a slow and gentle mode of conduct. This latter opinion prevailed: Anthony was received by the young king in a manner which afforded no hopes of displacing the Guises, or even of participating with them in the government: Francis's answers were cold, ungracious, and harsh; nor did he ever
admit

FRANCIS THE SECOND.

and dreading left some attempt should be made upon it, published an edict, forbidding any one to carry fire-arms, or even to wear any dress favourable to the concealment of such weapons. This order, calculated for their personal safety, and strongly expressive of their fears, was followed by a second, which was dictated by their interest. The king declared, that he would permit no person to hold two posts at the same time. Coligni, who to the high charge of admiral, joined the government of Picardy, resigned chearfully the latter, in the expectation that it would be conferred on the prince of Condé; but the Marechal de Brissac was recalled from his command in Piedmont, and invested with that employment. The Constable reluctantly, and after many delays, laid down his office of grand master of the houshold, bestowed on him by his late sovereign, and was succeeded in it by the duke of Guise.

admit the king of Navarre into his presence, except when the duke of Guise and the Cardinal were with him.—Thus repulsed, Anthony endeavoured to work upon the queen mother; but Catherine, versed in Italian wiles, duped the king of Navarre; and, partly by terror, partly by flattery, induced him to desist from any further remonstrances. He was then dispatched on the empty ceremony of conveying the young queen of Spain to Roncevaux in Navarre, at which place the duke of Alva came at the head of an embassy to receive the princess, and conduct her to Philip the second.

Animated

1559. Animated by an intemperate and sanguinary zeal, the ministers persuaded their weak sovereign that he only adhered to his father's maxims and conduct, in commencing a persecution against the Hugonots. Courts of ecclesiastical judicature, invested with inquisitorial powers, were erected, which took cognizance of heresy; and they were denominated the "Chambres ardentes," from the severity of the punishments which they inflicted. The strictest search was made to discover offenders; crimes of the most improbable and flagitious nature were imputed to them in their nightly assemblies; and a death of ignominy and cruelty was decreed for their adherence to Calvinism. The rigour of the prosecutions was not confined to the capital, but was imitated in the provinces; and this unhappy body of men being forced into resistance, and actuated by despair, began to attempt to defend themselves against their oppressors.

The great number of troops which had been disbanded at the late peace, and the many military adventurers whom the cession of the duchy of Luxembourg and the restitution of Piedmont had left unemployed, afforded the Calvinists the means of raising forces in case of necessity, and was another cause that contributed to the commotions which soon followed. The court, which then resided at Fontainebleau, was crouded with soldiers

soldiers of fortune, who importunately demanded 1559.
some recompence for their services. The Cardinal of Lorrain, to whom they principally addressed their petitions, being unable to satisfy them, and apprehensive of some conspiracy among this multitude, published an edict, by which all persons, who had any favour to ask of the king, were commanded instantly to withdraw themselves, on pain of being hung up on a gibbet, which was expressly erected for that purpose in the forest of Fontainebleau. A proceeding so inhuman and despotic, irritated extremely all those against whom it was directed, and alienated from the duke and Cardinal many brave officers, who were before devotedly attached to the house of Guise.

Francis's health in the mean time, enfeebled by distempers, gave alarming symptoms of decay. A quartan ague, with which he had been indisposed during several months, made him totally unfit for any application to business of state; and when this disorder left him, his face was covered with pustules, which evinced the diseased state of his blood. He was therefore carried to Blois, in hopes of receiving benefit from the change of air, and from the methods usually practised to abate the acrimony of scorbutic habits. A report even prevailed, and was generally believed in the neighbourhood of Blois, that the blood of infants was procured, to make

November.

1559. make him a bath. The same story had been asserted of Louis the eleventh during his last illness, though probably without foundation. From the remedies administered, of whatever kind, the young king however derived some temporary benefit and relief.

Dec. Meanwhile the severities against the professors of the Reformed religion were redoubled at Paris. Anne du Bourg, one of the five members of the parliament, whom Henry the second had committed to the Bastile a few weeks before his death, was brought to his trial, and adhering pertinaciously to his opinions, was 20th Dec. capitally condemned. His execution was hastened by the assassination of the president Minard, one of his judges; to whom he had particularly objected, and who had been zealously active in the seizure and conviction of the Calvinists *. The authors of this crime were never discovered; but Robert Stuart, a native of

* Anne du Bourg was a man of distinguished talents and erudition. The unexpected death of the late king Henry the second had protracted his trial; and as the Elector Palatine, and many other protestant princes of the empire interposed in his behalf, it is probable that his life might have been granted to the requests of such powerful intercessors, if the assassination of Minard had not irritated the commissioners who presided on his trial. This magistrate, returning from the "Palais" to his own house on the 12th of December, about six in the evening, was attacked and

of Scotland, and who was afterwards in the battle of St. Denis where he mortally wounded the Constable Montmorenci, was suspected and seized on that account. He claimed the young queen's protection, to whom he declared himself related by blood; and when Mary disowned his alliance, and would extend no mark of her favour towards him, Stuart found resources in his own firmness and intrepidity: he underwent the most excruciating pains of the torture without making any confession, and was therefore absolved and dismissed.

1559.

Driven to despair by the ill-judged tyranny of their persecutors, and opposing the undaunted spirit of religious conviction to the superior power of their enemies, the Calvinists began secretly to unite for their common preservation. Neither Louis prince of Condé, nor Coligni, though notoriously proselytes to the new opinions, had however as yet declared themselves their chieftains. A gentleman of the province

1560, February.

---

and murdered by three ruffians: Du Bourg was suspected, from some obscure and indirect menaces which he had thrown out against Minard, to have been privy to this attempt; and the supposition tended to accelerate the sentence pronounced, by which he was condemned to be strangled, and his body consumed to ashes. Du Bourg suffered this punishment in the "place du Greve," at Paris, to which he was drawn in a sledge, and put to death at thirty-eight years of age.

of

1560. of Perigord, named John de Bary la Renaudie, was notwithstanding commissioned by the principal persons among them, to collect a number of people under proper leaders, who by different roads should meet at Blois; and, having presented a petition to the king, should seize on the persons of the duke of Guise and Cardinal of Lorrain, as enemies to the kingdom and public tranquillity. The secret was divulged, and information of the conspiracy sent to court from many quarters *. The Guises, warned of the coming storm, took every measure necessary to avert it: Francis was removed from

* Davila and De Thou agree in all the principal and leading features of this memorable conspiracy. La Renaudie was a gentleman of an antient family, brave even to intrepidity, and of a ruined fortune, having been not only cast in a law-suit, but condemned to a severe fine and banishment, for having produced fictitious titles. He retired to Geneva and Lausanne, where he imbibed the doctrines of the Reformation, and became known to a number of French, who had fled into Switzerland to avoid persecution. By these he was regarded as their deliverer; and returning into France, he traversed many provinces of the kingdom under a feigned name. Nantes was appointed for the general rendevous; and the 1st of February 1560 was named by La Renaudie for the time of assembling, as the parliament of Bretagne would be then sitting. Every precaution was there taken to secure the success of this desperate enterprize; the respective destination of the principal conspirators was settled, and the 15th of March appointed for their general union at Blois, where the court then resided.

It

from Blois to the castle of Amboise, as a place 1560. more capable of defence, and immediately issued letters, commanding the prince of Condé's and the admiral's attendance, who obeyed. The duke of Guise's title of lieutenant-general of

> It would seem that the princes of Guise received various tho' obscure intimation, that some insurrection was to be dreaded. Davila says, it came from Germany; and De Thou confirms this opinion. The first authentic detail of the conspiracy was, however, brought to court by Avenelles, a protestant lawyer, at whose house in Paris La Renaudie lodged, and to whom he had divulged this dangerous secret.— Avenelles, from what motive is uncertain, instantly gave information of the plot to Milet, the duke of Guise's secretary, and was by him carried to Blois, from whence the king had already removed to Amboise ; but the Cardinal of Lorrain not having instantly followed the court, Avenelles revealed to him every circumstance of the conspiracy. It is not only probable, but almost certain, that had the enterprize been successful, it was intended to seize, and possibly to put the Guises to death, as enemies to the kingdom ; and to declare the prince of Condé regent or administrator, granting at the same time a compleat toleration of the Reformed religion. These facts must be admitted ; but it is at least as indisputable, that the attempt was never extended to the person of the king, or of any of the royal family, as calumny pretended, with intent to render the Hugonots odious. Davila avows this truth, though he mentions the conspiracy with detestation : De Thou even goes further, and assures us, that the chiefs concerned in the enterprize only meant to liberate the kingdom from the tyranny of the house of Guise ; and that they even bound themselves by oath to defend the king and royal family with their lives and fortunes, against every attempt contrary to the laws.

the

1560. the kingdom, was confirmed; bodies of foldiery were ftationed on all the furrounding roads; and a company of mufqueteers, mounted on horfeback, was raifed to guard the perfon of the king.

15th March. Notwithftanding thefe judicious and neceffary precautions, the confpirators, marching in fmall bands, and only during the night, appeared unexpectedly at the gates of Amboife. The Cardinal of Lorrain, terrified at the approach of danger, betrayed the timidity which was natural to him; but his brother the duke inftantly prepared to meet it with becoming courage. His cool difcernment appeared confpicuoufly in this hour of trial; and he inftantly affembled the guards, the nobility, and the inhabitants. Sufpecting the prince of Condé, the duke committed to him the poft of one of the gates to defend; but took care to affociate with him the grand-prior, one of his own brothers, who watched all the prince's movements, and prevented him from lending the moft indirect affiftance to the enemy.

The Calvinifts were all difperfed, taken, or cut in pieces. La Renaudie, with a few defperate affociates, was met in the foreft of Chateau-Renaud by the Baron de Pardaillan, at the head of two hundred cavalry. He defended himfelf, notwithftanding the difparity of numbers, with a bravery heightened by defpair; but

but his followers being almost all slain, and no chance remaining either of victory or retreat, he spurred his horse up to Pardaillan, and thrusting a poniard through his vizor, laid him dead upon the ground. He himself fell soon after by a ball from a harquebusse; and his body being brought to Amboise, was hung during some hours on a gallows erected upon the bridge across the Loire.—All the inferior conspirators were treated with the same ignominy; their bodies were dragged at the tails of the horses, and afterwards placed on iron hooks round the walls of the castle, booted, and dressed as they fell in the field [*].

Some clemency might yet have been extended towards the chiefs. Olivier, the Chancellor, advised lenient and conciliating measures; even the Guises were in suspence whether to pardon or to punish; when a new, but unsuccessful attempt to surprise the town, (which was made by

[*] La Renaudie, though he found that the court had quitted Blois, and retired for protection to the castle of Amboise, which, from situation as well as from art might resist an attack, yet determined to proceed. Lignieres, one of the principal leaders in the conspiracy, having however betrayed his associates, and given the most exact information of the time and roads by which the different bands were to arrive, the Marechal de St. André and the duke of Nemours were sent out to intercept, and cut them in pieces. The baron de Castelnau, at the head of a considerable body of his followers, being invested in the castle of

1560. by La Mothe and Coqueville, two of the principal confpirators, who were not difmayed by the ill fuccefs of their friends,) gave a loofe to the utmoft feverity. All who were taken in arms, even though on their return home, were put to death; and a number not lefs than twelve hundred expired under the hands of the executioner. The ftreets of Amboife ran with blood; the Loire was covered with floating carcafes; and all the open places were crowded with gibbets, on which hung thefe unhappy wretches, who infected the air with a peftilential fmell.

The principal leaders were the laft who were led out to death. The queen-mother, with her three young fons, and all the principal ladies of the court, beheld this horrid fpectacle from the windows of the caftle, as a diverfion. Two of them, under the agony of the torture, accufed the

of Noifai by the duke of Nemours, furrendered on promife of life for himfelf and his affociates; but this capitulation was difregarded and violated. La Renaudie, who had received information of the danger in which Caftelnau ftood, endeavoured to arrive in time for his relief; but was met by Pardaillan in the woods near Amboife. After a brave, though ineffectual refiftance, the Calvinifts were routed; and La Renaudie, after having killed Pardaillan, was fhot through the thigh by that officer's page, and died fighting defperately to the laft. His troops were almoft all put to death upon the fpot. La Renaudie's body was hung upon a gibbet, with a label affixed to it, containing the words "Chef des Rebelles;" and his quarters were afterwards expofed on ftakes in the environs of Amboife.

prince

prince of Condé as their accomplice; but the Baron de Caftelnau, being confronted with them, denied it ftrongly, and in the moment before his head was fevered from his body, continued to affert the prince's innocence *.

1560.

Some fufpicions ftill remaining againft him, notwithftanding this depofition in his favour, he demanded permiffion to clear himfelf in full council before the king; and Catherine, ever endeavouring to hold the balance between the contending factions, as the line of conduct moft beneficial to her own interefts, granted his requeft.

The

---

* La Bigne, who was fecretary to La Renaudie, being put to the queftion, only afferted that it was commonly believed the prince of Condé would have put himfelf at the head of the confpirators, if the enterprize had been accompanied with fuccefs. This accufation, if fuch it could be properly termed, was confirmed by Raunay and Mazere, two of the leaders, previous to their execution; but the Baron de Caftelnau peremptorily contradicted their depofition.—This nobleman was of the moft amiable and honourable character, infinitely beloved by the whole court, and of a family which had done diftinguifhed fervices to the ftate. The ftrongeft entreaties were ufed to fave his life: Coligny, d'Andelot, and even the duke d'Aumale, though brother to the duke of Guife, yet interceded for his pardon.—The queen-mother inclined to clemency, and wifhed to fpare him; but Francis, inftigated by the two princes of Lorrain, was inexorable. Caftelnau fubmitted to the fentence of death with perfect compofure; but when the crime for which he fuffered was ftated to be that of high treafon, he burft into the moft indignant complaints:—

"If,"

1560. The prince, with that intrepidity which distinguished all his actions, vindicated his honour from the imputations cast upon it; and, after having given the lye to whoever should dare to maintain or assert the charge against him, he offered to engage with his accuser in single combat, as the most convincing proof of his adversary's falsehood. The Cardinal of Lorrain, who clearly saw at whom this defiance was levelled, made a sign to the young monarch to rise without reply; but his brother the duke, concealing his indignation under the mask of friendship, praised with warmth the prince's conduct, and offered himself to be his second, against whatever antagonist. Yet in private, it was his

"If," said he to his judges, "it be declared treason to have taken up arms against strangers who have violated the laws, and usurped the sovereign authority, let them be proclaimed kings!" Villemongey, one of the principal conspirators, being conducted to the scaffold, which was already covered with the bodies of his friends who had suffered, imbrued his hand in their blood, and holding it up to Heaven, "Behold!" exclaimed he, "righteous Judge, the innocent blood of those who have fought thy cause! thou wilt not leave their death unrevenged." The royal family, and all the ladies of the court were present at these affecting and inhuman spectacles. Only the duchess of Guise, Anne d'Esté (who was daughter of Reneë of France, the youngest child of Louis the XIIth) retired to her apartment to lament these executions, which she had vainly deprecated. The duchess, as well as her mother, were suspected of an adherence to the doctrines of the Reformation.

advice

advice to arrest the prince; but the queen-mother, who foresaw the annihilation of her own power by such an act, opposed and prevented its execution.

1560.

The Chancellor Olivier died at this time, of grief and horror excited by the cruel and sanguinary scenes to which he had been a witness *.

30th Mar.

---

* Olivier rose under the protection of Margaret queen of Navarre, and sister of Francis the first, to whom he had been Chancellor; and he was raised to the same high dignity by Francis the first himself in 1545. While he held this office, his integrity, firmness, and love of his country, rendered him beloved by all France. Henry the second deprived him of the seals on his accession to the throne, which were entrusted to Bertrandi, a man devoted to the duchess de Valentinois. Soon after the time when Olivier was recalled, and reinvested with his office under Francis the second, the emperor Ferdinand the first sent the bishop of Trent into France, to demand the restitution of Metz, Toul, and Verdun, which Henry the second had retained by the peace of Cateau, and which had been dismembered from the empire. Ferdinand chose the opportunity of a weak and tumultuous reign, such as that of Francis, in which to claim these fiefs; and he had besides commissioned the bishop his embassador to bribe such of the lords of the council as might be inimical to his demand. The chancellor, aware of Ferdinand's intentions, and vigilant to counteract them, opened the debate, and declared that it was incumbent to take off the head of that person who should dare to propose so pernicious and traiterous a measure, as the surrender of the cities and districts reclaimed by the emperor. This bold and honest declaration intimidated and overawed those who might otherwise have been for such a step, and preserved these valuable acquisitions to the crown of France.

1560. He was succeeded by Michael de l'Hopital, an able minister, and devoted to the queen-mother. His advice, though always temperate and judicious, yet confirmed her in that system of temporizing and intricate policy, and in those arts of division and disunion, which mark her character. She trembled left the Guises should obtain a complete victory over the princes of the blood, and therefore secretly supported Condé and the Hugonots. An assembly of the nobility was summoned with this view at Fontainbleau, whither the young king was carried; and to which came the Constable Montmorenci, Coligni, and a numerous train of followers. It was held in Catherine's own cabinet, Francis himself being present. The admiral advancing, threw himself on his knees before his sovereign, and presented him a petition unsigned, in which a toleration was demanded for the professors of the reformed religion; adding, that though no names were affixed to it, yet whenever his majesty should be pleased to signify his pleasure, it would be instantly subscribed by an hundred and fifty thousand persons. The Cardinal of Lorrain opposed the indulgence requested by Coligni, with that impetuous and commanding eloquence by which he was distinguished; and expressions of so much asperity passed between the princes of Lorrain and the admiral, as to oblige Francis to impose silence on the two parties. No decisive resolution was taken; but

20th Aug.

the states were ordered to assemble in the month of December ensuing, and a national council was proposed, in hopes of finally adjusting these religious differences.

1560.

Neither the king of Navarre nor prince of Condé were present at this conference, they having previously retired into Guyenne, where they were engaged in concerting measures to dispossess the Guises of their power and offices. The person whom Anthony employed as his confidant and messenger, named La Sague, having imprudently communicated the commission with which he was charged, to one of his friends named Bonval, this man betrayed the trust reposed in him, and gave information of La Sague's errand. He was immediately seized at Estampes, by order of the queen-mother, on his return into Gascony, together with a number of letters which he carried. The terror of the torture induced him to confess the method of discovering their contents; and those of Francis de Vendome, Vidame of Chartres, a personal enemy of the duke of Guise, were regarded as peculiarly criminal. He was one of the most brave and gallant lords of the court, and had even been so particularly acceptable to, and favoured by Catherine, as to give rise to suspicions very injurious to her honour*. As he was how-

Septem.

ever

---

* The protestant writers, who detested Catherine of Medicis, have not failed to accuse her of gallantries, among

her

1560. ever now become equally an object of her hatred, she caused him to be carried to the Bastile; and he was transferred some time after to the palace of the Tournelles, where he died either of chagrin, or of the consequences of his debaucheries.

Bouchard, Chancellor to the king of Navarre being likewise seized, and actuated by the same timidity as La Sague, accused the prince of Condé of having endeavour'd to seduce his brother to engage in treasonable practices. Notwithstanding this act of undisguised hostility on the part of the court, Anthony and Louis, after long irresolution and many delays, finally embraced the dangerous resolution of attending the states which were convoked at Orleans. Francis himself, quitting Fontainbleau on account of the danger to which his person was exposed in so defenceless a place, removed to the

---

her other faults and crimes. Jurieu particularly names the duke of Nemours, the Vidame of Chartres, and the Marquis de Mescouet, as her lovers; and declares her to have been criminally intimate with all these noblemen. Impartial justice must, however, acquit her from such imputations. Ambition, not love, was her predominant passion; and her conduct towards Mademoiselle de Limeuil, when seduced by the prince of Condé, of which I shall have occasion to speak particularly hereafter, was very opposite to any such libertinism.—Mezerai, and Le Laboureur, only blame her love of pleasures, without any reflections on her honour, which are certainly to be distrusted as false aspersions.

palace

palace of St. Germain. His health was even in 1560. ſo precarious and declining a ſtate, as to induce the Guiſes to order public prayers for its reſtoration; but as it was neceſſary for him to open the deliberations of the ſtates in perſon, the young king proceeded towards Orleans, eſcorted by a thouſand horſe, and accompanied by the queen-mother, and Charles duke of Orleans, his brother. He entered that city in a 18th Oct. ſort of military pomp, to which the nation had been little accuſtomed, and which had more the appearance of a conqueror triumphing over rebels, than of a king ſcarcely yet attained to manhood, and who could neither have forfeited or alienated the affections of his people.

Meanwhile the princes of Bourbon ſet out to attend the aſſembly of the ſtates: their friends adviſed them to appear well armed, and well accompanied; but the mandate which the Guiſes iſſued in the king's name, forbidding them to bring any other followers than thoſe of their own houſehold, together with the confidence which they repoſed in their own high rank, and relation to the royal blood, made them deſpiſe and neglect theſe ſalutary precautions*. Various informa-

---

* Davila, the great directing hiſtorian of theſe times, beautifully lays open the artifices which the Guiſes uſed to draw the two brothers into the ſnare. Louis, ſays he, conſcious that his co-operation in the late conſpiracies and commotions

1560. informations and intimations of a very alarming nature met them on their way towards Orleans. They were assured that Francis and his mother, hurried on by the impetuous counsels of the duke of Guise and the Cardinal, had been either induced or compelled to adopt the most sanguinary measures; but the two princes, notwith-

commotions might be ascertained from the papers and persons lately seized, peremptorily refused to trust himself in the power of his enemies: but Anthony, either more innocent, or more credulous, and deeming it impossible that an Italian woman and two strangers would venture to arrest and capitally punish the first princes of the blood, inclined to attend the states. While they fluctuated in this state of uncertainty, the Count de Crussol and the Marechal de St. André were dispatched by the young king, to induce them by the strongest assurances of amity not to delay their journey; but Condé still remained firm in his first determination. This report being made by the Count de Crussol on his return to court, the Marechal de Termes was sent into Gascony, and ordered to levy a body of troops, which might invest them in Bearn, where they were unprepared for their defence. At the same time, the queen-mother, ever effecting her schemes by dissimulation, prevailed on Charles, Cardinal of Bourbon, brother to Anthony and Louis, to add his entreaties to her own, and assured him of the good intentions of Francis. The Cardinal, credulous and relying on Catherine's assurances, instantly left Orleans, and proceeded to Bearn, where he implored the two princes his brothers no longer to refuse their obedience to the repeated orders of their sovereign. These united efforts were at length successful: the princes reluctantly left Pau, and with a slender train proceeded towards Orleans.

standing

standing thefe advices, continued their journey *. On their arrival at Orleans, they entered the royal prefence and faluted the king, who gave them a cold and ungracious reception. The inftant of their departure, two captains of the guard took them into cuftody. Anthony was only carefully watched; but the prince of Condé was committed clofe prifoner to a houfe erected purpofely in a public

---

* The king of Navarre confiding in his innocence, and trufting likewife to his high rank, refufed feven hundred gentlemen of Poiƈtou the permiffion to accompany him to Orleans, and forbad above fifteen hundred others, who had prepared to attend and efcort his perfon. Marillac, archbifhop of Vienne, confcious of the danger into which the two princes of Bourbon were precipitating themfelves, gave them the moft authentic information of the intentions of their enemies; but they difregarded all admonition.

As they advanced towards Orleans, their retreat was cut off by troops, who occupied the provinces behind them through which they muft have returned into Bearn; and no fooner had the court received certain advice of their being on the territory of France, than, as if that act had ferved as a fignal for taking off the mafk, Grollot, Bailiff of Orleans, who was fufpected of holding a correfpondence with Anthony, was committed to cuftody.

At Poitiers, Montpezat, the governor fhut the gates of that city againft the princes; but, on their inftantly fufpending their journey, and complaining of this infult by a meffenger whom they difpatched to court, the Marechal de Termes was fent to excufe it in the king's name, and they were received in triumph into Poitiers. Termes having executed this commiffion, followed them at fome diftance with a body of cavalry, to obferve their motions, till their final entry into Orleans.

square,

1560. square, and which was defended by some pieces of cannon *.

The

* The Marechal de Brissac first proposed in council to arrest the prince of Condé; and Francis signed the order, which was reluctantly countersigned by de l'Hopital, the Chancellor.

"I saw the two brothers Anthony and Louis," says Brantome, "when they arrived: the king of Navarre entered the court of the palace on horseback; the prince, on foot. Never did I see a man exhibit a more bold and fearless mien than did the latter; but on his return, when arrested, he appeared covered with astonishment. Anthony, who had thought to disconcert and terrify his enemies by his threats and appearance at court, was not less confounded and amazed."

Davila has related with equal accuracy and minuteness all the principal circumstances which preceded and attended the arrest of the two princes: they are too authentic and interesting to be omitted.—"When they entered the city of Orleans," says he, "they found all the streets lined with soldiers, thro' whom they passed to the king's lodging; but, the gate being shut, and only the wicket left open, the two princes were compelled to dismount and enter on foot. Scarce any of the persons whom they met, saluted them; and on being conducted into the royal presence, they found the young king seated between the duke of Guise and the Cardinal of Lorrain, surrounded by the captains of the guard. Francis received them with coldness, and then conducted them himself to the apartment of the queen-mother, the Guises not following: Catherine, with her accustomed dissimulation, and to preserve the appearance of impartiality, treated the princes with every demonstration of affection, mixed with sadness, and even shed tears on the occasion; but Francis, with looks of resentment, and in terms of

"reproach,

The admiral Coligni was in Orleans at this 1560.
time; but d'Andelot his brother, more cir-

" reproach, arraigned the prince of Condé, accused him
" of attempting to seize on the principal cities of his do-
" minions, and even of having plotted against his life,
" and that of his brothers. Condé, not in the least dis-
" mayed, boldly denied the accusation, and said that he
" would make his own innocence and the calumny of his
" enemies apparent to the whole world. ' To ascertain
" the truth,' answered Francis, ' it is necessary to pro-
" ceed by the usual modes of justice:' and instantly quit-
" ting the room, gave orders to the captains of the guard
" to arrest the prince of Condé.

" Catherine, affecting on this memorable occasion the
" utmost sympathy and concern, endeavoured to soothe the
" two princes, though she had previously consented to the
" act of seizing on Condé; who suffered himself to be led
" away, only venting his reproaches on himself for hav-
" ing been so deluded by the good faith and credulity of
" the Cardinal his brother, as to venture himself in the
" power of his enemies. Anthony remained with the queen-
" mother, who threw the whole odium of the prince's arrest
" on the duke of Guise, and endeavoured to remove all
" participation in it from herself. After a long conversa-
" tion, the king of Navarre was conducted to an apartment
" prepared for him in a house adjoining to the palace in
" which Francis resided; and where, tho' he was permitted
" the liberty of conversation, he was in every other respect
" a prisoner."

Philip de Maillé Brezé, and Chavigni, captains of the body guard arrested the prince of Condé; he was then led to a tower of brick, erected for the purpose, and on which were mounted some pieces of cannon. Iron bars were fixed to the windows; and the door was closed up, only an opening being left in it by which to convey to him provisions and necessaries.

cumspect,

cumspect, and foreseeing the danger, had retired into Bretagne.—Magdalen de Roye, mother to the princess of Condé, was arrested at her own house of Anici in Picardy, by Tannegui de Carrouge, who sent her prisoner to the castle of St. Germain; and Grollot, bailiff of Orleans, had been already taken into custody.

The Chancellor, and five judges, who were appointed to interrogate the prince, waited on him in prison for that purpose. In no degree dismayed by the violence exercised against him, he refused to plead before such a tribunal; and demanded a public trial by the whole parliament, peers, and king, to which he was entitled by his high dignity. This spirited and intrepid behaviour did not however disconcert his enemies, or delay the proceedings against him, which were continued without interruption. He stood on the brink of destruction; while the Guises, already anticipating the fall of this powerful rival, and intoxicated with their own success, observed scarce any deference towards the queen-mother whom they secretly suspected, and whom they intended to divest of all influence or authority.—Catherine saw the error which she had committed, in uniting herself with the princes of Lorrain against Anthony and Louis; but it was too late to retract, and the

evil

FRANCIS THE SECOND.

evil was beyond a cure *. The condemnation 1560. and execution of Grollot were univerfally regarded as preparatory to that of the prince of Condé; when an unexpected and great event, big with the moſt important confequences, averted the blow, and fnatched him from the impending deſtruction.

The king, to avoid being prefent at Grol- 17th Nov. lot's execution, had gone out to the chace. On his return from that diverfion he was at-

* The duke of Guife and the Cardinal of Lorrain publicly boafted, fays Davila, that " at two blows only " they would cut off the heads of herefy and rebellion." Permiſſion was refufed the prince of Condé to fee either his wife or brothers; but he was allowed to write to them. Anthony would, in all probability, have been involved in the fate of his brother, as the princes of Guife muſt naturally have dreaded the revenge due to the execution of Condé. The 25th of November was regarded as the day fixed on for that melancholy fpectacle, and his death feemed equally imminent and inevitable. Davila draws a mafterly and ſtriking picture of the queen-mother's conduct during the time of the prince of Condé's trial and imprifonment. She anxioufly defired to appear innocent of the crime, to which fhe had notwithſtanding previoufly confented: fhe wore a face of forrow and diſtreſs: fhe continually fent for the admiral Coligni and his brother the Cardinal de Chatillon, on pretence of finding fome expedient to extricate the king of Navarre, and the prince of Condé: fhe even fent the duchefs of Montpenfier to Anthony, with kind and condoling meſſages. " So exquifitely," adds Davila, " did " fhe diffemble, that even thofe who knew her beſt, yet " hefitated in pronouncing whether fhe was fincere or not " in her affectation of concern."

tacked

1560. tacked with a heaviness in his head, which at the end of some days was followed by a suppuration, and an imposthume in his ear*. The symptoms did not at first appear mortal, or alarming; but the Guises apprehensive of the event, and dreading lest their prey should escape, pushed on the trial of the prince with an unprecedented and indecent haste. The customary forms, observed in capital cases were omitted, and he was at last condemned to lose his head.

The Chancellor, ever averse to the violent measures pursued, and seeing that Francis's complaints assumed every hour a more dangerous appearance, artfully delayed affixing his signature to the order for the prince's execution. Yet among all the nobles and great personages with which the court was crowded, (so despotic was the influence of the princes of Lorrain, and so servile the devotion paid them) only the Count de Sancerre had the courage to refuse ab-

* Davila says that "Francis being under his barber's "hands, was suddenly seized with an apoplectic or faint-"ing fit, and that his attendants immediately laid him on "the couch without signs of life. His senses returned "after some time; but it was evident from the na-"ture of the attack, and the effects which it left, that "he could not long survive." De Thou calls it an abscess which the king had in his head, and which beginning to suppurate thro' his ear, was attended with the most fatal symptoms. Mezerai speaks of it in similar terms; but adds, that during the first five or six days it was not regarded as mortal, or even dangerous.

solutely

folutely to fign it, though three repeated orders 1560. of the king were brought him for that purpofe. Whether Francis himfelf had affixed to it his fign manual or not, is a fecret of ftate never divulged, and on which hiftorians differ.

In the mean time the phyficians, from the nature of the fymptoms which they obferved in the young king, and a gangrene which had begun to manifeft itfelf, declared him near his end. The Guifes, confcious of the critical fituation in which their daring conduct had involved them, and believing that their own perfonal fafety was infeparably connected with a fteady adherence to the principles which they had hitherto purfued, remained firm in their determination to put the prince of Condé to death. Placing their confidence only in the profecution of this meafure, they even endeavoured to induce Catherine to join them in arrefting the king of Navarre, and conducting him to a fimilar fate; but fhe, too wife to be rendered fubfervient to their ambitious purpofes, and emancipated by the profpect of Francis's death from the tyranny which they had exercifed over her, refufed to confent to, or to permit of fo fanguinary a proceeding*. She faw herfelf exactly

in

---

* Monfieur de Thou exprefsly afferts that previous to the young king's attack on the 17th of November, the Guifes, apprehenfive that if Anthony was left alive, he

would

1560: in that situation to which she had long aspired. The approaching minority left the regency open

would revenge the prince of Condé's death, took the decisive resolution of causing him to be assassinated. Their consciousness of being the objects of the public hatred for their despotism and tyranny, confirmed them in this desperate and criminal purpose, which was absolutely debated, and finally settled in a secret council. The misguided king, who was to be made the instrument of so foul and base an assassination, committed in the person of the first prince of the royal blood, consented to it; and it was agreed on, that he should command the attendance of Anthony in his own cabinet, the Guises being present, where, feigning to have discovered new proofs of his treasonable practices, he should reproach the king of Navarre in the severest manner. As they naturally imagined that this latter prince would reply in terms of warmth and generous indignation, they meant to take advantage of that circumstance, and to dispatch him in the confusion, under pretence of his having threatened Francis's life. Anthony received information of this barbarous project from some of the adherents of the Guises themselves: he was at first undecided what conduct to hold; but reflecting that he was absolutely in the power of the Guises, who could effect their purpose in any way which they chose, he boldly resolved to prepare himself for the worst, and to dispute his life with his own sword, if attacked. In this perilous and awful moment, he called to him Reinsy, one of his gentlemen; "If they kill me," said he, "carry my shirt all bloody, to my wife and son! "They will read in my blood what they ought to do to "revenge it."

' Anthony then entered the apartment where the young king Francis the second was seated, and approaching him, kissed his hand with profound submission. Softened

by

open to her ambition, while both parties paid her the moſt aſſiduous court, as to the common arbitreſs of their lives and fortunes. In the anticipation of her ſon's death, ſhe took with the moſt cool perſpicuity and maſterly addreſs, the neceſſary precautions for ſecuring to herſelf the firſt place in the government under Charles, the immediate heir to the crown, and who was only ten years and five months old. Anthony promiſed in writing to cede to her the regency, which belonged to

by this behaviour, and affected by the preſence of Anthony, the king changed his reſolution, and omitted to give the ſign previouſly ſettled, at which the ſurrounding attendants were to fall upon the king of Navarre. It is pretended, adds De Thou, that the duke of Guiſe, finding his project abortive, exclaim'd with a voice full of indignation, "Oh! le timide et lache enfant!"

This ſtory, which powerfully arreſts the imagination, conveys an aſtoniſhing idea of the daring and criminal lengths to which the princes of Guiſe carried their projects of vengeance and aggrandizement. We cannot wonder at the irreſolution of a prince of ſeventeen years of age, refuſing to ſtain the majeſty of the throne with ſo atrocious a deed of blood; but we are loſt in aſtoniſhment at the unprecedented boldneſs of the perſons who could dare to propoſe to their ſovereign ſo flagitious and unmanly an aſſaſſination. Though Davila does not relate this anecdote, yet he expreſsly aſſerts that both before the king's attack of illneſs, and at the time when his death was regarded as imminent and certain, the Guiſes implored the queenmother to put the king of Navarre to death before Francis's eyes were cloſed.

1560. him of right, as first prince of the blood; and the Guises swore to serve her in every manner, for and against whomever she commanded *.

Amid these intrigues and cabals, Francis the second breathed his last, on the eighteenth day

* De Thou and Davila perfectly coincide in their account of Catherine's conduct during the last hours of her son Francis's life. The Guises urged her to put both the princes Anthony and Louis to death, as the only certain means of securing the regency to herself, and providing for the tranquillity of the new reign. The duchess of Montpensier opposed this sanguinary advice, and represented to the queen-mother, that by following it she would confirm the power of the princes of Lorrain, and become their slave, instead of their arbitress. Catherine hesitated long between these different lines of conduct, endeavouring to gain time, giving out that there were yet great hopes of the young king's recovery, and intending eventually to conform to circumstances. De l'Hopital, the chancellor, confirmed her in this system of procrastination; and at last, when the symptoms of Francis's disorder appeared to indicate his imminent and inevitable dissolution, he strongly advised the queen to spare both the princes of Bourbon, and even to enter into a private negotiation with the king of Navarre. In pursuance of this salutary counsel, Catherine dispatched the prince-Dauphin of Auvergne, son to the duchess of Montpensier, to bring the king of Navarre privately in the night, to her own chamber: they there conferred together; and after the queen had again disclaimed all participation in the trial and intended execution of the prince of Condé, she assured Anthony of her desire to join with him to repress the exorbitant power of the house of Guise. This interview and compact took place only a few hours before the death of Francis the second.

from

from his seizure, and aged only seventeen years 1560. ten months and a half, of which he had reigned 5th Dec. about a year and five months *.

We know not with certainty what qualities he possessed, or might have discovered, if he had attained to manhood; but his capacity appears to have been very mean and weak, and his bodily infirmities encreased these mental defects. Some French historians have absurdly given him the epithet of "The king without vice." Voltaire has drawn

* The critical nature of Francis's death, so opportune for the preservation of the prince of Condé, and so fortunate to Catherine of Medicis whom the Guises had deprived of all influence, gave rise to reports of poison. "Le La-"boureur," and several other writers, have accused Ambrose Paré the king's surgeon, and a Scotch valet de chambre who was a Hugonot, with having poisoned Francis's night-cap exactly at the place which answered to, and covered the imposthume in his ear; but De Thou, infinitely more worthy of credit, denies and disproves this assertion. That historian expresly attributes his death to the weakness of his constitution, and to hereditary maladies derived from his mother.

Davila seems to incline likewise to the belief that he died a natural death, yet mentions the opinion generally received of his having been poisoned. "The young "king," says he, "had always been troubled with pains "and defluxions in his head, from his infancy. An im-"posthume formed itself over his right ear; and that "bursting, so great a quantity of matter fell into his "throat, that it stopped up the passage, and prevented "him either from speaking, or receiving any sort of
H 2 " nourishment.

1560. drawn his portrait more spiritedly and more justly, in his Henriade.

> "Foible enfant, qui de Guise adorait les caprices,
> "Et dont on ignorait les vertus et les vices."

His continence has been made the subject of encomium; but to the feeble state of his health and early youth, this virtue may be chiefly attributed; besides that his attachment to his confort Mary was extreme, and both her beauty and accomplishments such, as to challenge the warmest homage of the heart.

Francis's funeral was indecently neglected, ambition and intrigue occupying the whole court. Catherine, who had been ostentatiously magnificent in the obsequies of her husband, was equally remiss in those of her son; while the Guises, on whom he had heaped so many fa-

---

"nourishment.—Most people," continues Davila, "believed at the time, that his barber had conveyed poison into his ear; and it was even reported, that the physicians had discovered evident signs of the fact. The sudden nature of Francis's seizure, and the extraordinary crisis in which he expired, would have given universal credit to the accusation, even among men of the best understandings, if the disorder which terminated his life had not been known to have grown up with him from his cradle."

After the testimonies of these two last historians, we cannot hesitate to believe the king's death natural, and almost inevitable, from his hereditary weakness and complaints.

vours, and to whom he had confided such unlimited power, by a conduct which marked them with the basest ingratitude, did not shew him this last and slender token of respect. They excused themselves, under the frivolous pretext, of remaining to console the young queen, their niece; but in reality with intent, by their presence and authority, to controul and over-awe their enemies.

Among so many lords and bishops who were assembled at Orleans, only Sansac and La Brosse, who had been Francis's governors, and Guillard bishop of Senlis, who was blind, followed his corpse to St. Denis. Upon the cloth which covered his coffin, a billet was found, containing this severe and pointed sarcasm, " Tanne- " guy du Chatel, où es tu?" It alluded to the funeral rites of Charles the seventh: Du Chatel had been that monarch's favourite and chamberlain, but was afterwards banished from court. On Charles's death he instantly returned, and as a mark of his gratitude and affection to a master whom he had loved, was said to have buried him at his own private expence, with a royal magnificence.

Francis the second left no issue, legitimate or illegitimate, and the crown descended to Charles his brother.——Mary, queen of France and Scotland, makes no figure in her husband's reign. Subservient to, and awed by the daring genius

1560. genius of her uncles, the princes of Lorrain, she performed only an inferior part. They made use of her charms and influence over the young king, to bend him to their wishes and measures. In a court of such gallantry, where her beauty was adored, she could not however escape some malignant and false reflections on her character; but they do not deserve to be mentioned, and much less to be refuted.

The Constable Montmorenci, who had been repeatedly ordered to appear at Orleans, but whose distrust and caution rendered him slow, hastened his march on the news of the king's death [*]. He arrived on the third day after that event, accompanied by six hundred horse; and making use of the authority which his high charge conferr'd, he drove the guards from the gates of the city; threatening to hang

---

[*] Davila, usually so exact, and on whose authority we may rely with an almost implicit faith, expresly asserts, "That the prince of Condé was condemned to be beheaded "before the royal palace, previous to Francis the second's "seizure; and that the execution of the sentence was only "delayed, in hopes to draw Montmorenci and his sons "into the net, and to involve the king of Navarre in the "same common destruction." So that the Constable's delays were chiefly instrumental to Condé's preservation. It is impossible not to be amazed at the bold and nearly successful plan of the duke of Guise and cardinal of Lorrain, thus at one blow to cut off by a solemn and public trial, two princes of the blood, and the first officer of the crown.

them

them up, if they kept the king invested in full peace, and in the centre of his kingdom *.

Meanwhile, the prince of Condé escaped amidst these unexpected changes, Francis's death having unloosed his fetters. With a magnanimity and courage becoming himself, he notwithstanding refused to quit his prison, till he knew who had been his prosecutors and accusers; but no person dared to avow himself as such. The Guises declared that every step had been taken by the late king's express and particular command; but they did not produce the royal order, in consequence of which measures

so

---

* Davila says, that Montmorenci suspected the intentions of the Guises to such a degree, that no invitations or artifices could allure him to venture himself in their power. He returned from Paris to Chantilli, under pretence of the gout; and when he began his journey a second time, he purposely delayed his progress, on the plea of his advanced age and infirmities.

His sons pressing him to hasten to court, and assuring him that the Guises and the queen-mother would equally dread offending him; he replied, that " those in whose power the " government then was vested, would act as they pleased; " that the states could not be assembled without some cause; " and that a little time would unfold all these dark and " mysterious proceedings."

Nothing could have been more artful and masterly, than the address which the queen-mother exerted, in flattering and gaining the Constable, whom she termed the arbitrator and moderator of all things. Loyalty to his sovereigns, and

1560. so violent had been pursued. Thirteen days afterwards the prince quitted Orleans, accompanied as a mark of honour, by those very soldiers who had served as his guard, and retired first to Ham in Picardy, and thence to La Fere, both which places belonged to his brother Anthony, king of Navarre.

unshaken allegiance to the throne, were the leading features of Montmorenci's character, on which Catherine relied.—When he arrived at the palace, where the young king (Charles the ninth) resided, at Orleans, he did homage to his new sovereign with tears in his eyes, and exhorted him not to be disturbed at the present commotions, since he himself, and all good Frenchmen, were ready to lay down their lives for the preservation of the crown and kingdom. Catherine then entered into a long conversation with him; and by those blandishments of which she was so compleat a mistress, worked upon his feelings of public spirit and regard to the interests of the state, till the Constable, won to her purposes, consented to be the common mediator between the princes of Bourbon and the Guises. Catherine secured by this means the regency for herself, and attached Montmorenci to her son, independent of either of the two great factions.

CHAPTER

CHARLES THE NINTH.

CHAPTER THE TENTH.

Reflections on the situation of affairs at the accession of Charles the ninth.—Catherine of Medecis secures to herself the regency.—Formation of the " Triumvirate."—Pernicious policy of the regent. — Assembly of the states. — Massacre of Vassy.—Duplicity of Catherine.—The young king carried to Paris by Anthony king of Navarre.— Commencement of the civil wars.—Prince of Condé declared chief of the Hugonots.—Vain attempts to produce an accommodation.—Siege of Rouen.—Death of the king of Navarre.—Battle of Dreux.—Consequences of that action.— Siege of Orleans.—Assassination of the duke of Guise.—Account of the circumstances attending it.—His funeral, and Character.—Conclusion of Peace.—Death of La Cipierre.—Character of the marechal de Retz.—The prince of Conde's amours, and second marriage. — Charles the ninth attains to majority. — Administration of Catherine.—Interview of Bayonne.—Commencement of the second civil war.—Ineffectual enterprize of Meaux.—Battle of St. Denis.—Death of the Constable Montmorenci.—Circumstances of
that

that event. — Character of the young king. — Second pacification.

1560.
Dec.

THE circumstances in which Charles the ninth succeeded to the crown, were such as seemed to indicate the future tempests which shook his throne; nor do the annals of any nation present us with a reign producing events of a more calamitous nature. Religion, a sacred name, but prostituted to the purposes of interest or policy, served as an ostensible pretext to cover the ambition, and the other real causes, which conspired to involve the unhappy kingdom in all the horrors of civil war.—An historian of sensibility cannot even relate these disastrous circumstances, without feeling the utmost commiseration and distress. That inveterate animosity, that sanguinary spirit, which ever characterises theological disputes, actuated and inflamed the whole community. All the provinces became in turn the theatre of war and rapine; while the dreadful night of St. Bartholomew, stained with blood, and veiled in darkness, completes the mournful picture. An event which stands unparalleled in the history of mankind, and which must impress with horror, in ages the most remote!

The young king Charles the ninth, who ascended the throne in this critical and perilous juncture, was as yet of an age too tender to

interfere

interfere perſonally in the adminiſtration of affairs, and could not, during many years, extend any effectual or permanent redreſs to the accumulated evils of the ſtate. Catherine of Medecis, only anxious to lengthen the term of her ſon's minority, and of her own regency; ever intent on projects for the enlargement and the continuance of that authority with which ſhe was inveſted, ſowed diviſion and diſcord among the principal nobility. Oppoſing, with Italian refinement, one party to another, negligent of the public tranquillity, and ſolely attentive to her own private intereſts, ſhe ſacrificed every conſideration to her thirſt of power. Even the feelings of a parent could ſet no bounds to this tyrannic paſſion; and Charles, tho' her own ſon, yet from the moment that he conceived the deſire of reigning without her aid, was regarded by her as the moſt inveterate enemy. As yet however ſhe had not this event to dread, Francis the ſecond's premature end having placed her in the firſt poſt of government. The ſtates, aſſembled at Orleans, were opened with a ſpeech from the chancellor de l'Hopital, in which he exhorted them to toleration, unanimity, and an oblivion of paſt diſſentions. Counſels the moſt wiſe and ſalutary, but unhappily impracticable amid the furious zeal of contending parties!

- Some attempts were made while the ſtates were ſitting, to deprive the queen-mother of
the

1560.

13 Dec.

1560. the regency, which she had assumed by a sort of political violence; but the weakness of Anthony king of Navarre, and her own address, soon extinguished all appearance of opposition. She then dissolved the assembly, whose deliberations she feared might tend to diminish the prerogatives of the crown; and convoked them to meet anew at Poissy in the month of May ensuing.

1561. The court having retired to Fontainbleau, February. Louis prince of Condé repaired thither with a slender train. Desirous of justifying himself from the imputations cast upon him in the late reign, he demanded permission to prove his innocence before the king, which was granted; the Chancellor pronounced him guiltless of the crimes laid to his charge, and he was re-admitted to his seat in council.

Unaffected by the elevation of their enemies, and the unexpected reverse of fortune which had befallen them, the princes of Lorrain still maintained their ground. Equally supporting, and supported by the ancient religion, they yet preserved a prodigious influence, and spread terror among their opponents. In vain did the king of Navarre, though invested with the title of lieutenant-general, and though aided by the Constable and the Colignis, attempt to humble, and compel the duke of Guise to relinquish a part of his authority, as grand master of the houshold: Anthony was himself reduced,

duced, after an ineffectual ſtruggle, to renounce his pretenſions.

1561.

Juſtly alarmed at ſo powerful a combination between the princes of the blood, Montmorenci and his nephews, the regent exerted herſelf to diſſolve a confederacy, which ſhe feared might affix limits to her own power. The Conſtable was long uncertain and irreſolute which party he ſhould join. His eldeſt ſon Francis, Marechal de Montmorenci, eſteemed one of the moſt prudent lords of the kingdom, and cloſely connected with the Hugonot party, endeavoured to retain his father on that ſide; but Henry d'Amville, his ſecond ſon, and Magdalen of Savoy, Montmorenci's own wife, were attached to the oppoſite faction *. Catherine, regardleſs of the engines which ſhe made ſubſervient to her meaſures, and anxious to ſucceed by whatever means, recalled Diana de Poitiers again to court, and ordered her to try her powers of perſuaſion upon the Conſtable. She ſucceeded: he declared at length in favour of the Guiſes; and

a private

* Henry, ſecond ſon of the Conſtable Montmorenci, and the favourite of his father, was early diſtinguiſhed by his courage, and roſe after the extinction of the houſe of Valois, under Henry the fourth, to the dignity of Conſtable of France. He was one of the moſt accompliſhed noblemen of the courts of Henry the ſecond and Francis the ſecond; and after the death of the laſt of thoſe princes, he followed Mary, queen dowager of France and queen of Scotland,

when

1561. a private union of interests was established between the duke, the Marechal de St. André, and himself, which obtained the name of " the Triumvirate *."

15th May. The ceremony of Charles's coronation, which these intrigues and disputes had hitherto delayed, was at length performed at Rheims, with
the

when she returned into her own dominions. He was tenderly attached to her; and Mary was so sensible to his passion, that it was believed had he been at liberty, she would have married him; but d'Amville had been already married in 1558 to Antoinette de la Marck, grand-daughter of the celebrated duchess de Valentinois. His elder brother Francis dying without issue, Henry succeeded in 1579 to the possessions and titles of the house of Montmorenci. By Louisa de Budos, his second wife, he was father to Henry, last duke of Montmorenci, equally amiable and unfortunate, who was put to death at Toulouse by the cardinal de Richlieu, after the combat of Castelnaudari, in 1632.

* This was the last public act of the celebrated duchess of Valentinois; and she again retired, after this proof of her influence over Montmorenci, to the castle of Anet. She survived it about five years, and at length died, in the sixty-seventh year of her age, on the 26th of April, 1566. Her body reposes under a marble mausoleum, in the centre of the choir of the great chapel of Anet, which she had herself constructed. She was the most extraordinary instance of beauty and powers of pleasing, preserved even in the winter of life, which occurs in modern history; unless Ninon de l'Enclos may be supposed to form an exception.
—It was by no means the intention of the queen-mother, in detaching the Constable from Anthony king of Navarre and his own nephews the Colignis, to force him to so strict a
union

the accustomed magnificence. This splendid pageantry could not however in any degree heal the wounds of the state; and Catherine's ambiguous conduct, which tended to spread universal jealousy and distrust, encreased and irritated the public disorders. Fearful that she might be oppressed by the superior power of the three great united lords, and incapable of detaching them from their new confederacy, she attempted to balance their political weight by another of equal importance. In consequence of this determination, she immediately made proposals to the king of Navarre, for establishing a more close and intimate alliance between them, which might conduce to their common support. Anthony gladly embraced these offers; but while, in compliance with her promises to him, she affected to protect and favour the reformed religion, she secretly prevailed on the Constable to complain of those very innovations. Not sufficiently powerful to annihilate and compress by force the numerous parties,

---

union with the house of Guise and the Marechal de St. André. She had hoped to attach Montmorenci to herself and to the young king her son, independantly of either of the great factions; but she was deceived in this expectation. The union of "the Triumvirate" was studiously concealed from Catherine, who dreaded and trembled at that powerful combination.—Davila and De Thou equally agree in their account of the principal facts respecting this transaction.

she

1561. she substituted cunning and artifice in its stead; but her abilities, though great, and equal to almost every undertaking, yet fell short of this purpose. After having fomented the sparks of civil discord, she vainly flattered herself that she could extinguish them at pleasure, or direct their fury; they blazed to the destruction of her son, and to the ruin of his kingdom.

A feigned reconciliation took place about this time between the duke of Guise and the prince of Condé; after which they embraced in the royal presence, and made professions of the most sincere and cordial amity*. The king of Na-

* Mezerai says, that the Constable was the author of this pretended reconciliation; because, conceiving it unbecoming his own honour openly to ally himself with the duke of Guise, while the prince of Condé was that nobleman's enemy, he requested of the queen-mother to undertake the accommodation of their differences.

The young king in consequence commanded their attendance at St. Germain-en-Laye, where the court then resided, and ordered them mutually to forget their past animosities. The duke of Guise protested that he had not advised the imprisonment of the prince of Condé; who replied, that "whosoever was the person from whom that advice " came, he regarded him as a villain and a traitor." The duke answered that he was equally of that opinion, and that the prince's observation no way affected him. This scene having been acted, they embraced; and the king enjoined them to observe in future a strict and cordial friendship. Catherine then invited them both to a magnificent entertainment, which she gave as a testimony of her satisfaction at this auspicious event.

varre,

varre, in the assembly of the states, was again so weak as to renounce his claim to the regency. Catharine, who intimately knew the human heart, who ever addressed herself to its passions, and conquered by flattering its propensities, had enslaved Anthony by a new allurement, peculiarly calculated to retain him in her obedience. Mademoiselle du Rouet, one of the most beautiful maids of honour in her train, served as an instrument to fascinate the easy prince; and her ascendency over a temper yielding, voluptuous, and indolent, was only extinguished with his life.

1561.

The states meanwhile were opened with great solemnity at St. Germain; the young king, though only ten years of age, seated on his throne, with the queen-mother, and his sister the princess Margaret on his left hand, being present at the debates. As the admiral Coligni had been principally instrumental in prevailing upon the king of Navarre not to contest the regent's power, she in return avowedly patronised the Calvinistical doctrines and followers. This pretended partiality, which was the result not of conviction, but of the most profound political hypocrisy, was equally displayed by Catherine at the disputation of Poissy; a vain attempt made to reconcile the religious differences, and in which the Cardinal of Lorrain on one side, and Theodore Beza on the other, declaimed with equal violence

August.

Sept.

1561. violence and eloquence, in defence of their respective tenets.

Dec.

Disgusted at the loss of their credit, as well as at the preference shewn to the Hugonots, and covering their dissatisfaction at Catherine's conduct under the pretext of attachment to their religion, "the Triumvirate" quitted the court. Still however, attentive to their great political interests, they exerted every artifice which might win the king of Navarre, and bring him over to their party.—The Guises first proposed to him a divorce from his wife Jane d'Albret queen of Navarre, and his marriage with their niece, the young queen dowager, Mary of Scotland. Finding that from attachment to his son Henry, prince of Bearn, he disapproved and rejected this offer, they pretended to have received promises from Philip the second of Spain, of ceding to him the island of Sardinia, in compensation for the kingdom of Navarre. Anthony, deceived by this ideal advantage, at length united himself to his natural enemies, and became the dupe of their artifices, in contradiction to his honour and real interests *.

The

---

* It is to Davila alone that we can have recourse, amid this chaos of opposite and continually shifting measures, for any clear or certain explication of the sources, from which sprung the different actions related.—According to that great historian, who appears to have traced beyond any other writer,

the

The voluntary retreat of "the Triumvirate" 1562.
having left the prince of Condé and Coligni un- January.
disputed

the silent workings of the heart, Anthony's change of conduct is not to be attributed, in any degree, either to religious or to patriotic motives. Interest, ambition, and rivalship, were his sole directing principles; to which indolence, and a pacific temper, added strength. His partiality to the Calvinistical tenets had been shaken at the dispute of Poissy, from the little agreement which he found in the ministers of that persuasion on the articles of belief, and their reasons of dissension from the Romish church. He was offended with the behaviour of the admiral Coligni, who affected, and attempted to govern him in every particular; but above all, he was stung with the preference given to his brother among the Reformers. The prince of Condé's open detestation of the Guises; his personal courage, and his avowed protection of the Hugonots, had made him in reality the hero of the party. The king of Navarre's interests were likewise very different, as he was the first prince of the blood, and might entertain no very distant or chimerical hopes of the crown. All these reasons account for his confederacy with the Guises.—De Thou, though he does not analyze with equal accuracy and perspicuity the motives to Anthony's conduct, yet accounts for it upon similar principles. He adds, that Manriquez, the Spanish ambassador, instructed by his court to deceive the king of Navarre with false promises and expectations, effected his purpose by flattering or corrupting the two favourites of that prince, Lenoncourt, bishop of Auxerre, and d'Escars. They engaged to endeavour to induce him to declare himself protector of the Catholic religion in France; in return for which Philip was to put him in possession of the kingdoms of Sardinia and Tunis. Anthony was completely deceived by these flattering prospects, and entered into the closest union with "the Triumvirate."—Jane d'Albret, his wife,

1562. disputed masters of the court, Catherine issued a new edict, highly favourable to the Hugonots. She even affected to regulate her measures by their advice, and shewed them every mark of perfect confidence; but these encouraging appearances were only calculated to deceive, and were followed by the most dreadful convulsions. The queen had favoured the Calvinist party merely from her apprehensions of the tyranny of the king of Navarre and " the Triumvirate;" who, though they seemed to have quitted the court, waited only for an opportunity to resume their authority. Condé and Coligni foresaw the storm; they knew the queen's duplicity, and prepared to ward off the dangers with which they were menaced. Anticipating the hostilities which they conceived to be imminent and inevitable, they applied to the Protestant princes of the Germanic empire, and received from them assurances of support.

Meanwhile the duke of Guise, at the pressing instances of his friends, and peculiarly of Anthony king of Navarre, set out on his return to court; when a fatal accident which happened on the way, hastened the rupture between

---

no sooner found that he had abandoned the party and religion of the Calvinists, than she immediately withdrew from court, carrying with her Henry and Catherine her children, and retired into Bearn, where she educated them in the doctrines of the Reformation.

the

the two factions, and began the bloody quarrel. While he ſtopt at the little town of Vaſſy in Champagne, and was employed in hearing maſs, a crowd of Calviniſts, aſſembled in a barn, interrupted and diſturbed his devotions by their hymns. A diſpute ariſing among the duke's domeſtics and the Hugonots, he ran eagerly himſelf to prevent it; but in this attempt he received a blow upon the cheek with a ſtone; and his attendants ſeeing his face bloody, drew their ſwords, and killed above fifty, beſides near two hundred others, who were wounded in the fray *.

1562.

1 Mar.

The prince of Condé, who had accompanied the young king and court to the palace of Monceaux

---

* If we may credit Davila, the duke of Guiſe had no intention to injure or moleſt the Hugonots, while occupied in an act of their religion; and the account which he gives of this unfortunate maſſacre, inclines us to imagine that the duke regretted, and exerted every endeavour to prevent the ſcene of blood which took place. He was on his way from Joinville to Paris, accompanied by his brother the Cardinal, a train of gentlemen, and an eſcort of two hundred lances, when the unuſual noiſe of bells, as he paſſed through the village of Vaſſy, incited the pages and lacqueys to advance, partly from curioſity, and partly from deriſion, to the ſpot from whence the ringing proceeded. A congregation of Calviniſts being there aſſembled, and hearing that their great enemy the duke of Guiſe was in the town, ſome of them began the diſpute by throwing ſtones at his attendants; who inſtantly betook themſelves to their arms, and a dangerous quarrel

ceaux near Meaux, having immediately demanded juſtice and reparation for the maſſacre, Catherine,

quarrel enſued. The duke no ſooner received intelligence of it, than ſpurring his horſe into the crowd, he reprehended his followers, and entreated of the Hugonots to retire; when a blow from a ſtone, which ſtruck him on the left cheek, and which cauſed a confiderable effuſion of blood, compelled him to quit the place. His attendants, irritated at the wound which their lord had received, attacked the houſe into which the Hugonots had retreated for ſecurity, killed above ſixty of them, and ſeverely wounded the miniſter, who eſcaped by climbing over the tiles into one of the adjoining houſes. When it was over, the duke ſummoned the magiſtrate of the place into his preſence, and ſeverely reprimanded him for permitting theſe licentious and illegal aſſemblies of the people. On his attempting to juſtify himſelf, by pleading the royal edict lately iſſued in favour of the Calviniſts, the duke laid his hand on his ſword, and replied angrily, " This ſhall " ſoon cut the bond of that edict, though never ſo ſtrong."

De Thou's narration of the maſſacre of Vaſſy, differs in ſome material circumſtances from that of Davila; peculiarly in that leading feature of it, which exculpates the attendants of the duke of Guiſe.—De Thou, on the contrary, charges them expreſsly with having commenced the fray, by riding up, and inſulting the Hugonots, who were aſſembled at their devotions, with every injurious and opprobrious epithet; but he allows that the duke himſelf exerted every poſſible endeavour, though unfortunately to no purpoſe, to ſtop the fury of his followers and ſervants. He draws a very affecting picture of the unhappy wretches who were victims on this occaſion to the merciless rage of the duke's attendants: women and children, who made the air echo with their cries, were ſhot at, till none remained alive to ſatiate their vengeance. The miniſter, named Leonard Morel, was wounded,

as

rine, distressed at this peremptory requisition, promised ample satisfaction to the prince. She issued an order to the king of Navarre, commanding him to provide for the safety of her son and of the kingdom; enjoined the duke of Guise to repair instantly to her, unattended; and commanded the Marechal de St. André to set out without delay for his government of Lyons. Not one of the three obeyed her mandate. Anthony repulsed the Hugonot deputies with threats, who were sent to lay before him their

as were two hundred others, and sixty were killed upon the spot.

De Thou seems to impute in some degree this inhuman carnage to the duchess dowager of Guise, Antoinette de Bourbon, mother of the duke and cardinal; whose residence being in the neighbourhood of Vassy, she had frequently complained to her son the duke, of the meetings of the Calvinists so near her castle, and had requested him to deliver her from such a scandal.—Very different, adds this great historian, was the conduct of the young duchess of Guise, Anne d'Esté, who had derived from her mother Renée, daughter to Louis the twelfth, a partiality towards the Calvinists. She followed the duke her husband in a litter; and hearing the cries of the unhappy people, she instantly apprehended the cause of it, and dispatched a messenger to her husband, to implore mercy for the Hugonots. The duke had already rode up to the spot, and was exerting himself to terminate the quarrel, when the wound which he received on his cheek gave an immediate loose to the violence of his attendants.——These are the principal circumstances of this unfortunate massacre, from whence we may date the origin of the civil wars.

complaints:

1562. complaints: the duke of Guife replied, that he had no leifure to come yet to court, being otherwife employed: and St. André, more infolent, informed her majefty to her face, that in the prefent critical fituation of affairs, he could not abandon the perfon of his fovereign.

The duke of Guife arrived foon after at Paris, attended by twelve hundred horfe. Terrified by his approach, and dreading left he fhould, in conjunction with the other confederates, deprive her of the fupreme management of affairs, the queen took a ftep the moft pernicious, and productive of future calamities. She wrote to the prince of Condé, who had retired to his own houfe, recommending to him, in terms fo touching and pathetic, herfelf, the kingdom, and her fon, adding, that the combined nobles held her in captivity; that fhe gave him the moft plaufible and juft pretence to arm his affociates. He availed himfelf of thefe letters to excufe his proceedings; but being as yet too feeble to oppofe enemies fo numerous and powerful, he withdrew a fecond time to his feat of La Fertè-Aucou, near Meaux.

March. The queen meanwhile, accompanied by the Chancellor, had carried the young king to Fontainbleau. She beheld the awful picture of a civil war in full view, which her own ambiguous and interefted policy, directed only to preferve the authority of regent, had greatly conduced to accelerate;

rate; and she would yet most willingly have averted by any means whatever, so deplorable a calamity. Her own interests made her wish to prevent the effusion of blood; and, conscious that her junction with either party must be the signal of open hostility, she still anxiously hoped to remain in a state of neutrality, and to hold the balance; but this middle line of conduct was become impracticable. The duke of Guise, with a prodigious train, calculated to inspire terror, having arrived at Fontainbleau, Catherine again summoned the prince of Condé secretly to her assistance. She vainly flattered herself that his presence would restore her to freedom, and render her the common arbitress; but the evil genius of France had decreed otherwise, and all her schemes became abortive.

The prince appeared immediately in arms, and passed the river Seine at St. Cloud, in his way to join her. Though his forces were too few to terrify the confederate lords, they instantly availed themselves of the occasion to render themselves masters of the king's person, which act of violence they pretended was necessary, to prevent his falling into the hands of the Hugonots. The king of Navarre brought the regent this melancholy intelligence, and Catherine hesitating, Anthony informed her that he was come to conduct his sovereign to Paris, where he would be in safety; adding with a sort of brutality, that

" if

"if she did not chuse to accompany him, she might remain alone." He even allowed her no time to deliberate upon this important and decisive measure. Charles himself, too young to oppose the violence offered him, turned towards his mother, as if to know her sentiments: she dared not utter a word; and the young king, bursting into tears of impotent resentment and indignation, suffered himself to be conducted weeping to Melun, and from thence to the capital*. No

* Davila has given the most satisfactory and interesting detail of Catherine's conduct during this whole transaction. It is beyond a doubt, that she yielded to a force which she was unable to resist; and that she exerted every artifice to induce the king of Navarre and "the Triumvirate" to leave herself and the young king at liberty. She even used so many powerful arguments to incline them to permit her to remain at Fontainbleau, where the court would at least have had the appearance of being free, that the king of Navarre and the Constable were on the point of yielding to her entreaties, if the duke of Guise had not dissuaded them from any such compliance.

De Thou says, that in a council which was held by " the Triumvirs," the Marechal de St. André proceeded to such lengths of violence, as to propose to throw the queen-mother into the Seine, if she should dare to oppose or impede the journey to Paris. He adds, that Catherine had prepared a boat, in which she meant to carry off her son Charles the ninth during the night, previous to their departure from Fontainbleau; but that she found it impossible to deceive the vigilance of Montmorenci.—"The queen mother," says Davila, "perceiving it in vain to attempt any resistance to the peremptory requisition of the Catholic lords and of Anthony,

CHARLES THE NINTH.

No alternative, except open war, remained to the prince of Condé. Deceived as he apprehended, by the queen, and seeing his enemies in poffeffion of the king's perfon, he deemed it too late to retract, or even to fufpend his enterprize. Setting off therefore with the utmoft expedition for Orleans, accompanied by two thoufand cavalry, he rendered himfelf mafter of the city, after a vigorous oppofition *.

1562.

2 April.

Confcious

---

thony, inftantly refolved to yield with grace; and mounting on horfeback with the king and her two younger fons, being furrounded by " the Triumvirate" and their attendants, reached Melun that night; from whence they proceeded on the following day to the Bois de Vincennes, and arrived on the third day at Paris." The young king, continues Davila, was feen by many to weep on that occafion, being confcious that he was treated as a prifoner; the regent, perplexed in mind, forefeeing a civil war, and finding all her projects overthrown, fpoke not a word, but obferved a gloomy filence; while the duke of Guife, regardlefs of the king's tears, or of the queen-mother's diftrefs, was heard publicly to fay, that " the good is always good, whether it pro-
" ceed from love, or from force."——Thefe are the moft interefting circumftances of that memorable tranfaction.

* Louis, prince of Condé, was only at a fmall diftance from the court, when intimation arrived of the Catholics having carried Charles the ninth to Paris. Aftonifhed at this intelligence, the prince checked his horfe, and remained a confiderable time motionlefs, and filent. He perceived the critical fituation in which he ftood, while all the troubles and difafters of the future war rofe before his imagination. He had not yet paffed the Rubicon.—As he revolved in his mind

thefe

1562. Conscious that the measure which he had embraced was decisive and irretrievable, he proceeded to form regulations for the military and civil conduct of his followers; and as in war only his future safety could be found, he neglected no precautions becoming a general, to ensure success. He was proclaimed chief of the party by unanimous consent; the pretext for their having taken up arms, was declared to be the release of the king and his mother from the captivity in which they were held by " the Triumvirate ;" and he immediately dispatched mes-

these considerations, Coligni, who had been behind, overtook him, and they conferred together some minutes. At length, the prince seemed to have taken his ultimate resolution; and after a deep sigh exclaimed, " Affairs are arrived at " that pass, that it is necessary for us to drink, or to be " drowned!" So saying, he proceeded instantly towards Orleans, at the head of near 3000 horse; and as d'Andelot, Coligni's brother, had already attempted to render himself master of that city, in which endeavour he was vigorously opposed by Montcreau the governor, the alarm was communicated for many miles by the incessant firing, and ringing of the bells. Condé redoubled his haste, on hearing these proofs of the attack made by d'Andelot, and galloped at full speed till he reached the gates of Orleans, where he arrived at a most critical moment, as d'Andelot, overpowered by numbers, was on the point of retreating without success. The unexpected arrival of the prince at the head of such a body of cavalry, decided the fortune of the day, and rendered him master of Orleans.——It is Davila who relates these particulars of the commencement of the civil war.

sengers

fengers to the German princes, requesting their aid in the great caufe of religion. 1562.

This conduct was the fignal of revolt and fedition throughout the whole kingdom. The Hugonots, excited by their leader's example, having expelled in many places the Catholics, the cities of Rouen, Blois, Poitiers, Tours, and Lyons, fell into their hands; but their ungovernable zeal carried them every where to the moft violent and fanguinary exceffes. Animated with the frenzy commonly characteriftic of new and oppreffed fects, they refpected no places or profeffions, however facred; while the prince of Condé in vain attempted to reftrain thefe licentious practices, as he was neither heard nor obeyed amid the fury of religious animofity.

The Chancellor de l'Hopital, who alone in this tumultuous and melancholy period, preferved a calm and equal temper, yet laboured to avert the tempeft. He beheld France ready to be plunged into a civil war, heightened by every circumftance of mutual hatred, and inveterate antipathy. He felt for his bleeding country a parent's and a patriot's fenfations, and he prevailed on the queen to exert her endeavours for an accommodation *. Catherine wifhed

it

---

* Davila and De Thou perfectly coincide on this point, and affert, that the Chancellor exerted every poffible endeavour to prevent and avert a civil war. When the king of Navarre

1562. it with equal ardour, though from motives of a far inferior nature. She saw the prince of Condé already in poffeffion of half the kingdom; fhe dreaded left the confederates fhould imitate the precedent, and the king be finally left between the two factions, without places, revenue, or dominions.

Stimulated by confiderations fo forcible to an ambitious mind, fhe undertook the arduous tafk of conciliating the rival parties. Not difcouraged by ill fuccefs, and confcious of her own talents in negotiation, fhe made repeated and mafterly attempts to detach the prince of Condé from Coligni and the Hugonots. More than once, her addrefs and perfuafions had nearly proved fuccefsful: fhe allured him by the moft feducing propofals, promifed that " the Trium-

Navarre and " the Triumvirate " had fecured the perfon of Charles the ninth by bringing him to Paris, they fummoned a council at the palace of the Louvre, where the duke of Guife propofed to declare war with the prince of Condé and the Hugonots. De l'Hopital oppofed this violent meafure very ftrongly; and the Conftable having faid, that the queftion in agitation was not of the refort of perfons of the long robe, the Chancellor replied, that " if he and his " profeffion were not acquainted with the art of making " war, they at leaft perfectly well knew under what cir" cumftances it could be made with equity."—In confequence of this upright and fpirited anfwer, the Chancellor was excluded from the further deliberations of the council of ftate, and the moft violent refolutions were embraced in that affembly.

virate "

virate" should quit the court, and a general freedom of religious sentiment and worship be granted to his followers. An interview even took place between the prince and the queen-mother, at Toury near Orleans; and though unsuccefsful in its effect, Catherine still continued her efforts to produce an accommodation*. Acting in person, and not through the medium of delegates; mistress of all the winning arts which enslave the human mind; ever attacking the heart and its favourite propensities, she at length engaged him to give his word that he would quit the kingdom, if his enemies confented to relinquish the administration. "The Triumvirs," from whom she had previously obtained a promise to that effect, instantly performed

1562.

June.

---

* The queen-mother, by the mediation and endeavours of the bishop of Valence, having induced the prince of Condé to agree to a conference at Toury, a small place about ten leagues from Orleans, they met on the day appointed. The king of Navarre accompanied Catherine, and each party was escorted by thirty-six horsemen; Henry d'Amville commanding the escort of the queen, and the count de la Rochefoucauld that of the prince. To prevent any quarrel, the two bands were stationed at eight hundred paces from the town, and they remained more than half an hour in their respective posts; but gradually approaching, they at length joined, and embracing with warmth, they mutually lamented the hard destiny which thus armed them against each other, and which pointed their weapons against themselves. A more affecting spectacle,

1562. performed it, and retired to Chateau-Dun. Catherine having therefore summoned the prince to the observance of his agreement, he affected to obey; and a second interview took place between them at Talsy, only six miles distant from either camp, where Condé made his feigned submissions to Charles and the queen. But Coligni, who reposed no confidence in her honour, and who beheld the Hugonots in the most extreme peril if their chieftain abandoned them, by his remonstrances and representations, broke this treaty, which was on the point of being accomplished, and led him back to his expecting partizans *.

27 June.

The

cle, or one more calculated to display the fatal spirit and effects of civil discord, history scarce ever has commemorated. Meanwhile Catherine, the king of Navarre, and the prince of Condé held a conference of two hours, during which the queen affected the greatest concern at her inability to comply with Condé's demands. Anthony, on the contrary, treated his brother with severity, and rejected all his propositions for peace with the utmost asperity. The interview terminated ineffectually, and only served to exasperate the two princes of Bourbon against each other. De Thou is very minute in his relation of all the circumstances of this interview: Davila is more succinct in his account of it, nor does he seem to have known or apprehended, that the king of Navarre was present at, and a party in the private conversation which took place between Catherine and the prince of Condé.

* Nothing can be more evident, than that neither " the Triumvirate," or the Hugonot lords sincerely meant to
terminate

The war, so long suspended by the queen's 1562.
negotiations, now began in all its fury: the
duke of Guise and the Constable being sent
for in great haste, returned to the camp, and
the royal army, in which was the queen and her
son Charles the ninth, after having taken July and
Blois, Tours, and Bourges, which were aban- August.
doned to plunder, laid siege to Rouen. Mont- 27 Sept.
gomeri, whose fatal tournament with Henry
the second has rendered him so famous in the
annals

terminate their differences by an accommodation. Davila, who is very exact and diffuse in his delineation of the principles of conduct in each party, expressly asserts, that the whole plan was concerted between the prince of Condé and Coligni, previous to the visit made by the former to the queen-mother and the king, at Talsy. Nor do " the Triumvirs" appear to have been at all more sincere in their affected renunciation of power, and voluntary secession from court; for, tho' they quitted the army, and left the person of the sovereign free, yet they only removed to Chateau-Dun, five leagues from the royal camp, where they remained, with intent to watch the prince's conduct. Catherine had previously obtained a promise subscribed by Condé, in which he engaged to quit the kingdom, provided that " the Triumvirate " likewise retired from court, and laid down their authority. This engagement, into which he had imprudently entered, on a presumption that his enemies never would accede to, or fulfil their part of the conditions, had so far committed the prince of Condé, that it was impossible for him to refuse to venture his person by paying his duty to the young king, and to the queen-mother. He accordingly went, accompanied with a very slender escort, to Talsy, where, as the court had only the ordinary guards,

Vol. II.   K   he

1562. annals of France, commanded in it, and made a most vigorous defence. Honourable terms were offered him repeatedly, which he as frequently refused. The queen, by the Chancellor's entreaties, thrice prevented the duke of Guise from storming the place; but as the besieged rejected obstinately every proposal of an accommodation, it was at length permitted *. The city

he was under no apprehension of being detained by violence. A scene of mutual duplicity then took place, the queen urging the prince to leave the kingdom, at least for a short time; and he procrastinating and postponing any final determination. While this illusory negotiation was performing, Coligni, and the other great Hugonot chiefs arrived, as pre-concerted, under pretence of paying their respects to the king; and affecting indignation at the prince's too easy concessions, hurried him away by violence, mounted him on horseback, and carried him back to their own camp.——De Thou agrees with Davila in most of these particulars, which, however, he relates in a manner less unfavourable to the prince of Condé and his party.

* Among the many great qualities which Catherine of Medécis possessed, and which are rarely found in women, was her courage: it approached to the noblest heroism. During the siege of Rouen, she went every day to the fort St. Catherine, where the most bloody attacks were made; the duke of Guise and the Constable remonstrating with her on the danger to which she exposed her person, "Why," answered she, "should I spare myself more than you? Is it that I have less interest in the event, or less courage? True, I have not your force of body, but I have equal resolution of mind!"—What grandeur of sentiment, had it been guided by principles of virtue! The soldiers gave her the title of "Mater Castrorum," in imitation of the Romans.

was

was carried by assault, and the pillage lasted two days without intermission. Montgomeri, with a few desperate attendants, and a party of English whom Elizabeth had sent to his aid, escaped in a boat upon the Seine, and broke the chains which were stretched across the river at Caudebec.

1562.

26 Oct.

Anthony king of Navarre met with his death at this siege; he was wounded in the trenches, by a ball from a harquebuſſe, in the shoulder, on the day intended for the assault. His emulation of the duke of Guise, and his own personal courage, carried him ever into the most dangerous situations. When the city was taken, tho' much indispos'd, he caused himself to be carried by his Switzers through the breach, in a litter. The wound did not at first assume a mortal appearance; but his fondness for Mademoiselle du Rouet, one of the maids of honour to the queen-mother, and the pleasures in which he imprudently indulged himself with her, threw his blood into a violent agitation, and brought on a fever. The uneasiness of his mind inducing him to embark upon the Seine, for the village of St. Maur near Paris, he was seized with a shivering and cold sweats, which announced his approaching end. The boat in which he had embarked, stopping at Andely, he soon after breathed his last, at forty-two years of age. That irresolution which distinguished him through life, equally accom-

15 Oct.

17 Nov.

1562. panied him in the article of death: he received the sacrament after the forms of the Roman Catholic communion; but his dying professions evinced his attachment to the Reformed religion. He ordered those who were around his bed, to carry his strictest injunctions to Jane queen of Navarre, on no account to trust either herself or her children at court; to be ever upon her guard; and to fortify her places*.

While

---

* Davila's account of Anthony's wound, and the circumstances of his decease, is somewhat different from that of most other historians.—" The king of Navarre," says he, " had
" gone out to reconnoitre the breach, when he received a
" musket-ball in his shoulder, which breaking the bone,
" and tearing the nerves, he dropped down upon the spot
" as dead. This accident obliged the commanders to de-
" lay the assault; the soldiers and attendants bore him to
" his tent, and the surgeons immediately dressed his wound,
" in presence of the young king, his mother, and all the
" generals. It was their unanimous opinion that he could
" not live, on account of the great size of the orifice, and
" the depth which the ball had entered." He makes no mention of Mademoiselle du Rouet; but says, " That the
" king of Navarre not being able to support the extreme
" and violent pain which he underwent, was resolute, not-
" withstanding the remonstrances and entreaties of his phy-
" sicians, to go up the Seine to St. Maur, whither he was
" accustomed frequently to retire, on account of the pu-
" rity and salubrity of the air. His brother the cardinal
" of Bourbon, the prince of La Roche-sur-Yonne, Louis
" Gonzaga, and several other persons Catholic and Hugo-
" not, accompanied him; but he was scarcely arrived at
" Andely,

While success attended on the royal troops before Rouen, the kingdom became a scene of desolation,

" Andely, when his fever, which the motion of his journey
" had irritated, encreasing, he became delirious, and soon
" after expired."—Davila mentions his varying religious belief, even in the article of death. He ever speaks of Anthony in terms of approbation, mixed with compassion; and says, that he was not calculated for the tempestuous scenes in which he was compelled to act a part. His candour, sincerity, and gentleness were ill adapted to the universal dissimulation and fury, which characterised his associates in power. Davila adds, that his death happened at a time when experience had so ripened and matured his judgment, that it would probably have produced events widely different from the ideas preconceived of him.

Brantome says, that he was of a fine stature, and much superior in personal dignity and appearance, to any other prince of the house of Bourbon: He confirms Anthony's uncertainty and fluctuation between the two religions. — De Thou describes very circumstantially every particular respecting the progress of his wound. The ball had pierced too deep into the king of Navarre's shoulder, to be found or extracted, tho' the surgeons made repeated incisions and attempts for that purpose. The flesh returned in great quantity, and closed up the orifice: he appeared, however, to be on his recovery, when on a sudden he was seized with a violent fever. New operations being performed, in order to cut away the flesh which had grown over the wound, a quantity of matter was found to have formed, the discharge of which weakened, without giving him relief. He continued, notwithstanding, adds De Thou, to flatter himself with the hope of a speedy recovery: he fed his imagination with the delusive prospect of possessing the island of Sardinia, which Philip the second had always held out as a bait

1562. defolation, rapine, and blood through all the provinces; the contending parties, inflamed with civil and religious rage, being equally guilty of the moſt barbarous exceſſes. A mi-

bait to delude this eaſy prince. Entertainments and play occupied his time; and he kept conſtantly by his bedſide a young lady, maid of honour to the queen, whom he paſſionately loved, and whom Catherine had intentionally placed about him, to ſerve as her inſtrument in governing the king of Navarre.—His two phyſicians, Vincent Lauro, and La Meziere, were of different religious perſuaſions, and each endeavoured to influence the dying prince's mind and conduct. In compliance with the exhortations of the firſt, who was a Catholic, he received the Viaticum, and con-feſſed himſelf at Rouen, in preſence of the prince of La Roche-ſur-Yonne. Yet the queen coming to viſit him, and adviſing him to hear ſome pious book read, he liſtened with great attention to the book of Job, which his Calviniſt phyſician had brought; and this man reproaching him with indifference for his tenets, Anthony aſſured him that if he recovered, he would publicly embrace the profeſſion of Lutheraniſm, as eſtabliſhed by the confeſſion of Augſbourg.— De Thou ſays, that during the time when La Meziere was reciting to Anthony the prayers uſed by the proteſtants for dying perſons, the Cardinal of Bourbon, brother to the king of Navarre, remained at the other extremity of the boat; but, when he found the king approached his laſt moments, he brought in a Dominican monk, difguiſed in a ſecular habit. The expiring prince ſeemed for ſome inſtants to liſten to the diſcourſe of the friar; then, ſuddenly turning to his Italian valet-de-chambre, who was at his bed's head, he charged the ſervant to exhort the young prince of Bearn, his ſon, to preſerve his loyalty and fidelity unſhaken to the king of France; and ſoon afterwards he expired.

nute recapitulation of these calamities would present a picture too humiliating to human nature, though the pen of history is compelled to hold them up to view, however reluctantly, for the instruction and detestation of future ages.

1562.

Louis prince of Condé at length took the field, with twelve thousand men. He had determined, in contradiction to the advice of Coligni and d'Andelot, to march directly to Paris, expecting that the consternation which he should strike into the inhabitants and the queen, would reduce them to terms of accommodation. In this hope he however found himself deceived: Catherine, skilled in all the subtleties of delay, and of negotiation, engaged him in repeated and fruitless conferences, only calculated to give the Parisians time to recover from the panic into which they had been thrown by his sudden appearance. While she tendered him fallacious conditions of peace, she seduced his bravest captains, and prevailed on them to quit his cause. Condé, convinced how futile and dangerous were all the regent's offers, after several vain attempts upon the capital, decamped, and began his march into Normandy. "The Triumvirs" followed close upon his steps; and, having come up with him unexpectedly near Dreux, an engagement became unavoidable.

Nov.

10 Dec.

The Hugonots had in the beginning the whole

20 Dec.

whole advantage, the impetuosity of their charge bearing down all opposition. The Constable, who commanded in chief, being wounded in the face with a pistol-ball, and his horse falling under him, was taken prisoner; a part of the cannon of the royal army was seized, and the rout appeared to be universal. But the duke of Guise, cool and unmoved, had not yet engaged: he regarded the battle with the most serene composure, and watched the moment in which it might be retrieved. Though never possessed of any military rank higher than that of a captain of gen-d'armes, his great and distinguished capacity rendered him more respected than were the first commanders of the age. Observing that the Hugonots were dispersed and already engaged in plunder, he fell upon them, and put them instantly to flight. The prince of Condé, who disdained to turn his back, and who was ever found in the front of danger, was surrounded and made prisoner by Henry d'Amville, the Constable's second son, after having been wounded in the right hand. Coligni rallying his forces, retired precipitately, under cover of the night; and so far from being vanquished, he would have returned to the combat the ensuing day, if his German auxiliaries had not refused. He retreated therefore towards Orleans, unpursued by the

the Royalifts, and carrying with him his captive, Montmorenci*.

The

---

* It is evident from De Thou's defcription, that the prince of Condé was furprized, and in a great degree compelled to hazard a general action at Dreux. That hiftorian agrees with Davila in all the leading and important particulars of the engagement. Robert Stuart, who has been already mentioned in the reign of Francis the fecond, was the perfon who made the Conftable prifoner. The duke of Guife having recovered the honour of the day, and regained the battle at a moment when the rout was univerfal in the royal camp, the prince of Condé was in turn borne reluctantly away by his flying troops; but his horfe having been wounded in the leg, fell under him; and while he was endeavouring to remount himfelf, d'Amville arrived, and compelled him to furrender. Coligni made the moft vigorous and repeated efforts to retrieve the day; and after the unfortunate charge of the royal troops under St. André, in which that Marechal was taken prifoner and killed, he had nearly again obtained a victory. It was referved for the duke of Guife a fecond time to tear the laurels from the Hugonot leaders: he attacked the admiral in flank, who then yielding to the difparity of numbers, retreated flowly, in the beft order, without quickening his ordinary march, and even carrying off two pieces of the royal cannon. The action lafted four hours, and near eight thoufand men were killed on both fides, of which number the Hugonots owned to have loft only three thoufand.

The moft exact detail of this celebrated engagement is likewife to be found in Davila. He allows that the prince of Condé's negligence chiefly involved the Hugonots in the neceffity of fighting; the Conftable having taken advantage of his fecurity and want of precaution, to pafs his whole army over the river Eure by moon-light, on

the

1562. The field of battle, and the whole glory of the day, remained undisputed to the duke of Guise; but if his masterly conduct in the action gained him the applauses of the court and the adoration of his troops, his behaviour to the prince of Condé did him likewise immortal honour. The duke received him with the utmost politeness, lodged him in his own tent, and even divided with him his bed, no other

the preceding night. Coligni first discovered this error and its consequences, of which he sent immediate information to the prince; who might still have avoided a decisive action; but his great spirit would not permit him to retreat before the Catholics. The admiral fought with dauntless resolution, and with his own hand laid dead upon the ground Gabriel de Montmorenci, fourth son to the Constable, and the Count de Rochefort. The Switzers alone remained firm and immoveable, tho' they were surrounded and repeatedly charged by the whole Hugonot army. Davila attributes all the merit of the victory, very deservedly, to the duke of Guise. D'Andelot, one of the most intrepid chieftains in the Hugonot army, had been obliged to retire from the field, being ill of an ague, which rendered it impossible for him to continue there, or to take any part in the action.—The prince of Condé, all covered with sweat and blood, was conducted by d'Amville to the duke of Guise's tent at Blainville, where they supped together, and afterwards divided the same bed.——These are some of the most interesting facts of the battle of Dreux, as enumerated by Davila; who however represents the victory on the one side as more compleat, and the defeat on the other as more universal, than they appear to have been, as related by De Thou.

being

being procurable at the time. The prince himself afterwards declared, that during the whole night he could not close his eyes, while the duke enjoyed the soundest sleep by his side.— In this engagement fell the Marechal de St. André, one of "the Triumvirate *."

At the beginning of the engagement, as the advantage was entirely on the prince of Condé's side, numbers of the royal army fled even to Paris, and published that all was lost. The duchess of Guise, who was usually attended by a prodigious crowd of courtiers and votaries, remained almost alone. The queen-mother, prepared for every event, careless of the fate of religion, and viewing all objects through the medium of policy and interest, received the news with

---

* St. André was a polite and gallant nobleman, much regretted by his party. Brantome has given us the minutest particulars of his death. The battle was already gained, says he, when intelligence arrived, that a body of four hundred Hugonot cavalry had rallied, and prepared to renew the attack. St. André was mounted on a horse, which spent with fatigue, fell in the onset, and had not strength to rise. At that moment, a gentleman on the opposite side, named Aubigné, or Bobigné, whose estate the Marechal enjoyed by confiscation, came up, and discharged a pistol-ball through his head, which instantly killed him. His body was not found till the next morning, in a ditch near the spot where he fell.

Davila only mentions very briefly that the Marechal de St. André was mortally wounded; but De Thou circumstantially relates the origin and cause of Bobigné's detestation and vengeance

1562. with extreme compofure, and is reported only to have faid, "Eh bien! il faudra donc prier Dieu en François!"—It was to her indifferent, provided that fhe retained poffeffion of power, whether Condé or Guife ultimately prevailed; whether the Catholic, or the Calviniftical doctrines gained the pre-eminence. When the fucceeding day corrected the error, and brought certain intelligence of the victory obtained by the royal forces, fhe from a confequence of the fame principles, was concerned and mortified; her difcernment compelling her to forefee that it eftablifhed the duke of Guife's authority, and reduced her to a more compleat fubjection. She notwithftanding endeavoured to conceal her feelings; ordered rejoicings to be made for the

---

geance on that nobleman. His refentment appears to have been too juftly founded, as St. André had repaid the deepeft obligations conferred on him by Bobigné, with ingratitude, perfidy, and rapacity. After having availed himfelf of the pecuniary affiftance of Bobigné to the greateft degree, he had the cruelty and the bafenefs to procure for his own ufe the confifcation of his effects; and to this injury St. André even added perfonal indignities and infults. Bobigné, thus doubly affronted and degraded, fwore revenge, and waited the opportunity of fatiating his vengeance, which he fully obtained. De Thou confeffes that the Marechal, though adorned by nature and by fortune with their choiceft prefents, and though alike calculated to fhine in the cabinet or in the field, was become equally an object of hatred and contempt, by his profligacy, injuftice, and infatiable avidity, to which vices he juftly fell a victim.

defeat

CHARLES THE NINTH. 141

defeat of the Hugonots; and conferred upon the duke the supreme command of the army, with which he had already been invested by his troops. 1562.

Coligni meanwhile, on whom his forces had likewise conferred the post of general, passed the Loire at Beaugency; and having left his brother d'Andelot in Orleans with two thousand men, in expectation of that city being invested by the royalists, marched into Normandy, where he might receive the queen of England's promised supplies. After having waited upon the sea coast some weeks in anxious suspence, and hourly menaced with the cries of the German auxiliaries, who loudly demanded their arrears, the expected succours arrived under the conduct of Montgomeri, who brought an ample supply of money, troops, artillery, and ammunition. The admiral's precautions for the security of Orleans were justly founded; as notwithstanding the severity of the winter, and the strength of the city, the duke of Guise was determined to commence the siege. The queen mother accompanied him, carrying with her the prince of Condé, who was shut up in the castle of Onzain, under the custody of d'Amville, who had made him prisoner. Though d'Andelot, one of the most intrepid and experienced captains of the age, animated by the important charge confided to his care, exerted every effort of courage and military skill to defend the place; yet the supe- 1563.
January

rior

1563. rior genius and conduct of the duke had already rendered him master of the bridge acrofs the Loire, and of the fuburbs. Coligni, occupied in reducing Normandy to fubjection, was not able to march to its relief, in time to have afforded it an effectual aid; nor can there be any doubt that Orleans muft have furrendered in a few weeks, if the fatal accident of the duke of Guife's death had not fnatched the Hugonots from the imminent and unavoidable danger.

A gentleman of Angoumois, named John Poltrot de Meré, was the author of this deteftable affaffination. He was of the Reformed religion, which he had pretended to renounce; and the duke had received him with his accuftomed courtefy and liberality of fpirit. Poltrot had long watched the favourable opportunity to give the blow. The duke of Guife being accuftomed to go every day in perfon to vifit the works, and to infpect the advances made, as he returned in the evening, without his armour, only attended by one gentleman, and mounted on horfeback, the affaffin, who waited for him, dif-
18th Feb. charged three balls into his left fhoulder. Every affiftance of art was procured, but he died at the end of eight days *.

The

* Davila fays, that the duke was fhot by Poltrot on the 24th of February, in the evening, being the feaft of St. Mathias; that the affaffin was mounted on a fwift jennet, and difcharged three balls into his right fhoulder, all which paffing

The queen-regent, fearful left she should be
suspected as instrumental or privy to his death, 1563.
caused

sing through his body, laid him on the ground, as dead.
He agrees with Brantome in many of the particulars respecting the duke's death; and adds, that he expired on the third day from that on which he received the wound.

De Thou coincides with the historians already mentioned, as to all the leading facts. He is very minute in his account of Poltrot, and mentions many curious circumstances relative to that fanatic, which tend to hold up in the strongest point of view, the atrocious spirit of the times, where devotion and the most flagitious crimes were continually found united in the same person and character. In his interrogatory before the queen-mother and the principal lords of the court, Poltrot, among many other facts which he confessed, and which evince the force of that gloomy and sanguinary enthusiasm by which he was actuated, declared, that " only
" a few moments before he killed the duke of Guise, he had
" dismounted from his horse in a neighbouring wood, and
" on his knees had urgently besought the Lord to turn his
" mind, and to change his resolution, if it arose from the sug-
" gestions of the evil spirit."—Many similar instances occur in the history of these melancholy times, when the human mind was under the dominion of the most inveterate errors, heightened and inflamed by the acrimony of religious differences. Jacques Clement, the Jacobin friar, who stabbed Henry the third in 1589, received the sacrament, and passed the day in prayer, previous to an act of regicide and assassination.

Brantome, who served under the duke of Guise, and was at the siege of Orleans, has given the most minute account of the circumstances of this assassination. On the evening when the duke was killed, says he, only Monsieur de Rostain accompanied him, and he had just passed the river in a little boat, which constantly waited for that purpose. Poltrot immediately fled on discharging his pistol;
and

1563. caused herself to be interrogated in his chamber, before his own family, and a number of the nobility. Poltrot had endeavoured to secure himself by flight; but after having wandered the whole night in the woods on horseback, he found himself in the morning at the bridge of Olivet, only a league from Orleans; where exhausted with fatigue, he entered a house to repose himself, and was taken while asleep by one of the duke's secretaries.

When questioned with respect to the motives that had urged him to the commission of so foul a crime, he declared it to have arisen solely from zeal for his religion. As to his instigators, he accused several, but without uniformity; and among others the admiral. Coligni highly resented and denied the imputation, which must have stigmatized him with indelible infamy to his own adherents, and to the latest posterity. He even demanded of the queen, that the criminal's punishment should be delayed till they could be personally confronted, and the falsity of the accusation demonstrated. These justifications and solemn protestations did not, however, convince the family of Guise of Coligni's innocence. Henry,

---

and affecting to be a pursuer of the assassin, cried out, "Take him! take him!"—The duke perceiving himself dangerously wounded, only said, "L'on me devoit celle-la; mas je crois que ce ne sera rien." They carried him to his own quarters.

son to the expiring duke, and then in very early 1563. youth, vowed an immortal hatred, and imprecated vengeance on the admiral's head, as his father's murderer. He satiated this unrelenting desire of revenge many years afterwards, at the fatal massacre of St. Bartholomew *.

The

---

* Brantome, though devotedly attached to the house of Guise, yet does not absolutely accuse the admiral as the concealed author of the duke's death. He only drops some ambiguous intimations that Coligni knew of Poltrot's designs, without exposing himself to the infamy of a discovery, in case of the assassin being taken. He however pretends, that the duke himself suspected Coligni, and pardoned him, when expiring.—Davila says, that the admiral and Theodore Beza were universally believed to have persuaded Poltrot to commit this crime. They constantly denied the charge, and dispersed long justifications of their innocence over all Europe; but the Catholics, and the house of Guise still believed them guilty, and anxiously waited for an occasion of revenge. Davila expressly declares, that Poltrot persisted invariably in the same assertions, and confirmed, when under the torture, the accusations of the admiral and Beza, which he had first voluntarily made.—De Thou seems to leave the matter more in doubt; he says, that Poltrot, though he had twice repeated on oath, and signed the deposition by which he accused Coligni of having urged him to the commission of the crime, yet on being afterwards put to the torture, retracted this accusation, and exculpated Coligni; then again he repeated the same assertion. The admiral, De Thou allows, wrote in the most pressing terms to the queen, beseeching her to delay Poltrot's execution, denying the crime imputed to him, or any participation in it, and demanding to be personally confronted with the assassin.

I cannot

The duke of Guife, perceiving that his end approached, prepared himfelf for it, as became a hero. That magnanimous and exalted intrepidity, that mild and equal ferenity of temper, which had fhone eminently in his life, was equally vifible in his dying moments. He recommended to the duchefs his wife the education of their children; and he exhorted Henry, his eldeft fon, to preferve an inviolable fidelity to the king. Mindful of his honour, and defirous to clear his conduct from the afperfions which had been caft upon it, he vindicated himfelf from any intention to commit the maffacre of Vaffy; and lamented in the moft pathetic terms, that unhappy event, which had lighted up the deftructive flame of civil difcord. With earneft entreaties he implored the queen, as the common mother of her people, to terminate the quarrels which defolated France; and pronounced the man an enemy to his country and his fovereign, who fhould venture to offer her any other counfel.

I cannot quit the fubject of Francis duke of Guife, without mentioning a circumftance refpecting him, which marks the trueft magnanimity and patriotifm.—When previous to the ftorm of the breach at Rouen, he harangued his foldiers and put himfelf at their head, he ardently recommended to them three things; to refpect the chaftity and honour of the women; to fpare the lives of every Catholic without diftinction; and to fhew no mercy or quarter to the Englifh auxiliaries, their ancient and inveterate enemies.

The

CHARLES THE NINTH.

The funeral honours paid to him after death, were scarce less than royal, and are equalled by nothing in the French annals, except those which Turenne received above a century afterwards. His body was carried in melancholy pomp to the Chartreux at Paris, and from thence to the church of "Notre-Dame," where he lay in state; immense crowds of weeping citizens following the procession. He was at last deposited with his ancestors at Joinville, in Lorrain.

1563.

18thMar.

Poltrot was adjudged by the parliament to suffer the same punishment inflicted on traitors or regicides, and was torn in pieces by horses. At his execution, it is said that he still accused the admiral, as privy to the commission of the crime: and though the whole tenour of Coligni's life and conduct seems to refute this imputation, though a candid and impartial mind must refuse to admit so insufficient a testimony, yet we too well know what degrading and unnatural violations of honour and justice, the spirit of religious zeal, inflamed and heightened by personal animosities, can induce mankind to commit.

Francis duke of Guise appears to have been one of the greatest characters of the age in which he flourished, whether regarded as a warrior or a statesman. His errors, and even his faults and vices, were more the result of situation than of sentiment; and his towering ambition, tho' not justified, is yet palliated and diminished by

1563. the sublime qualities which he possessed from nature, and by the peculiar circumstances which gave them scope and exertion. His death must certainly be considered as a misfortune to France; since he alone set some limits to the restless and intriguing genius of Catherine, henceforth liberated from all constraint, and without a rival in authority.

The queen shewed her deference to the duke of Guise's dying advice, by the immediate overtures which she made for a pacification. It was 19thMar. soon concluded by the mediation of the Constable and prince of Condé, on terms not unfavourable to the Hugonots; though the admiral, on his arrival from Normandy, reproached the prince in very severe expressions for his hasty compliance with the propositions, at a juncture when their great adversary's death gave them reason to expect the most flattering reverse of fortune.

Orleans was evacuated by the Calvinist troops; and the Seigneur de la Cipierre, one of the most accomplished, virtuous, and amiable lords in the kingdom, was appointed governor of the city. He was already in possession of a post perhaps the most important which could be entrusted to any subject; that of preceptor to the young king. No man was more calculated to execute its high duties: he endeavoured to instil the most elevated and glorious sentiments into his royal

royal pupil; and he would probably have inspired Charles, who possessed lively parts and a quick perception, with the love of virtue, and the feelings of a great monarch; but his death, untimely, and before these noble seeds could sink deep into Charles's bosom, deprived his country of so inestimable a treasure. All the miseries of this unhappy reign, are probably in a great measure to be imputed to that inauspicious event.

Albert de Gondi, Marechal de Retz, a Florentine, and a devoted creature of Catherine, was placed by her in the charge which La Cipierre had occupied. Destitute of principle, dissolute in his manners, cruel from temper, dissembling, and master of every little art of sordid policy, he corrupted and perverted the many shining qualities with which nature had liberally endowed the king. The unfortunate prince was ruined while yet in early childhood, and all the high expectations to which he had justly given birth, were defeated and rendered abortive.

During the tranquillity which succeeded to the late troubles of the state, Catherine, with her usual duplicity endeavoured to sow distrust and jealousy between the prince of Condé and Coligni. To the former she made the same fallacious proposals, which she had used with so much success to Anthony his brother; but Louis was not to be deceived by her infidious offers, and she attempted in vain to diffolve the intimate connection which continued to fubfift between him and the admiral.

The prince of Condé, gallant and amorous, was more affailable on the fide of love, than on that of policy. No nobleman of the court had received fuch flattering proofs of female attachment, or was more generally acceptable to women. Margaret de Luftrac, widow of the Marechal de St. André, long difputed the poffeffion of his heart with Ifabella de la Tour de Turenne, known in hiftory under the name of " La Belle de Limeüil." Each of thefe contending rivals gave him the moft romantic teftimonies of their love: the firft prefented him with her eftate and caftle of St. Valeri, magnificently furnifhed; the latter carried her paffion yet farther, and facrificed to him her chaftity and honour. She was even brought to bed in the queen's wardrobe; and Catherine, to whom fhe was diftantly allied by blood, and to whom fhe immediately belonged as a maid of honour, ordered her to be inftantly conducted to a convent *.

The

---

* Almoft all the French writers have been very minute and circumftantial in the relation of this fingular anecdote, and Even Davila did not deem it unworthy a recital.—" It was Catherine's favourite fyftem of policy," fays he, " at the conclufion of the firft civil war, to engage the prince of Condé
" in

CHARLES THE NINTH.

The admiral, who was conscious that these irregularities in the chief of his party reflected a disgrace on all its adherents; and who dreaded left some one of the prince's amours might prove too strong for the weaker ties of ambition or religion, remonstrated with him so forcibly on the pernicious consequences of his continual engagements and gallantries, that he prevailed on him to put an end to them by a second

" in all those effeminate pleasures which might insensibly
" enervate his mind, and imperceptibly diminish the natural
" activity of his disposition. She peculiarly endeavoured, by
" the donation of honours and ample possessions, to give him
" a distaste for the fatigues of a camp. To accomplish this
" end, she prompted and encouraged the Marechale de St.
" André, who inherited from her father and her husband
" prodigious riches, to attempt the conquest of the prince's
" heart; but though he accepted her splendid present, he de-
" spised her person, and remained proof against all her
" attacks."—To Mademoiselle de Limeüil he was more deeply attached; and Davila makes no scruple to declare that Catherine was not ignorant, though she affected to be so, that he had obtained from her the last favours.—De Thou coincides with the historian already mentioned, in all the principal circumstances of this story. " The queen-
" mother," says he, " having first vainly attempted to se-
" duce the prince of Condé by the same fallacious prospects
" of ambition, which had succeeded with his brother the
" king of Navarre, and peculiarly by the pretended promise
" of the island of Sardinia, attacked him thro' another chan-
" nel, with more success. Having remarked that the prince
" betrayed a partiality towards Mademoiselle de Limeüil,

1563. second marriage with Frances, sister to the duke of Longueville.

Meanwhile the Catholics and Hugonots forgetting their inveterate animosities, and animated by the love of their common country, joined to retake Havre-de-Grace from the English, to whom it had been ceded during the war. The place soon capitulated, and its surrender was followed by a final accommodation between the two crowns, which took place a few months afterwards.

28 July.

" one of her maids of honour, Catherine herself induced
" and engaged her to omit no means of augmenting his
" passion. The princess of Condé, his wife, was so deeply
" affected by his infidelity, that it produced her death.
" Mademoiselle de Limeüil then flattering herself that the
" prince would marry her, granted him the last favour; but
" becoming with child, the queen expelled her from court,
" and she was abandoned by her lover.—The Marechale de
" St. André conceived the same chimerical project, and
" was equally deceived in her expectations."—It is said
that the prince's wife, Eleanor de Roye, died a martyr to her
jealousy and chagrin at her husband's amours. Mademoiselle
de Limeüil was married afterwards to Geoffry de Causac,
Seigneur de Fremon.

The prince of Condé's gallantries and libertinism gave occasion at the time to the following Vaudeville, or satirical sonnet;

" Ce petit homme tant joly,
" Toujours cause, et toujours rit,
" Et toujours baise sa mignonne :
" Dieu garde de mal le petit homme!"

Catherine,

Catherine, who had always amused the prince of Condé with promises of admitting him to a participation in the government, and who knew not how longer to exclude him, determined on a singular expedient. The Chancellor de l'Hopital, who had withdrawn from court during the league of the triumvirate, but who had been recalled by the regent, was the author and adviser of the measure. The young king, Charles the ninth, entered at this time into the fourteenth year of his age. By the famous edict of Charles the fifth, made in 1363, it was necessary that he should have completed the year, before he attained to majority; but as the queen, by the declaration of his being no longer a minor, knew that she should retain unmolested the supreme power in her son's name, she procured an act to be registered in the parliament of Rouen, which declared the king's minority to be expired *. That of Paris refused to receive or confirm this edict; but

1563,

15 Sept.

Charles,

* No measure of the administration of Catherine of Medecis was more able, or more artful, than that of anticipating her son's majority, by which, under the appearance of resigning, she in effect continued and augmented her authority. Charles addressed the parliament of Rouen from his throne, on that occasion, surrounded by all the princes of the blood, and environed with the insignia of royalty. His speech was full of fire, and in a tone of command, which was highly consentaneous to his character. When he had

1563. Charles, inftructed by his mother, reprimanded them in terms fo peremptory and fevere for their audacious temerity, that after a confiderable delay, it paffed that affembly.

1564. Magnificent in all her plans, the queen caufed the palace of the Tournelles, in which her hufband Henry the fecond had expired, to be entirely demolifhed; and began to erect in its place, the more fplendid one of the Tuilleries. She employed in its conftruction the moft celebrated architects of the age, and rewarded them as became a fovereign, with the nobleft liberality. All the branches of polite literature felt her patronage; and Italy, her native country, was ranfacked to enrich and adorn the kingdom over which fhe reigned. She piqued herfelf on the unbounded reverence which fhe paid to the memory of Francis the firft, in whofe court fhe had paffed her early years, and whofe character

had finifhed his harangue, the queen-mother rofe, and declared that fhe then with infinite joy reftored to her fon the adminiftration of his kingdom. As fhe prepared to take the oath of allegiance and fidelity, Charles defcended from his throne, uncovered himfelf, and went to meet her: Catherine embraced him on her knees, and the king declared that he fhould defer more than ever to her advice and counfels. Being again feated on his throne, the princes of the blood, and principal lords of the court, were permitted to kifs his hand, and to do him homage. The edict which declared the king's majority was then read publicly by the proper officer, and inftantly afterwards folemnly regiftered.

fhe

she wished or affected to imitate. Elegant and luxurious in her taste, refined and delicate in all her projects far beyond the genius of the century in which she flourished, Catherine of Medecis forms one of the most extraordinary characters which is to be found in the history of mankind.

1564.

The continual complaints which were made by each party, of the infringement of the peace, strongly proved the uncertainty of its duration; and the family of Guise loudly demanded justice against Coligni, as the supposed author of the late duke's assassination. A contest between Francis de Montmorenci, the Constable's eldest son, who was governor of Paris, and the cardinal of Lorrain, had nearly lighted up again the fatal brand of civil commotion throughout the kingdom.

The queen therefore from a variety of motives, resolved to carry her son on a progress through his dominions. It was supposed that a principal inducement to this journey, was to form an estimate of the Hugonot forces and real strength, by an inspection of them in person; to which was added the desire of shewing the young sovereign to his subjects, and awakening their loyalty and fidelity by his presence, and their knowledge of his character. Catherine, however, who always concealed her political designs under the mask of pleasure,

endeavoured

1564. endeavoured to attribute to vanity and affection what originated in deeper motives. All her magnificence of difpofition was betrayed in the preparations for Charles's journey: a train of courtiers and ladies attended his perfon; and Henry duke of Anjou, the eldeft of the king's two brothers, as well as Margaret his fifter, afterwards queen of Navarre, accompanied their mo-

April. ther. After having vifited Sens, and Troyes in Champagne, at which latter city Charles concluded a folemn treaty with Elizabeth queen of England, from whom he at the fame time received the order of the Garter, he continued his progrefs to the city of Bar. The duke of Lorrain, and his wife the duchefs Claude, who was fifter to the king, met him at that place, and entertained him with the utmoft magnificence. Paffing through Burgundy to Lyons, he was compelled to quit that city on account of the plague, and to remove to the town of Roufillon in Dauphiné, where he was vifited by Emanuel Philibert, duke of Savoy. At Marfeilles he made a public entry, and returning by Avignon, he paffed the Rhone into Langue-

1565. doc. The court, after vifiting the principal cities of that province, and making fome ftay in Touloufe and Bourdeaux, arrived at Bayonne in the fummer of the following year, where

June. took place the celebrated interview between Charles and the queen of Spain, Elizabeth, his fifter.

CHARLES THE NINTH.

sister. The princess was conducted by a splendid train, at the head of which was the duke of Alva, and the Count de Benevento. The duke of Anjou, with a number of the young nobility passed the frontiers, and met his sister at Arnani in the Spanish Navarre. Catherine of Medecis, from impatience to embrace her favourite and beloved daughter, crossed the river Bidassoa which separates the two kingdoms; and on the opposite side Elizabeth was met by the king himself, who gave her his hand to conduct her out of the vessel.

1565.

10 June.

The young queen was received with prodigious pomp at Bayonne, and the interview lasted above three weeks. Every beautiful and brilliant entertainment, every gallant and elegant diversion, which Catherine's fertile genius and uncommon capacity could invent or procure, was exhibited to testify her joy on this occasion, and to inspire the Spaniards with the highest ideas of the magnificence of her court. Pleasure seemed to engross all present, and to have banished from this scene of festivity the sterner passions; but it was the queen's peculiar characteristic, to cover her schemes of ambition or vengeance under the mask of dissipation. A gallery, constructed to join the house in which she resided, with that of her daughter the queen of Spain, served to facilitate the secret conferences which it is said she held with the duke of Alva, on the subject of reducing and extirpating the Hugonots *. Some uncertain and ambiguous informations of this powerful confederacy for their destruction, were circulated abroad, the suspicion of which was confirmed by Catherine's character and subsequent conduct. Distrust necessarily succeeded, nor could any caresses of the king or court dispel their apprehensions. At the termination of the interview of Bayonne, the queen-mother conducted her son to Nerac, a little city of Gascony, in which Jane queen of Navarre had fixed her residence and established her court, on account of its distance from the Spanish frontiers, where even her person was not safe from the perfidy and enterprizes of Philip

* De Thou gives credit to the suspicion of measures having been concerted at Bayonne for the extermination of the Protestants; though he seems to rest the proof of such an intention chiefly on the assertion of the Calvinist writers themselves. Jean Baptiste Adriani, who was the continuator of Guicciardini's history, confirms the accusation, and adds, that the conferences between Catherine and the duke of Alva were held at the desire of the Pope; that it was determined to renew the Sicilian Vespers, and not to spare even the persons of the highest quality or distinction. It is even pretended that the city of Moulins, where an assembly of the principal nobility was convoked to meet in January 1566, was destin'd to be the scene of this tragedy.—Davila expresly avows Catherine's intention of cutting off the heads of Heresy, and destroying the Hugonots. He only says, that the duke of Alva was of opinion to employ the most violent

CHARLES THE NINTH.

Philip the second, who had attempted to seize on and deliver her over to the Inquisition as a heretic.

1565.

After a short stay in Nerac, the court continued its progress through Angoulesme and Tours, to Blois, where Charles passed the winter; and early in the ensuing year repaired to Moulins. An assembly of the nobility was held in that city, where a constrained reconciliation, destitute of mutual forgiveness, took place between the admiral and the family of Guise; which was followed by another, not more sincere, be-

Nov.

1566.
January.

lent and sanguinary measures; while the queen-mother, consulting the genius of the French nation, reluctant to imbrue her hands in the blood of the first nobility and princes of the royal family, dreading a renewal of the civil commotions, and fearful of the dismemberment of the kingdom by the introduction of English and German auxiliaries, leaned to more gentle and temporizing councils.— Nothing can be better established than the secret consultations for the destruction of the Hugonots, during the interview of Bayonne, tho' it is difficult to say how accurately the precise and minute features of that plan were traced. Francis de la Noue, a protestant writer, asserts, that the prince of Condé and Coligni received exact information of the intention to massacre themselves, and their adherents, at the assembly of Moulins. It is certain that they conceived a general and well-founded suspicion of the hostile and treacherous designs of the court, from the time of the interview at Bayonne; and that it laid the foundation of the renewal of the civil war in little more than two years afterwards.

1566. tween the cardinal of Lorrain and the Marechal de Montmorenci.

New sources of war disclosed themselves every day. The edicts of toleration and protection, repeatedly issued in favour of the Reformed religion, were violated in all the provinces with impunity; while the government indirectly encouraged these proceedings, and afforded no redress to the grievances of the Calvinists. They carried the complaints of their oppressions to the admiral and the prince of Condé; but it was long before either of those chiefs could be induced to resume the sword. The latter yet hoped to be appointed lieutenant-general of the kingdom, as his brother the king of Navarre had been; and both of them peculiarly dreaded impressing their young sovereign, who was now advancing fast to manhood, with sentiments unfavourable and hostile to themselves and their party. They twice dismissed the delegates sent by their adherents, after having advised and enjoined them rather to submit to any indignities or persecutions, than to have recourse to so dreadful a remedy as rebellion, and a renewal of the calamities of which they had already been witnesses: but the intimation which they soon afterwards received, that it was determined to seize on them both, to detain the prince in perpetual imprisonment, and to put Coligni to death, obliged them to think of taking more

decisive

CHARLES THE NINTH.

decisive and vigorous measures. In a great assembly of the Hugonot nobility and leaders, which was held at the castle of St. Valeri, it was agreed to suspend all acts of hostility or violence till they had received more certain intelligence of the intentions of the court; but in a subsequent council summoned at Chatillon, d'Andelot, who was ever of opinion to embrace the most daring and decided measures, strongly urged an immediate and open renewal of the war. His remonstrances prevailed; and it was resolved to attempt to gain possession of the young king, which could only be effected by cutting in pieces the Swiss guards, who attended on and protected his person *.

1567.
May.

This

---

* Brantome, who was certainly well informed in the court intrigues, declares the war to have been principally caused by the prince of Condé's disappointed ambition. He had flattered himself with the lieutenancy of the kingdom; but Catherine, unable longer to delude him with promises, tutored her favourite son Henry, and inspired him with the desire of filling that high office. At a supper in the abbey of St. Germain-des-Prez, the young prince most severely and haughtily reprimanded Condé for his audacity in presuming to aspire to a post, which he had resolved to possess himself. Brantome says that he was present, and heard the conversation. Condé perceived from what hand the blow came; he saw all his expectations blasted; he beheld himself duped by the queen, and sought for revenge by unsheathing the sword. The writer of Louis duke of Montpensier's

1567.
Sept.

This enterprize was not difficult, as Charles, with the queen his mother, refided fecurely at the palace of Monceaux, where he held a grand chapter of the order of St. Michael. The Switzers, difperfed in the furrounding villages, might have been feparately furprized, and eafily put to the fword; but Catherine having received intelligence of the enemy's approach, and fufpecting their intentions, retired haftily with her fon into the city of Meaux. She then difpatched the Marechal de

Montpenfier's life afferts the fame fact, and Davila confirms its authenticity.

This laft hiftorian, with his ufual impartiality and difcernment, has laid open, with great exactnefs, the many latent principles which produced the fecond civil war. He accufes the partizans of both religions with being principally acceffory to it, by their reciprocal injuries and animofities. He attributes it to the young king's high and unconcealed refentment of the prefumption and encroaching fpirit of the Hugonots; to the prince of Condé's ambitious and reftlefs temper; to the fears of the Calvinifts on account of the fuppofed fchemes for their deftruction planned at Bayonne; to the march of the duke of Alva, at the head of a numerous army, along the frontiers, for the purpofe of fubjecting the revolted fubjects of Philip the fecond in the Low Countries; to the continual infractions of the peace by the Catholics, and the wanton outrages committed by them on the Hugonots; to Coligny and d'Andelot's haughty and unfubmitting fpirit; to Catherine's hypocrify and dangerous diffimulation; and laftly to the Cardinal of Lorrain's violent counfels.—All thefe conjoined caufes, operating on minds already inflamed with mutual animofity, and incapable of being reftrained, again involved the kingdom in new commotions.

Montmorenci

Montmorenci with some unmeaning proposals, 1567. only calculated to gain time, while the Switzers assembled for the king's defence.

A council was held, on the measures requisite to be pursued in this critical juncture. The Constable, cautious and provident of his royal master's safety, wished if possible not to expose him to the hazard of an uncertain combat. The Chancellor, touched by the great and salutary considerations of the public tranquillity, and conscious that the young king would be irritated to the highest degree by so audacious an attempt, which must infallibly produce a second civil war more cruel and inveterate than the first, joined Montmorenci in advising the king to remain at Meaux. Unhappily for France, the cardinal of Lorrain opposed these lenient counsels, and prevailed. At the break of day therefore, Charles quitted the city, surrounded by the Switzers, in the centre of whom he was placed; but before they had advanced two leagues, the prince of Condé appeared in sight with near five hundred horse. The Constable, dreading the shock of so determined a body commanded by such leaders, and rendered distrustful by age, after having sustained the repeated shocks of the Hugonot cavalry, sent the king forward with only two hundred horse by a private road, and he arrived safely at Paris the same evening. Condé, who was ignorant of this precaution, charged the Switzers repeatedly, 30 Sept.

1567. repeatedly, but in vain: they suſtained the attacks unmoved, and after having harraſſed them a conſiderable way, he at length retired *.

Ineffectual

* Davila's account of the enterprize of Meaux is very circumſtantial, and ſomewhat different from that of Mezerai, and moſt of the other French hiſtorians.—He attributes the advice of marching to Paris, not to the cardinal of Lorrain, but to the duke of Nemours. He adds that the Conſtable's opinion would notwithſtanding have prevailed, if Fifer, general of the Switzers, had not requeſted to be admitted to the young king's preſence, and aſſured his majeſty, that his troops would open him a paſſage through the enemy with the point of their pikes, if he would entruſt his perſon to their protection. This offer was accepted, and the march began at day-break. Charles, the queen-mother, the foreign ambaſſadors, and all the ladies of the court were received into the center of the Swiſs battalion. The Count de la Rochefoucault, and Andelot, having joined the prince of Condé and the admiral, they made a furious attack on the rear, but were received on the Swiſs pikes with great intrepidity. The king gallantly ſpurred on his horſe to the foremoſt ranks, followed by all the noblemen who attended him; and when he arrived ſafe in the capital, the Pariſians ſhed tears of joy for his preſervation. The whole merit of this action and eſcape was due to the bravery of the Switzers.

De Thou is by no means ſo minute as Davila in his narration of the particulars attending the enterprize of Meaux. He ſays, " that the queen-mother aſſembled the council in the
" duke de Nemours' chamber, who was confined to his bed
" by the gout; and that contrary to the advice of the Con-
" ſtable and the Chancellor, it was there determined to en-
" deavour to reach Paris. In conſequence of this reſolution,
" Charles, accompanied by about nine hundred gentlemen,
" quitted Meaux at midnight, and proceeded towards the
" capital,

CHARLES THE NINTH.

Ineffectual conferences succeeded; but both parties, inflamed with animosity, were incapable of listening to any terms of peace; and the Hugonots, though few in number, having attempted to block up and distress the capital, Montmorenci, however reluctant, yet compelled by the murmurs of the Parisians, marched out to give them battle. The prodigious inequality of numbers insured him the victory; but the glory of the day remained to Condé and Coligni, who with a handful of troops, could venture to engage a royal army so much superior *.

1567.
October.

The

" capital, escorted by the Switzers."—Mezerai and De Thou equally accuse the Cardinal of Lorrain, as the promoter of the war, by his violent and injudicious counsels.

* The action, says Davila, began about noon, and the superiority of the Hugonots in cavalry chiefly contributed to their success in the commencement of the battle. Though the royal army was so much superior to that of the enemy in numbers and in artillery, yet only the horse were engaged on both sides, the infantry of the Constable not being able to keep pace with the squadrons of cavalry, and being almost totally thrown out of the engagement. The prince of Condé was opposed to the Constable's division, which he entirely routed; but his horse was killed under him, and he with great difficulty recovered another. Coligni commanded the van on that day; and being mounted on a fiery Turkish horse, was once so much engaged among the enemy, that he was borne away in their flight, and narrowly escaped being taken prisoner. D'Andelot, who had been stationed on the other side the Seine, at Passy, could not join his friends in time to be present at the battle, on account of the bridges

1567.
10thNov.

The engagement was fought in the plains of St. Denis, and was rendered famous by the Conſtable's death, who exerted during the action all the courage and activity of a young ſoldier. Wounded in five places, he yet continued to defend himſelf with undaunted intrepidity, till Robert Stuart diſcharged a ball into his reins which proved mortal. Even then, he had vigour enough left to drive the pommel of his ſword into Stuart's mouth, with which he beat out ſeveral of his teeth. His ſon Henry d'Amville reſcued, and diſengaged him from the enemy. Fainting with loſs of blood, he ſunk down upon the ground; but the firſt uſe that he made of his ſpeech when recovered, was to demand if there yet

acroſs the river having been all demoliſhed. The Hugonots took the advantage of a very dark and rainy evening to cover their retreat; and the Catholics, though victorious, yet did not purſue them, on account of the loſs of their general.

In all the principal circumſtances attending the battle of St. Denis, De Thou and Mezerai concur with Davila.—The Conſtable only meant originally to drive the prince of Condé from his poſts round Paris, by which he diſtreſſed and ſtraitened the capital; but ſtung with the complaints and outcries of the Pariſians, who even dared to inſinuate ſuſpicions injurious to his fidelity and loyalty, Montmorenci at length marched out, aſſuring the diſcontented citizens, that "he would on that day evince his ſteady adherence to "the crown, and return either dead or victorious."—The royal army conſiſted of ſixteen thouſand infantry, and three thouſand cavalry, beſides fourteen pieces of cannon; whereas

that

yet remained sufficient day to pursue the Hugonots. It was long before he would even permit himself to be carried off the field, on which he obstinately resolved to expire. " Tell the king " and queen," said he, " that I die with the " highest pleasure in the discharge of the great " duties which I owe them; and that I have " at length found that honourable end, which I " have fought under their predecessors in so " many battles!"—Yielding at last to the importunate solicitations of his sons and surrounding friends, he suffered himself to be carried to Paris, where Charles and his mother visited him, and wept his approaching end. A Franciscan

that of the Calvinists only amounted to twelve hundred foot, and fifteen hundred horse. Yet, encouraged by the season of the year when the days were so short as not to allow the Catholics, even if victorious, to pursue their triumph, the prince of Condé determined to give battle to the Constable. The Switzers did not maintain their reputation for courage in this engagement, but gave way when charged by the prince and the admiral. A report having been spread that Coligni was taken prisoner, Catherine of Medecis caused very strict search to be made after him in Paris, among those whom she suspected to be capable of concealing his person.—D'Andelot, having repaired the pontoons upon the Seine, passed that river at St. Ouen the same evening, and joined his friends. All the honour of the action must be confessed to have remained with the Calvinists, who, notwithstanding the prodigious disparity of numbers, had maintained so unequal a contest. About seven hundred persons fell on both sides, principally from among the cavalry.—It is De Thou who enumerates these particulars.

1567. friar tormenting him with admonitions and exhortations in his laſt moments, Montmorenci beſought him to ceaſe thoſe needleſs remonſtrances: " Doſt thou imagine," ſaid the Conſtable, turning himſelf towards the monk with a ſerene countenance, " that I have lived to near four-
" ſcore years, without having yet learned to die
" a ſingle quarter of an hour *?"

In

* " The Conſtable," ſays Davila, " though overpowered
" by the fury of Condé's and Coligni's attack, yet con-
" tinued to fight deſperately. He had already received
" four ſlight wounds in the face, and one very large one on
" the head, with a battle-axe. While he was attempting
" to rally his diſordered troops, Robert Stuart rode up to
" him, with a piſtol levelled at his head." ' Doſt thou not
'" know me?' ſaid Montmorenci, ' I am the Conſtable of
'" France.' ' Yes,' anſwered Stuart, ' I know thee well,
'" and therefore I preſent thee this.'—So ſaying, he diſ-
" charged a piſtol ball into the Conſtable's ſhoulder, who
" fell; but while falling, he daſhed the hilt of his ſword,
" which he had held faſt in his hand, though the blade was
" broke, into his enemy's mouth. So violent was the blow,
" that it beat out three of Stuart's teeth, fractured his jaw-
" bone, and laid him inſtantly ſenſeleſs on the ground. All
" his followers abandoned Montmorenci; and the Hugonots
" were carrying off his body, when the duke of Aumale and
" d'Amville having routed the van commanded by Coligni,
" came up and reſcued the Conſtable. They then carried him,
" ſenſeleſs and dying to Paris, where he expired on the
" enſuing day, with undaunted compoſure and magna-
" nimity."

Davila ſpeaks with perfect impartiality of his character.—
" Montmorenci was," ſays he, " a man of great capacity,
" mature

In him expired the last remaining obstacle to Catherine's authority, and she saw herself delivered from every rival who could henceforth oppose or impede her designs. She possessed an ascendancy the most unlimited over her son's mind, and governed in effect, though not invested with the title of regent. Notwithstanding that the Constable had been always uniformly unsuccessful in war, and was accounted the most unfortunate general

1567.
11 Nov.

" mature wisdom, and long experience. Those who judged
" of him dispassionately, allowed that he was a valiant
" soldier and a dutiful servant; but a bad friend, and ever
" entirely governed by his own interest." The Constable was in his seventy-fifth year, when he was killed: his funeral rites were conducted with unusual pomp and solemnity. De Thou coincides with Davila in every important circumstance relative to the death of Montmorenci.

Robert Stuart was afterwards taken prisoner at the battle of Jarnac, and being brought before Henry duke of Anjou, the Marquis de Villars besought the prince's permission to put him to death, as an offering to the manes of Montmorenci. Henry long refused to consent to so base a murder; but at length, overcome with the importunity of the Marquis, he turned his head aside, and said, " Well then—be " it so." Stuart, with animated entreaty, represented to him how ignominious and dastardly an action he was about to authorise, and endeavoured to awaken his compassion and sense of honour; but all was ineffectual: he was led a little on one side, disarmed, and put to death, in the very hearing of the duke. Even Brantome, corrupt as he was, speaks with honest indignation and abhorrence of this infamous act, exactly similar to that of Montesquiou and the prince of Condé.

of

1567. of his age; though his bigotry, his severity, and imperious manners rendered him little an object of love, or even of veneration; yet we cannot help lamenting the veteran commander, who had fought under Gaston de Foix at Ravenna, and who had been succeffively the friend and favourite of two monarchs, Francis and Henry. He alone could have inspired the young king with the desire of reigning himself, without his mother's pernicious counsels; and his death left her genius full scope to exert all its destructive influence.

The post of Constable was not filled up after the death of Montmorenci, nor would the king confer so high a dignity even on his own brother Henry, though strongly urged to that purpose by Catherine of Medecis. Several lords of the court requesting it for themselves, Charles, jealous of his authority, and deeming this charge too great and near the throne, refused to confer it on any subject. "I want no person," said he, "to carry "my sword: I am well able to carry it myself." Yielding however with reluctance to the entreaties and expostulations of the queen-mother, in favour of her beloved son Henry duke of Anjou, the king constituted him Lieutenant General of the kingdom, tho' he was then scarcely sixteen years of age. Charles's character, as he approached to manhood, began gradually to unveil and disclose itself. He possessed almost all the qualities

requisite

CHARLES THE NINTH.

requisite to constitute a great monarch, had they 1567. not been corrupted and depraved by the most flagitious examples and instructions. Dissimulation, cruelty, and ferocity were either familiarised to him by constant habit, or even inculcated into him as virtues. Catherine, only anxious to reign, endeavoured to prevent her son from feeling his own powers, and of consequence emancipating himself from the state of tutelage, in which he had hitherto been detain'd.

Meanwhile the Hugonot army, far from being vanquished, and reinforced by d'Andelot, who had joined the prince of Condé, advanced towards Paris, and even attacked the suburbs of 11thNov. that capital. They were at length repulsed, though not without considerable slaughter on both sides; and then retiring in defiance of the royal forces, they effected their junction with Casimir son to the elector Palatine, who led to 1568. their assistance a body of German auxiliaries. 11th Jan. The city of Rochelle declared in their favour, and La Noue, one of their generals, made himself master of Orleans; but the prince of Condé was repulsed before Sens, by Henry the young duke of Guise. His combined troops however formed a numerous army, and in hopes of being again able to invest or distress the capital, he laid siege to the city of Chartres. The February. success of the enterprize was doubtful; but while he remained before the place, new propositions of

peace

1568.
2d March.

peace were tendered by Catherine. They terminated in the treaty of Chartres, concluded on terms nearly similar to the preceding pacification; but the Hugonots, who were dissatisfied with it, as fraudulent and dangerous, gave it the denomination of " La Paix boiteuse et mal-assize," from the two principal negotiators of it on the part of the king; one of whom, the Marechal de Biron, was lame, and the other, Henry de Mesme, was lord of the land of " Mal-assize." It produced however, a temporary suspension of hostilities, though it could neither procure a solid peace or diminish that mutual distrust and aversion which the opposite parties nourished against each other. We now proceed to the yet more bloody scenes of this calamitous reign.

CHAPTER

CHAPTER THE ELEVENTH.

Attempt to seize the prince of Condé.—Third civil war.—Battle of Jarnac.—Death of Condé.—Characters of the admiral Coligni, and of Jane, queen of Navarre.—Siege of Poitiers.—Battle of Moncontour.—Arrival of the king in the camp before St. John d'Angeli.—March of Coligni.—Conclusion of peace.—Treachery of the court.—Marriage of the king to the archduchess Elizabeth.—Her character.—Festivities at court.—Policy of Catherine of Medecis.—Reflections.—Dissimulation of Charles and the queen-mother.—Arrival of Coligni at the court.—Commencement of disunion between the king and Henry duke of Anjou.—Contrast of their characters.—Affiance of Henry, prince of Navarre to Margaret of Valois.—Death of Jane, queen of Navarre.—Circumstances attending it.—Determination of Coligni to remain at Paris.—Margaret of Valois.—Her nuptials, and character.—Attempt to assassinate Coligni.—Dissimulation of Charles.—Resolution taken to exterminate the Hugonots.—Terrors and irresolution of the king previous to the massacre.—Death of Coligni.—Deaths of the Hugonot chiefs.

chiefs.—Detail of the principal circumstances attending the massacre of Paris.—Conduct of Charles.—Fourth civil war.—Siege of La Rochelle.—Character of the duke of Alençon.—Remorse of the king.—Election of the duke of Anjou to the crown of Poland.—Carousals at court.—Charles's impatience for his brother's departure.—Mary of Cleves.—Her character, and amour with the duke of Anjou.—Quarrels between the king and his mother.—Henry, duke of Anjou begins his journey.—Illness of Charles.—Suspicions on that event.—Arrival of the king of Poland at Cracow.—He abandons himself to grief.—New commotions in France.—Change in the king's conduct.—Conspiracy of the duke of Alençon, discovered.—Progress of Charles's indisposition.—Intrigues of the queen mother to secure the regency.—Execution of La Mole and Coconas.—Circumstances of the king's last illness.—Death of Charles the ninth.—Enquiry into the causes of it.—His character, issue, and funeral.—Conclusion.

1568. SUCH was the sanguinary zeal which animated the partizans of either religion in these unhappy times; and such was the perfidious system of policy pursued by Catherine of Medecis, that no permanent accommodation could take place throughout the kingdom. Scarce any of the conditions stipulated by the late treaty of Chartres were observed; while mutual rage armed the hands of Catholics and

Hugonots

Hugonots against each other. Alternate insults and acts of violence were committed in many of the provinces, which strongly evinced how little either party could be restrained by edicts of toleration; the professors of the reformed religion were attacked, or massacred with impunity; and the treacherous intentions of the court itself soon appeared too visibly to be mistaken.

The prince of Condé not daring to trust himself in the power of his enemies, had withdrawn to the castle of Noyers in Burgundy, which belonged to him in right of his second wife Frances de Longueville, and whither Coligni likewise repaired. While they remained in this retirement, a soldier was one day surprized in the act of measuring the fossé and walls, as if with an intent to ascertain whether they might be successfully attacked; and on being questioned, this man confessed that he was sent by the court, who meant to seize on the prince and all his family. The queen, who had hoped to take the great leaders of the Calvinists unprepared, no sooner found that her designs were discovered, than she ordered the royal troops to enter Burgundy. Condé and the admiral, who saw the project concerted for their destruction, were sensible of the extreme peril in which they stood, and that no safety was to be found except in immediate flight. It was not easy to evade the many detached bodies of soldiers, already posted

July.

1568.
23d Aug.

19th Sept.

to intercept their paſſage; but neceſſity dictated the attempt as the ſole means of preſervation, and they therefore left Noyers, only eſcorted by a hundred and fifty cavalry, in the centre of which were placed their wives and children. Fortune favoured their enterprize; an unuſual drought enabled them to ford the Loire; and after having traverſed a number of hoſtile provinces, thro' continual and imminent dangers, they arrived ſafely at Rochelle *.

The conduct of the court breathed undiſguiſed hoſtility and revenge; nor were any heal-

---

* Mezerai, Davila, and De Thou, all relate the circumſtances of Condé's and Coligni's flight from Noyers, in nearly ſimilar terms. It was a ſpectacle worthy of compaſſion, to ſee a prince of the blood compelled to abandon his reſidence, and to fly from the deſtruction which impended, incumbered with a numerous family, and ſcarcely accompanied by any eſcort which could protect him againſt his enemies. Three of his children were ſtill in the cradle: the princeſs of Condé herſelf, and the two families of Coligni and d'Andelot, as yet in very early youth, or in their nurſes' arms, followed the march, and augmented the difficulties of their flight. Scarcely had they paſſed the Loire at Sancerre, when the count de Tavannes, at the head of a body of forces, appeared on the oppoſite bank; but a ſudden inundation prevented him from croſſing the river, and as by miracle, ſaved the prince. Continuing his route through the provinces of the Limouſin and Poictou, he arrived at length at Rochelle, where Jane d'Albret queen of Navarre joined him ſoon afterwards with her two children, Henry and Catherine. That princeſs was followed by all the principal Hugonot nobility and commanders.

ing

ing measures embraced amidst the fury which 1568.
seemed to possess and actuate the government.
The Chancellor de l'Hopital, too mild and virtuous for the manners of a corrupt administration, and suspected of a partiality to the Hugonots, was deprived of the seals, disgraced, and confined to his house at Vignan near Estampes: his office was soon afterwards conferred on John de Morvilliers, Bishop of Orleans. Henry duke of Anjou, only sixteen years of age, was placed by his mother at the head of the royal army, though the Marechal de Tavannes superintended and principally directed its operations. The young prince having joined his forces, a general en- Novemb. gagement was expected, but the advanced season of the year prevented it, and obliged both commanders to retire into winter quarters.

In the ensuing spring they again took the 1569. field, and after many unsuccessful attempts, the duke of Anjou at length compelled the Hugonots to a decisive action. The scene of war lay in the province of Angoumois, on the banks of the river Charente; and the fatal day of Jarnac, 13March, in which the royal army was victorious, put an end to the prince of Condé's life *.

In

---

* The victory of Jarnac must be entirely attributed to the prodigious disparity of numbers, as the Hugonot infantry were almost all absent from the field of action, and only the cavalry disputed the day, with a courage and constancy which approached to frenzy. The duke of Anjou having passed

1569. In that memorable battle, he behaved with almost unexampled heroism and courage. His arm

passed his army in the night unobserved, across the river Charente, Coligni was first attacked. The prince of Condé, who lay at some distance, galloped immediately to his assistance, made a masterly disposition, and sustained long, with far inferior strength, the whole fury of the Catholic army.

D'Andelot, who had been left with only a hundred and twenty horse to delay the enemy, and give time to Condé to range his soldiery, performed this dangerous commission with his accustomed intrepidity and success; filling the place in which he had taken his stand, with confusion and carnage. At the beginning of the attack he rode up to the duke de Monsalez, who headed the first squadrons of the Catholic horse; and lifting up with his bridle hand the vizor of his helmet, discharged, with the other, a pistol into his face, and laid him dead on the ground.—Overborne by numbers, d'Andelot at length gave way, and retired to the main body.

Here the engagement was renewed with incredible obstinacy, the admiral and his brother in the left wing, maintaining the combat for near an hour, against the young duke of Guise. But the royal army being continually supplied with fresh troops, Coligni's own standard beat to the ground, and the van completely routed, they deemed it unavailing to continue the fight, and provided for their safety by retreat. In the right wing, the Counts of Montgomeri and La Rochefoucault disputed with equal courage the glory of the day; but were at last compelled to quit the field with precipitation.

Only the prince of Condé remained, incapable of turning his back, tho' encompassed by superior numbers. He was in the centre, and had encountered, in the beginning of the action,

arm was in a scarf at the time when it began; 1569. and as he marched up at the head of his troops, his brother-in-law the Count de la Rochefoucault's horse reared, and broke his leg. Unmoved by so painful an accident, and disdaining to betray any emotions unbecoming his high station in that important moment, he coolly turned to those around him; " Learn," said he, " that unruly horses do more injury than service, in an army!"—An instant after, previous to the charge, addressing his followers, " French nobility," said he, " know that the " prince of Condé, with an arm in a scarf, and

action, the duke of Anjou's own squadron. Repeatedly broken and charged through by the royal forces, he yet rallied his men, and returned to the engagement. Even when almost deserted after the retreat of his adherents, and totally surrounded by the opposite army, he fought with invincible courage. His horse being killed under him, and himself wounded in many places, he yet continued to defend and ward off the blows aimed at him, with one knee upon the ground, till Montesquiou put an end to his life.

The duke of Anjou behaved with the utmost bravery in this action, and shewed a dauntless spirit above his years. His horse was killed under him, and he once narrowly escaped himself, fighting valiantly at the head of his squadrons. After the prince of Condé's death, no farther resistance was made; it became a flight, and evening which drew on, in some measure befriended the conquered Hugonots.—All these particulars are drawn from Davila; and many others are omitted, less interesting. De Thou coincides with the above-mentioned historian, in all the principal circumstances respecting this engagement.

1569. "a leg broke, fears not to give battle, since you attend him!"

The fortune of the day was unfavourable to the Hugonots; and the prince of Condé, thrown from his horse, was surrounded and taken prisoner. Overcome with fatigue and wounded, they seated him at the foot of a tree; when Montesquiou, captain of the duke of Anjou's Swiss guards galloped up to the spot. Having demanded who he was, and being informed, "Tuez, tuez, mordieu!" said he; and drawing out a pistol, discharged a ball into the prince's head, which instantly killed him. The cool and merciless barbarity of this assassination, committed upon a man wounded and defenceless, after the heat of the action was past, excited universal abhorrence; and the enormity of the crime was rendered more conspicuous, from the high rank of the person put to death. The duke of Anjou neither avowed nor punished it; but he permitted the prince's body to be laid upon an ass, and carried to the castle of Jarnac, where he went himself to lodge*.

Thus

---

* Though Davila does not speak of the prince of Condé's death, as of an assassination, yet as such it must be regarded, and the French historians are unanimous on this point. Davila, however relates the circumstance of his being carried across a *pack-horse* to the castle of Jarnac, to the joy and savage diversion of the whole army, who jested at this melancholy and affecting spectacle; tho' he adds, that the duke of Anjou would not suffer any indignity to be offered to his body,

in

Thus fell the firſt Louis prince of Condé, by 1569. the hand of an aſſaſſin, rather than of a warrior. The

in conſideration of the prince's alliance to the blood royal. He owns all the ſublime and ſhining qualities of Condé, and only laments that they were obſcured by rebellion.

De Thou, after relating the deſperate bravery with which the prince continued to diſpute the field, even after the retreat of the admiral, and notwithſtanding the diſparity of numbers, ſays, that " Condé being at length left almoſt " alone, and his horſe falling upon him, in that ſituation, " he recognized two officers of the royal army, named Ti- " ſon d'Argence, and St. Jean. Having raiſed the vizor of " his helmet that he might render himſelf known, he ſur- " rendered to them, under their promiſe to ſave his life ; " but Monteſquiou riding up while the prince was ſpeaking " to them, inſtantly diſcharged a ball into him from be- " hind, of which he expired."

De Thou celebrates with the warmeſt panegyrics, his valour, liberality, eloquence, talents, and numerous virtues, in which he was equalled by few of the princes his cotemporaries, and excelled by none. He reprobates the indignities offered to Condé's remains, diſhonouring only to thoſe by whom ſuch inſults were permitted. He inſinuates plainly, that Monteſquiou acted by ſecret orders, and that he did not commit ſo baſe an aſſaſſination without knowing that it would meet with approbation. He even mentions a ſingular circumſtance highly tending to corroborate this ſuſpicion : " The duke of Anjou," ſays de Thou, " after the " engagement, communicated to thoſe perſons who were in " his confidence, his determination to cauſe a chapel to be " erected over the ſpot on which the prince of Condé was " killed. This idea had been ſuggeſted to him by ſome " eccleſiaſtics ; but he relinquiſhed it on the advice of Car- " navalet his preceptor, who repreſented to him that it

" would

1569. The unhappy circumstances of the times had in some degree necessitated him, though allied by blood to the crown, to unsheath his sword against his sovereign; and the great talents for military enterprize and command which he possessed, rendered him the hero of his own, and the terror of the opposite party. There is too much reason to believe, that Henry duke of Anjou authorized and commanded the captain of

" would confirm the opinion already entertained in both
" armies, that Montesquiou had assassinated the prince by
" his express directions."

" We found him," says the writer of the duke of Montpenfier's life, " lying across an ass; and the Baron de Mag-
" nac asked me if I should know him again? but as he had
" one eye beat out of his head, and was otherwise much
" disfigured, I knew not what to answer. The corpse was
" brought in before all the princes and lords, who ordered
" the face to be washed, and recognized him perfectly.
" They then put him into a sheet, and he was carried be-
" fore a man on horseback to the castle of Jarnac, where
" Monseigneur, the king's brother, went to lodge."

Brantome has likewise given us many interesting circumstances of this tragical event. " The prince," says he,
" fought with a courage heightened by despair, on that
" day; but he was soon beat to the ground by superior
" numbers. It had been recommended to the duke of An-
" jou's favourites to kill Condé at all events; and Henry
" himself did not disguise the joy which he felt at the exe-
" cution of his orders. After the action was over, he chose
" to gratify his eyes with the sight of the dead body; and
" it was then thrown, in derision, across an old she-ass, the
" head and legs dangling down on either side. It even re-
" mained

of his guard to put him to death. He was not naturally cruel; but the prince had been his rival for the lieutenancy of the kingdom, and was peculiarly an object of his detestation: besides that in the person of Condé, they apprehended the whole Hugonot faction must infallibly be destroyed*.

Coligni, who with the broken remains of the

" mained during the ensuing night, in a room exactly under
" that in which the duke himself slept; and after having
" been exposed to the view of the whole army, it was re-
" stored to the duke of Longueville his brother-in-law, who
" interred him with his ancestors at Vendome. There was
" made on him this sarcastic epitaph,
   " L'an mil cinq cens soixante neuf,
   " Entre Jarnac et Chateau-neuf,
   " Fut porté sur une anesse,
   " Cil qui vouloit oster la Messe."
Brantome says, he intimately knew Montesquiou, and that he was a brave and gallant gentleman: at the subsequent siege of St. John d'Angeli, he was killed by a musket shot.

 * Voltaire, in his beautiful poem of the Henriade, introduces Henry the fourth pathetically lamenting the prince's death. It is to our Elizabeth that he relates the story; and the lines are so masterly and affecting, that I shall make no apology for their insertion. It is Henry himself who exclaims:
  " O! Plaines de Jarnac! O! coup trop inhumain!
  " Barbare Montesquiou, moins guerrier qu' assassin,
  " Condé deja mourant tomba sous ta furie;
  " J'ai vu porter le coup; j'ai vu trancher sa vie.
  " Helas! trop jeune encore, mon bras, mon foible bras
  " Ne put ni prévenir ni venger son trepas."

1569. cavalry, had retreated to St. John d'Angeli, naturally became by the death of the prince, the leader of the Calvinist forces. He was in every respect equal to, and calculated for this arduous station. More advanced in years than Condé, he joined the experience of a veteran commander, to the most intrepid courage, and the most distinguished military talents. Loyal to his prince even in the midst of rebellion; ardently zealous for the glory of his country, though a fatal necessity compelled him to appear in arms against it, Nature had designed him to promote its grandeur and prosperity. In happier times he would have been the guardian of France, enrolled among her heroes and patriots, her Condés and her Turennes. Less ambitious than the prince, he was ever ready to accept the overtures of peace; but more attached to the religious principles of Calvinism, and not seduced by love or pleasure to sacrifice and forget them, he steadily pursued these objects, for the defence of which he had first drawn his sword. Fertile in resources, vast and capacious in his projects, rising on his very defeats, and magnanimous in circumstances the most distressful, he long sustained with inferior force, the utmost efforts of his victorious enemies.

Jane d'Albret, queen of Navarre, a princess endowed with virtues and qualities of the most estimable kind, and inheriting from her mother Margaret

Margaret of Valois a ftrength of mind and elegance of genius rarely found, feconded the admiral's meafures for the protection and prefervation of the Hugônot party. She brought her fon Henry, as yet in very early youth, to Rochelle, where fhe harangued the troops, who formed a circle round her; and Coligni was immediately declared general of the forces, under the prince of Navarre and his coufin the young prince of Condé.

1569.

The intelligence of the victory at Jarnac, and the death of the Hugonot leader, were received at Paris with unufual demonftrations of joy. The king rofe at midnight to fing Te-Deum in perfon, announced it to all the fovereign princes of Europe, and fent the ftandards gained in the action to Rome, as a prefent the moft acceptable to the fovereign pontiff. The real advantages refulting from it to the royal party, were however very inconfiderable. Henry duke of Anjou was repulfed before Cognac; while Coligni, reinforced from every quarter, appeared again in the field, more terrible from his late ill fuccefs. The death of his brother d'Andelot, who died of a peftilential fever at the city of Saintes, was an event deeply regretted by all his adherents, who loft in him a chieftain eminent for intrepidity and martial fpirit.

27 May.

Meanwhile the admiral at the head of an army, faced the duke of Anjou in the Limoufin,

after

1569.
25 June.

25 July.

7 Sept.
3 Oct.

after having effected a junction with Count Mansfeldt, who led to his affiftance a large reinforcement of German auxiliaries. In the great fkirmifh of La Roche Abeille, the Hugonots were victorious; while the Count de Montgomeri, one of their moft active and enterprizing generals, reduced all the Province of Bearn to obedience, and extended his ravages even into Languedoc.

Coligni, encouraged by thefe profperous events, determined once more to pafs the Loire, and carry the war to the gates of Paris, as the only effectual means to procure a termination of it; but unfortunately he afterwards changed his refolution, and undertook the fiege of Poitiers. Henry, the young duke of Guife, fon to Francis, and not inferior to his father in genius, in courage or in ambition, had thrown himfelf into the place. Anxious to fignalize himfelf, and animated with an uncommon deteftation of the admiral, whom he ever regarded as his father's murderer, he made an obftinate and refolute defence. Coligni, compelled at length by the duke of Anjou's near approach, who had laid fiege to Chatelleraud, and finding his forces diminifhed by the lofs of above two thoufand men, retired without fuccefs from before the city. The battle of Moncontour, which followed only a few days afterwards, feemed to menace with total deftruction the Hugonot party,

party. The action lasted more than three hours; 1569. and victory declared a second time for Henry and the Catholics. Near nine thousand French and Germans of the vanquished side, were left upon the field; and scarce could Coligni, wounded in the face, and accompanied by about three hundred cavalry, who in some measure stopt the pursuit of the conquerors, secure his retreat to Parthenai *.

Any

* This was the most bloody and decisive engagement of any which was fought during the civil wars. It began two hours after sun-rise, at eight in the morning, and lasted till ten: Coligni, who knew that the Catholics were superior to his own forces in discipline still more than in numbers, would have declined a contest, the inequality of which was visible; but the clamours of his troops, and peculiarly of the German auxiliaries, who demanded their arrears, and refused to retreat before the Catholics, compelled him reluctantly to hazard the issue of a battle.

It was disputed with such incredible obstinacy and mutual antipathy, that the very sutlers, lacqueys, and pioneers of either camp took a part in the engagement, and each individual fought, as if on his personal exertion alone the fortune of the day depended. The event was long doubtful; but at length the Switzers in the royal army having cut to pieces the Germans, of whom out of four thousand, scarce two hundred remained alive, a general rout succeeded.

Henry duke of Anjou signalized his bravery, and appeared in the first ranks of danger; he narrowly escaped being killed more than once, having rushed into the thickest squadrons of the enemy (where the Marquis of Baden fell by his side) and exposed his person like a common soldier; but

the

1569. Any genius, except his own, must have sunk under so disastrous a reverse of fortune; but his mind, accustomed to adversity, and unshaken in every situation, seemed to rally and collect its powers in this moment of distress. On the very evening of the day upon which the battle was

> the admiral united on that day all the impetuous courage of youth, with the resources and ability of an able and experienced general. The Rhinegrave, who commanded the German troops in the royal army, encountered him in person; and firing a pistol into his face, beat out four of his teeth, and broke his jaw; but Coligni discharging his own into the Rhinegrave's vizor, laid him instantly dead upon the ground. He afterwards continued gallantly fighting, though the blood ran in such quantity from his wound, as to fill both his helmet and gorget.
> At length, seeing his troops dispersed on all sides, and flying before the conquerors; his voice quite spent, and scarce capable of being heard; being himself covered with blood, and sinking under fatigue, he found it in vain longer to dispute the field. Retiring therefore with the two young princes of Navarre and of Condé, who had remained at some distance during the combat, he gained Parthenai the same evening, at six leagues distance from Moncontour, only accompanied by 300 cavalry. The counts of Mansfeldt and Nassau, with about two thousand of their men, joined him at night, having retreated in good order, and stopped the pursuit of the conquerors. The duke of Anjou commanded quarter to be given to three thousand of the French infantry, who had thrown down their arms. Near two hundred colours were taken from the Hugonots.—These particulars are principally extracted from Davila, with whom De Thou and Mezerai agree in almost all the circumstances.

fought,

fought, though almoſt incapable of ſpeaking 1569. from the effects of his wound, he held a council of his chief officers; and diſpatched meſſengers nto England, Switzerland, and the German ſtates, to announce his perilous condition and late defeat. He demanded, as in the common cauſe of religion, an immediate ſupply of troops and money, without which the conſequences to his party muſt be the moſt fatal. He himſelf in perſon retired with the two princes of Navarre and Condé, into the province of Saintonge; and collecting the ſcattered fugitives diſperſed at Moncontour, meditated new oppoſition to the royal forces.

Had Henry inſtantly purſued the enemy broken and diſpirited by ſo many calamities, before they had ſufficiently recovered from their terror to reunite and appear again in the field; he would probably have deſtroyed them entirely, or at leaſt have rendered them incapable of farther reſiſtance: but the ſiege of St. John d'Angeli, 16 Oct. which he immediately undertook, prevented all the beneficial conſequences otherwiſe to have been expected from his late victory. Charles, who had long beheld his brother's glory with jealouſy, and who poſſeſſed equal or ſuperior courage, could no longer be reſtrained from appearing perſonally in the army. Catherine of Medecis, attached to the duke of Anjou with peculiar tenderneſs, and anxiouſly endeavouring

by

1569.

26 Oct.

by every means to exalt this her favourite son, tried in vain to withhold the king, and to oppose his determination. On Charles's arrival in the camp before St. John d'Angeli, he seemed to be transported with the scene: he was constantly present in the trenches, exposed his person like the meanest soldier, and declared publicly that he would gladly share his crown with Henry, so he might alternately command the forces*.

2 Dec.

After a siege of two months the city capitulated; but La Noue, and the count de la Rochefoucault yet sustained the party in Rochelle; while Coligni having assembled all his adherents near Saintes, began that celebrated march through

---

* Charles early saw with discontent, his mother's partiality to the duke of Anjou; he complained of it to her; and his temper, naturally impetuous and violent, could not bear this preference. Catherine on the other hand feared that Charles, who was endowed with great capacity for affairs, would not always be held in tutelage, and might at last dispense with her counsels, and deprive her of all power. Henry's indolence and submission secured her from those apprehensions, in case he should ever mount the throne.

An anecdote which Brantome mentions, very strongly proves the king's dissatisfaction at Henry's success, and early greatness. Soon after the battle of Moncontour, D'Orat the poet had presented him with some verses in his praise.—" It " is not to me," said Charles, " that these eulogiums are " due! I have not merited any panegyrics, or performed " any high exploits! To my brother they may indeed " justly be addressed, who is every day employed in acquir- " ing renown in arms."

so

CHARLES THE NINTH.

so many provinces, almost unexampled in modern history. In defiance of the inclemency of winter, of so many considerable rivers which intersected his course, of the royal generals and Catholic forces stationed to oppose his progress; he traversed all the provinces at the foot of the Pyrenees and Languedoc, returned along the banks of the Rhone, and appeared in Burgundy in the ensuing summer, after having carried terror through all the south of France*.

1570.

June.

Charles

* The march of Coligni thro' so many provinces, destitute of artillery, money, baggage, or ammunition; and the resources by which he maintained and supported his broken troops under such distressful circumstances, convey the highest ideas of his military talents. The princes of Navarre and Condé, early inured to the dangers and fatigues of a camp, accompanied him thro' the whole course of this perilous enterprize, and shared every calamity of their leader and their party. The Hugonots left bloody traces of their passage in all the provinces thro' which they passed; peculiarly in the environs of Touloufe. Having remained during the severity of winter near the shore of the Mediterranean, in the vicinity of Narbonne, they traversed Languedoc early in the spring, remounted the Rhone, and marching along the Loire, arrived towards the end of May in the province of Forez, at the little town of St. Etienne. Here Coligni was attacked with a malignant fever, which stopped the army three weeks, during which time the camp was plunged in the deepest consternation; but recovering, after imminent danger of his life from this distemper, he conducted his forces into Burgundy, where they re-appeared in the middle of June.

The following song, says Brantome, was commonly sung by

1570. Charles submitted with difficulty to permit the admiral thus to ravage his dominions, unpursued. He would even have followed Coligni immediately, had not the queen mother, who dreaded his assuming the command in person, prevented him by the remonstrances of the Marechal de Tavannes; who assured his majesty, that the troops were already too much exhausted and broken, to attempt any new enterprize in so advanced a season.

The re-appearance of Coligni in the heart of France, at the head of a formidable army; the combat of Arnay-le-Duc, where he had manifestly the advantage; the complicated ills under which the unhappy kingdom groaned; and the dread of future calamities yet more insupportable, at length produced a negotiation for the termination of hostilities. The duke of Anjou, whose health had extremely suffered from the fatigues of the preceding campaign, was retired under that pretext to the palace of St. Germain, and

25 June.

---

by the Hugonot soldiers, after Louis prince of Condé's untimely death, and on the succession of the admiral to the supreme command of the forces.

"Le prince de Condé,
"Il a été tué;
"Mais Monsieur l'Admiral
"Est encore a cheval,
"Avec La Rochefoucaut,
"Pour chasser tous ces papaux, papaux, papaux!"

Charles

CHARLES THE NINTH.

Charles had conferred the supreme command of the royal forces on the Marechal de Cossé. That general, whether from incapacity or want of inclination, obtaining no advantages over Coligni, peace so long and anxiously desired, was again re-established on terms not unfavourable to the Hugonots; and public tranquillity seemed once more to spread a calm over the state, which had been shaken and convulsed by so many intestine commotions. Charles solemnly swore to observe the treaty inviolate, and to protect the Hugonots in every right which it conferred; but all these flattering appearances concealed the most perfidious designs; and Catherine, who had been convinced by experience that Coligni and the Calvinists were not to be reduced by force, had already planned the fatal massacre, which she executed two years afterwards. All the intermediate period was employed in the most consummate dissimulation; in the deceitful arts of lulling to sleep the wretches destined to destruction. Only the vast and comprehensive genius of the queen-mother could have concerted a system of vengeance so enormously flagitious, and so unprecedented in the records of mankind. Like some minister of an angry Deity, she appears to have been occupied only in effecting the ruin of her people, and to have always marked her course with carnage and desolation.

1570.

15 Aug.

Pleasure and dissipation notwithstanding seemed to engage the whole court; and the marriage of Margaret of Valois, sister to the king, with Henry prince of Navarre, was already proposed by Catherine, with intent to strengthen and confirm the late union between the parties*.

The

* It is impossible not to enter with some minuteness and curiosity into the amours of Margaret of Valois, one of the most beautiful and accomplished, but dissolute princesses of modern times. It is said, so violent was her love of pleasure, that at twelve years old, she had sacrificed to it her honour. The young Entragues, and Charry, a captain in the royal guards, disputed the precedency in her affections, when she was about that age. Her warm and animated attachment to her own brother Henry duke of Anjou, gave rise to similar suspicions, which, indeed, her character, conduct, and writings all tend to confirm. Henry was handsome, amiable, and fond of women : the libertinism of the court authorised every debauchery. The duke of Guise was unquestionably beloved by Margaret with the most unbounded passion, which she herself does not disguise in her memoirs; and the duke of Anjou withdrew from her his confidence, when he found the duke of Guise master of her person and affections.

In the celebrated manifesto which Henry the fourth caused to be drawn up, and presented to the pope, as a justification of his conduct in soliciting a divorce from Margaret, he minutely enumerates her debaucheries, and successive lovers. It contains so astonishing and unparalleled an account of the queen's conduct, that I shall extract from it several particulars.

" The princess," says the manifesto, " was only *eleven* " years old, when she began to yield to the pleasures of love.

" Entragues

CHARLES THE NINTH.

The duke of Guise, who was in love with the princess, and beloved by her in turn, attempted to raise obstacles to this marriage, in hopes of obtaining her hand himself; but Charles, offended at his conduct, and resenting his presumption, gave orders to his own natural brother Henry Count d'Angoulesme, to put him to death, as he went to the chace; nor had the duke any other means of averting the blow, except

" Entragues and Charry were in turn favoured by her;
" and the former carried his proofs of attachment to such a
" length, as nearly to sacrifice to it his life. The prince
" of Martigues succeeded to their place, and was fondly
" beloved; but naturally vain, he could not conceal an in-
" trigue so flattering, and divulged the secret of their
" amours, which became universally known. He always
" wore on the most dangerous occasions, an embroidered
" scarf, which his royal mistress had given him, together
" with a beautiful little dog, presented by the same hand.

" The tears which she shed for this favourite's death,
" were dried by the duke of Guise; who became in turn
" her paramour, by the good offices of Madame de Carna-
" valet."—" On pretend," continues Henry, " que les
" ducs d'Anjou et d'Alençon troublerent cette intrigue;
" et qu'elle eut pour eux des complaisances, que le droit
" du sang n'autorisoit pas; mais je ne puis croire que sa
" debauche ait été jusqu'à cet exces."

All these lovers preceded the king of Navarre; and the manifesto continues the enumeration of her subsequent irregularities and gallantries, which almost exceed the bounds of credibility. Yet Henry, in the beginning of this extraordinary piece, which is opened with the greatest solemnity, calls on God to witness the veracity of his assertions, and the integrity of his intentions.

1570. by a speedy marriage with Catherine of Cleves, widow to the prince of Portien *.

The king being already entered into his twenty-first year, it was become advisable to marry him; and his mother, after having in vain solicited the hand of Elizabeth queen of England, fixed on the archduchess Elizabeth, daugh-

* Even Davila confirms the attachment of the duke of Guise to the princess Margaret; and says, that she long persisted peremptorily to refuse any other husband.—" One " night," adds he, " there being a ball at court, as the " duke was going into the great hall of the palace, dressed " with the utmost magnificence, and adorned with jewels, " he met the king, who had placed himself purposely at " the door. Charles, with an angry air, asked him, " Whither he was going?" The duke answered, " That " he came to serve his Majesty." " I have no occasion for " your services," replied he.—Henry saw the dangerous " situation in which he had engaged himself, and deter-" mined instantly to recover his sovereign's favour, by put-" ting it out of his own power to be longer obnoxious."

De Thou and Mezerai confirm, in the strongest manner, the unconcealed and reciprocal passion of Margaret and the duke of Guise, as well as the order issued by Charles the ninth to dispatch the duke, of which he received intimamation from Francis de Balzac-Entragues.—Davila adds, that it was commonly believed a promise of marriage had been exchanged by the lovers; but, that the duke of Guise, either from inconstancy, ambition, or desire of satiating his revenge upon Coligni, (whom it was requisite to draw into the snare by the lure of this marriage between the Prince of Navarre and Margaret) desisted from any further prosecution of his claims on the princess, and contracted another alliance.

ter

ter of the emperor Maximilian the second. The dukes of Anjou and Alençon, Charles's brothers, were sent to receive the new queen at Sedan; and he himself advanced to meet her at Mezieres, where the nuptials were solemnized. She was an amiable and virtuous princess, devout, humble and submissive. Her capacity, limited and slender, gave Catherine no alarm, and she was neither consulted in, nor privy to any of the sanguinary measures which were pursued during her husband's reign. Though agreeable in her person, and gentle in her manners, yet she never could attain any power over Charles's heart, and only possessed his esteem *.

1570.

26 Nov.

The

* Elizabeth of Austria, daughter of Maximilian the second, was born in June, 1554, and was only sixteen years of age at the time of her marriage with Charles the ninth. The duke of Anjou was sent at the head of a magnificent train of nobility, to receive the young queen at Sedan; to which city the king himself came incognito, to view her person, and then returned to Mezieres, where the marriage ceremony was performed with a royal splendor. She possessed all the characteristic superstition of the house of Austria, and carried her religious exercises to a length injurious to her health; but her conjugal affection, and sweetness of disposition, rendered her universally beloved. Brantome always mentions her with the warmest expressions of approbation, as one of the most virtuous and amiable queens who had ever appeared in France. He says that her person was more than merely agreeable: " Elle etoit une tres belle
" Princesse," adds he, " ayant le teint de son visage aussi
" beau & delicat que dame de sa cour, & fort agreable. Elle
" avoit

1570. The beautiful Mary Touchet, his miſtreſs, had long reigned in his affections without a rival; and the king, naturally conſtant, remained unalterably attached to her till the hour of his death *.

1571. Elizabeth was notwithſtanding crowned ſoon
25 Mar.

" avoit la taille fort belle auſſi, encore qu'elle l'eut
" moyenne aſſez."—This deſcription muſt certainly be allowed to convey an idea of a very pretty woman.

* Mary Touchet was daughter to the " Lieutenant Par-
" ticulier" of Orleans, and the time when Charles's attachment to her commenced, is not certain; but it appears from an anecdote related of her, that ſhe had acquired the higheſt influence over him before his marriage, ſince it is clear that ſhe dreaded no rival. Brantome ſays, that Elizabeth of Auſtria's portrait being ſhewn her, ſhe exclaimed, after having long and attentively regarded it, " L'Allemande
" ne me fait pas peur!"—Her perſonal and mental attractions were equally pre-eminent; but her aſcendency over the young king her lover never extended to affairs of ſtate, or enabled her to guide the counſels of the ſovereign, as the ducheſſes of Valentinois and Eſtampes had done under Francis the firſt, and Henry the ſecond. " I have ſeen her
" picture," ſays the author of the Anecdotes des Reines et Regentes de France, " done in crayons, and during
" the prime of her beauty. The contour of her face was
" round, her eyes finely ſhaped and lively, her forehead
" ſmall, her noſe juſtly proportioned, her mouth little and
" crimſon, the lower part of her face admirable." Such was the celebrated Mary Touchet! She was, by her marriage with Francois de Balzac-Entragues, mother of Henriette de Balzac, miſtreſs to Henry the fourth of France, and created by him marchioneſs of Verneuil. — Mary Touchet died at the advanced age of eighty-nine years, in March, 1638.

after

CHARLES THE NINTH.

after at St. Denis; and the queen-mother, whose magnificence and taste eminently appeared on these occasions, displayed all her talents for pleasure in the entertainments which were exhibited at court. The fictions of antiquity, as well as the allegories of Greek and Roman fable were called in, to embellish the representations. A refinement, superior to the progress which the human mind had made in the sixteenth century, and little, if in any degree inferior to the splendid productions of art and elegance afterwards displayed under Louis the fourteenth's reign, characterised all the amusements of Catherine. Her extraordinary and universal genius comprehended every thing in its embrace, and shone equally distinguished in the cabinet or at a banquet, whether directed to the destruction or delight of mankind. She even seems to have blended and united qualities the most opposite and discordant in their own nature. Her versatility of mind enabled her to pass with the easiest transition, from the horrors of war, to all the dissipations of indolence and peace; and we are forced to lament that a capacity so exalted, only produced from the principles with which it was actuated, more general and lasting evils to her kingdom, and to the world *.

The

---

* In the entertainments given at court on Elizabeth's coronation, the peculiar situation of the state was enigmatically

1571. The grand scheme of deceiving the Hugonot leaders and drawing them into the fatal snare, now totally occupied the queen-mother. She had tutored the young king her son but too well, and instructed him in all the lessons of a profound and pernicious dissimulation: His very virtues and great qualities were transformed under her baneful touch, into vices and crimes. His prudence, penetration, and discretion, she converted into a subtle and perfidious policy; his natural vivacity of temper became passion and fury; his courage degenerated into stern ferocity; and his heart, steeled against the impressions of benevolence and pity, was inflamed with a savage thirst of blood and vengeance.—For Catherine, there is no justifi-

tically pourtray'd under various forms, which exhibited a political mirror, under the appearance of an amusement. Charles the ninth was represented in the character of Jupiter; Catherine, in that of Juno; the young queen, in that of Minerva. The Hugonots appeared under the names of Typhon and the Giants. Even the vengeance of St. Bartholomew, already planned, was darkly alluded to in the mottos and devices chosen, of which the following was one, addressed to the king:

" Cadme, relinque ratem; pastoria sibila finge;

" Fas superare dolo, quem vis non vincit aperta."

The meaning of this remark is too evidently connected with the ensuing massacre to be mistaken; nor can we avoid being surprised that allusions so obvious should not have awakened more suspicion and distrust of the court, in the minds of the Calvinist leaders.

cation

CHARLES THE NINTH.

cation or apology to be fuggested; her name in distant ages will be pronounced with detestation, nor can the brilliancy of her genius, or the seduction of her captivating manners, preserve her from ignominy and abhorrence. But for Charles every heart of sensibility will form some excuse. Accustomed from his infancy to precepts and examples the most depraved, and encouraged to spill the blood of his subjects, as meritorious and acceptable to Heaven, he awoke too late from the fatal delusion, into which he had been plunged by his mother's maxims and advice. Death permitted him not to expiate his offences; and he expired in the flower of youth, an awful lesson to future times, that monarchs cannot with impunity violate the great and sacred duties of humanity!

Every artifice was used, and every appearance of perfect confidence was assumed, to convince the queen of Navarre and Coligni that the king and court were disposed to maintain the late peace inviolate. The Hugonot deputies were sent back, after a reception the most gracious, with the amplest confirmation of every article of the treaty. Count Ludovic of Naffau having quitted Rochelle in disguise, and waited on the king at Lumigny, was received by Charles with uncommon distinction, and loaded with favours. Teligni, son-in-law to the admiral, was dispatched to him with a request to lay aside all distrust,

1571.

August.

1571. distrust, and to repose himself on his sovereign's honour.

Confiding in this sacred pledge as he deemed it, and happy to give a proof of his implicit reliance on the sincerity and virtue of his prince, Sept. he came at length to Blois, where the court then resided. Charles embraced him, hung upon his neck, and kissed him: he gave Coligni the endearing epithet of his Father, and professed for him a filial deference and respect. He was re-admitted to take his seat in council, received from the royal bounty a donation of an hundred thousand livres, and all his estates were restored. After having permitted him to visit his castle Dec. of Chatillon, the king again recalled him, redoubled his caresses, bestowed on him numberless favours, and even carried his dissimulation to such a length, that the duke of Guise, and the more zealous Catholics took the alarm; and began to fear, lest Coligni should really effect that alteration in Charles's heart, which at first they knew was only assumed, to render the destruction of the Hugonots inevitable*.

When

* Never was dissimulation and treachery carried to a greater length, or more completely covered with the mask of affection, than on the occasion of Coligni's return to court. When the admiral embraced his sovereign's knee, the king raised him up, assured him that it was the happiest moment of his reign, and smiling added, " Enfin, nous " vous tenons; vous ne vous eloignerez plus de nous quand " vous

When the admiral withdrew a second time, the king yet kept up a continual and unreserved communication with him by letters. Charles re-assured him of his determination to complete the nuptials of his sister Margaret with the prince of Navarre; professed his intentions of shaking off the fetters in which his mother and the duke of Anjou had hitherto held him; and as the last flattering bait, declared that he would send an army into the Netherlands, to assist the revolted provinces against Philip the second, at the head of which he should himself be placed. Coligni, whose bosom glowed with the love of his country's glory, and a just indignation against Spanish bigotry and oppression, could not resist so animating a motive. He even persuaded the queen of Navarre to visit the

"vous le voudrez."—All acts of grace and favour were obtained by the admiral's solicitation, nor was there any thing too difficult to be effected by his powerful interposition. The Protestant leaders were constantly near the king's person, and all partook of the royal munificence. Davila says, that a young nobleman, named Villandry, who had offended Charles the ninth at play in so heinous a degree as to be condemned to die, and whose pardon the king had refused to his mother, to the young queen his wife, and to the duke of Anjou, was nevertheless instantly forgiven at Coligni's intercession, and even restored to his former familiarity with the king. Mezerai and de Thou confirm and recapitulate the many perfidious marks of dissembled kindness, shewn by Charles and the queen-mother to Coligni during his visit to the court.

king

1572.
April.

king and his mother at Blois, where she was received with an excess of honours, and diffembled fondness. The negotiation for her son's marriage was resumed, and finally concluded, only the dispensation from Rome remaining to delay the consummation of their nuptials *.

The reputation which Henry duke of Anjou had acquired by the two victories of Jarnac and Moncontour, the early glory with which he seemed to be invested, and the title to which he aspired of restorer and defender of the state,

* Similar demonstrations of affection and regard were shewn to the queen of Navarre and her son Henry, on their arrival at Blois, as had been lavished upon Coligni only a few weeks before. De Thou relates, that Charles having demanded of his mother, after his first interview with the queen of Navarre, whether he had not played his part well? Catherine replied, " You have undoubtedly begun well; " but that will be of little avail, unless you continue:" to which Charles answered, swearing, as was his custom, " I will take them all in a net, and deliver them over to " you."—The articles, and contract of marriage between Henry and Margaret, were signed on the 11th of April, and Charles stipulated to give a hundred thousand crowns of gold to his sister, as her dowry.—" Margaret," says Davila, " yielding at length reluctantly to her mother's solicita- " tions, and her brother's menaces, as well as from a regard " to her own honour, which began to be very much called " in question, though she did not absolutely consent to " marry the Prince of Navarre, yet no longer openly de- " clared her determination never to contract or submit to " that alliance."

justly

justly gave offence to Charles. He beheld himself obscured in Henry's superior lustre, and regarded him as his rival in fame, perhaps in empire. He saw, and resented his mother Catherine's unconcealed partiality for his brother; and these principles of aversion and discontent began already to display themselves. The queen-mother, who watched with peculiar tenderness over her darling son, and whose ambitious mind ever projected schemes of greatness for her children, turned her view towards the Polish diadem, and began her intrigues for procuring Henry's election to the throne of that distant kingdom. Though Sigismund Augustus, the reigning king was yet alive, Montluc, bishop of Valence, was sent into Poland to endeavour to gain the suffrages of the nobility, and he succeeded beyond expectation in his commission.

The duke of Anjou presented at this time the model of the most accomplished hero; nor can we be surprized, when we consider his many brilliant qualities, at Catherine's partial attachment to him. In his person he was beautiful and finely made, above any prince of the age; a majesty, tempered with sweetness, accompanied all his actions, and his courage had been distinguished in two great engagements where he had been uniformly victorious. A flowing, dignified, and commanding eloquence disposed all hearts to admire and love him; his presence and

1572. and demeanour announced a prince, nor had the houfe of Valois produced any, whofe perfon and manners were fo captivating in the eyes of mankind *.

The contraſt in many points of view between himſelf and the king, tended to diffuſe over him additional luſtre. Charles, endowed by nature with much greater qualifications, and better calculated for a throne; poſſeſſing vigour, capacity, difcernment, activity and judgment, was yet carried away by the impetuoſity of his paſſions, and prefented little to the view, except the unamiable part of his character.—Henry, under fo fair a form, and in full poſſeſſion of all the military renown which in fact was due to the wifdom and conduct of Tavannes, was yet deficient in that force of mind, and in thoſe kingly qualities with which his brother was endowed. Beneath that engaging appearance, was concealed

---

* Defportes, the moſt elegant poet of the time, defcribes him in thefe lines. It is the portrait of Adonis himſelf.

"Il eut la taille belle et le vifage beau ;
"Son teint étoit de lys, et de rofes pourpretés ;
"Et fes yeux rigoureux dardoient mille fagettes,
"On le prend pour l'amour!"——

Davila conveys a high idea of the duke of Anjou; and expatiates minutely on his uncommon perfonal beauty, courage, eloquence, and other dazzling or fublime qualities. He fays, that all mankind had their eyes fixed on him, and had conceived the greateſt expectations from his future conduct. Mezerai and De Thou confirm thefe eulogiums.

an

an effeminate indolence, an enervate softness, a prodigality without bounds, and an indulgence to favourites the most pernicious to his kingdom and himself.

The duke of Anjou had not, however, yet betrayed those errors and vices, which characterised Henry the third on his subsequent accession to the throne; nor could love and gallantry be ranked even among the list of faults, in a court so dissolute as that of Catherine of Medicis. The young prince was fondly attached to Mademoiselle de Chateauneuf, and equally beloved by her; and this connexion was only broken by the more violent passion which he afterwards conceived for the princess of Condé *.

Pius

---

* Renée de Rieux, commonly called Mademoiselle de Chateauneuf, was a Beauty of the most engaging kind. She was of the antient family of Rieux in Bretagne, and had been early taken into the houshold, and placed near the person of Catherine of Medicis, as a maid of honour to that queen. She possessed an elegance of form and manner peculiar to herself; and long after her retreat from court, it was thought a very high compliment to a young person, to say, " Qu'elle avoit de l'air de Mademoiselle " Chateauneuf."—Desportes, the Tibullus of the sixteenth century, celebrates her charms in many of his sonnets, addressed to her under the name of the duke of Anjou. After Henry the third's return from Poland, he designed to have married her to the Count de Brienne; but that nobleman quitted France, to avoid the marriage. She became

soon

1572.

April.

Pius the fifth, who at this time filled the papal chair, terrified at the intention of marrying the princefs Margaret to a Hugonot, which he apprehended would be highly injurious to the interefts of the Catholic religion, and uninformed of the defigns concealed under this alliance, ftill refufed and delayed the neceffary difpenfation. He even fuggefted to the young king of Portugal, the celebrated and unfortunate Sebaftian, to demand Margaret's hand; and difpatched the Cardinal Alexandrin as his nuncio into France, to prefs the acceptance of that propofal. Charles excufed himfelf from complying with the requeft, as having previoufly engaged his honour; but implored the legate to affure the holy Father of his filial obedience; and tenderly preffing his hands, added with warmth, " Oh! s'il m'étoit permis de " m'expliquer davantage *!"

Gregory

foon after the wife of a Florentine named Antinotti, whom fhe killed with her own hand in 1577; but it does not appear that fhe was punifhed, or even profecuted for this crime. Her fecond hufband was Philip Altoviti, baron de Caftelane, of whom mention has been made in a former note, and who was put to death in 1586 by Henry d'Angoulefme, natural fon to Henry the fecond. His widow died in great obfcurity fome years afterwards.

* De Thou minutely relates the efforts and expoftulations made by the legate, to induce Charles the ninth to retract his intentions of giving the princefs Margaret his fifter in marriage to the prince of Navarre; and adds, that the

nuncio

Gregory the thirteenth, who succeeded Pius the fifth in the papal see, having granted the dispensation, the day was fixed for the nuptials. Jane, queen of Navarre arrived at Paris with her son and the prince of Condé; but while she was engaged in preparations for the approaching ceremony, a malignant fever with which she was attacked, put an end to her life, after five

1572.
May.
5 June.
10 June.

nuncio persisting in his remonstrances on this point, the king replied, " Je ne puis pas, Monsieur le Cardinal, " m'expliquer avec vous; mais, soyez persuadé que le " Pape approuvera bientot le marriage qu'il condamne " aujourd'huy." Jerome Catena, who wrote the life of Pope Pius the fifth, relates, in addition to this anecdote, that Charles having taken off a diamond ring of great value from his finger, presented it to the cardinal, at the same time saying, " Receive this pledge of the promise which " I give you, not to defer the execution of my resolutions " against the heretics." The legate declined the acceptance of the ring, but assured his majesty, that " his word was the " most precious pledge which he could give to the sove- " reign Pontiff."
Davila allows that Charles made many ambiguous declarations of his design to the legate, promising affirmatively, that " all should terminate to the satisfaction of the " Pope, and the benefit of the Catholic religion;" but that every effort to pacify or satisfy the nuncio, was ineffectual. He relates the story of the ring, though not exactly as De Thou has done; but he says, that the cardinal refused the king's present.—Mezerai only mentions the dark and mysterious assurances made by Charles to the cardinal, intimating his intention to satisfy the Pope, and to punish his Calvinist subjects.

days

1572. days illnefs. The multitude, ever difpofed to attribute the deaths of great perfonages to violent caufes, fuppofed that poifon had been ufed for that purpofe; and a perfumer, named René, who had followed the queen-mother from Florence, of which place he was a native, has been accufed as the author of this crime. It is pretended that he even avowed himfelf as fuch, and boafted of it publicly. Some perfumed gloves, which Jane bought of him, were faid to have been the medium through which the poifon was conveyed, and Catherine of Medicis was fuppofed to be an accomplice in the tranfaction; but thefe fufpicions, on an impartial confideration of every circumftance, are probably ill founded. The phyfician and furgeon who opened her body, and who were both Hugonots, found no appearances to juftify fuch a conjecture; on the contrary, they declared her to have died of an abfcefs in her breaft; and there is every reafon to give credit to their depofition *.

Coligni,

* It muft however be confeffed that Davila afferts in the moft exprefs terms, that the queen of Navarre was poifoned. —" The firft blow of fo great a tempeft," fays he, " fell " upon Jane, whom the king and his mother thought fit to " take off by poifon; adminiftered, *as it was reported*, in " the trimming of a pair of gloves; but in a manner fo " imperceptible, and in fo nice a proportion, that after " having worn them for fome time, fhe was feized with a " violent fever, which put an end to her life in four days.—

" The

CHARLES THE NINTH.

Coligni, still irresolute, dreading Catherine's and Charles's treachery, and rendered even more distrustful

1572. July.

"The Hugonots instantly took the alarm, and began to suspect some unfair play; but to free their minds from these apprehensions, the king, knowing that the poison had left no traces except in her brain, ordered her body to be publicly opened. The vitals and intestines being found and untainted, the head was left untouched, under pretence of respect; and the surgeons then declared that she had died a natural death, caused by a fever." Notwithstanding this positive testimony of so great an historian as Davila, it may be justly questioned whether there are any poisons of so subtle a nature as only to affect the brain exclusively, and to cause death without leaving any symptoms on the body of their mortal tendency.

De Thou seems to discredit the suspicion of the queen of Navarre's death having been accelerated by any unnatural means. He says that she died of a fever, at the age of forty-three years, and some months; that reports of poison were spread, and René, a Milanese perfumer was accused as the person who had administered it; but that her body having been opened, no marks of violence were discovered, and that an abscess had formed itself in her left side.

Mezerai has strengthened the contrary opinion, by having said that the two persons who opened the queen's body did not touch her head, where it was supposed the poison had left traces too visible. D'Aubigné seems to make no question of her having been taken off by unnatural means. —Voltaire, on the contrary, has taken considerable pains to refute these assertions. "La Chronologie Novennaire" expressly declares, that Caillard her physician and Desnœuds her surgeon, *did* dissect her brain; which they found in a sound state.

KINGS OF FRANCE.

diftruftful by their careffes, long delayed his appearance at court, and retired to his caftle of Chatillon. New artifices were therefore employed for that purpofe; and an open commencement of hoftilities againft Philip the fecond in the Netherlands was permitted, as the

The queen had during her whole life been fubject to violent head-achs, attended with an itching; and fhe exprefsly requefted, that attempts might be made to afcertain the caufe, of this complaint, with the intention of relieving her children, if they fhould be attacked with the fame diforder.—Her defire was complied with; and the furgeons difcovered only fome little veficles full of water, between the brain and the membrane inclofing it, which they declared to have been the caufe of her malady.—Catherine of Medicis needs no fuppofititious crimes to blacken her character: Unhappily fhe committed too many, from which it is impoffible to juftify her.

Davila allows Jane to have been a great and accomplifhed princefs; he celebrates her courage, capacity, chaftity, and magnificence; adding, " That fhe would have been worthy
" of immortal praife, if fhe had not prefumed, without
" fufficient learning, to explore the profoundeft myfteries of
" divinity, and had not pertinacioufly adhered to the errors
" of Calvin."—D'Aubigné fays that " fhe had nothing of
" a woman about her except her fex; a manly mind, an
" elevated capacity, a magnanimity and fortitude of foul
" proof againft all the ftorms of adverfity."

De Thou concurs in thefe eulogiums on her capacity and grandeur of mind: he fays, that fhe ordered her body to be interred in the tomb of her father Henry d'Albret, without any funeral pomp; that fhe recommended to her fon Henry to perfevere in the doctrines of the Reformation; to love the princes of Condé and of Conti as his brothers; and above all, to maintain the ftricteft union between them and Coligni.

laft

last confirmation of the king's design to remain true to his past engagements. Conquered by this consummate piece of treachery, the admiral yielded against his better reason, and arrived at Paris, accompanied by a prodigious number of the Hugonot nobility, and followed by the young king of Navarre.

1572.

20 July.

The nuptials of Henry prince of Condé with Mary of Cleves, sister to the duchess of Guise, were meanwhile solemnized at the castle of Blandi near Melun; and those of Henry, now become king of Navarre by his mother's death, were appointed for the ensuing month. Every testimony of the most respectful and cordial friendship was studiously conferred on the Calvinist nobles, as well as on their leader, and every endeavour was used to dissipate their fears and suspicions.

Notwithstanding these external demonstrations of amity, the inhabitants of Rochelle dispatched repeated messengers, to implore Coligni not to rely on a king violent even to fury, and on the queen-mother, a faithless Italian, who was their irreconcilable and mortal enemy. Tho' conscious of the danger, he however remained immovable; and replied with the truest greatness of mind, that he would rather suffer himself to be dragged through the streets of Paris, than renew the horrors of a fourth civil war, and

August.

1572.
8 Aug.

and plunge his unhappy country into new calamities*. The Marechal de Montmorenci, either more clear-sighted or more cautious, obtained Charles's permission to retire to his castle of Chantilli, under pretence of an indisposition; and by that artifice saved both himself and all his family from the destruction intended for them by Catherine.

The nuptials of the king of Navarre with the princess Margaret were solemnized at the

---

* Davila says, that the admiral did not slight the solicitations repeatedly made to him to quit the court, from any feelings of a public nature; but that, elated with the honours shewn him, and intoxicated with his good fortune, he declared, that Charles and his council neither wished nor dared to attempt any thing against him and his adherents. It is however much more natural as well as pleasing, to think that Coligni was influenced by better motives: the other French historians attribute such to him; and we know that Davila, though one of the greatest writers of modern times, scarcely ever accounts for any action, or supposes it to have proceeded from disinterested and generous principles.

He relates an extraordinary anecdote, to prove the suspicions entertained among the Hugonots, relative to the king's sincerity. Langoiran, one of them, distrusting the appearance of affairs, determined at length to retire from Paris.—Coligni, when he came to take leave of him, asked Langoiran "Why he would not remain?" "Because," answered he, "I see that you are too much "caressed; and I choose rather to save myself with fools, "than perish with those who are too wise."

church

church of "Notre Dame" in Paris soon after*. The young queen was in the full bloom of her charms, and had just compleated her twentieth year. In her are said to have been united all the great qualities and virtues, with all the defects and vices of the family of Valois, from whence she sprung. The beauty of her person, captivating in the highest degree, inspired passion and desire in

---

* Davila enumerates with great exactness every circumstance attending these inauspicious nuptials. The cardinal of Bourbon performed the marriage ceremony, in presence of the whole court, and accompanied with a royal magnificence; but Davila expressly declares, that when the Princess Margaret was asked, whether she would take the king of Navarre for her husband? She did not answer a word. The king her brother having however, with his hand compelled her to bow her head, this act was interpreted as a consent on the part of the princess; though she always continued and persisted to assert, that to be deprived of the duke of Guise to whom she had engaged her promise, and to be united to his most inveterate enemy, were things to which her mind could never be reconciled. The young king of Navarre submitted notwithstanding, with a good grace, to all the marks of alienation visible in the conduct of his bride. The entertainments given by the court on this occasion lasted three days, and were more splendid than any ever exhibited at the nuptials of a princess of France. It is scarcely conceivable or credible, that only six days elapsed between the marriage of Charles's sister to the king of Navarre, and the massacre of St. Bartholomew.

the coldest bosoms. Her complexion was clear and animated, her hair of the finest black, and her eyes equally full of fire and languor. Her look, voluptuous and tender, indicated a heart framed for love; while full of grace and majesty in all her movements, and possessing like her mother, the art of disposing every ornament of dress with the most exquisite taste, she announced her high birth the instant that she appeared.

Her genius and imagination were equal to those of the first Margaret of Valois, queen of Navarre; and like that princess, she was celebrated by all the poets of her time, with the most flattering eulogiums. They addressed her rather as a deity than a mortal, and gave her the epithets of " Venus Urania," and " Celestis." Her munificence, her passion for glory, her protection of letters, her vanity, her unbounded attachment to the pleasures of love, were all striking features of the character of Francis the first, whom she intimately resembled, and whose memory she revered. Courteous and affable in her manners, like her father Henry the second, she was likewise of a temper yielding, flexible, and attached to favourites.

Capable of conducting the greatest affairs of government, but hurried away by her inclinations,

clinations, she only emerged by paroxysms from pleasure, and returned to it again from an incapacity of resisting its allurements. Mingling devotion with gallantry, and connecting the fervours of religion with the excesses of dissipation, she appeared, one while a penitent, stretched at the foot of the altar, and bewailing her past transgressions; at another, a refined voluptuary, devoted to all the enchantment of epicurean wantonness.

An unstudied eloquence, a graceful facility of expression characterised her in an eminent degree; but carried away by an enthusiasm which she could not restrain, her very virtues were carried to an extreme, and her vices were not concealed under any sort of decorum. Enslaved by constitution more than by passion, and criminal from habit rather than from principle; if genius, if generosity of sentiment, and superiority of talents could form the least apology for unrestrained sensuality, it would be in the person of Margaret queen of Navarre*.

The

* Margaret was born on the 14th of May, 1552. Brantome has exhausted all the powers of panegyric in his delineation of her character: Those which he bestows on her virtue might as well have been omitted; but the encomiums which he pays to her beauty and understanding she certainly merited. The assemblage of charms, accomplishments, and winning qualities which she possessed, rendered her almost irresistible. She sung and played on the

1572. The moſt ſplendid entertainments and demonſtrations of joy ſucceeded to the marriage of the king of Navarre, and were continued during three days; but amidſt this ſcene of feſtivity, the plan of the projected maſſacre was matured, and the circumſtances of it's future execution arranged. The intention of Charles and of the Guiſes extended only to the excluſive deſtruction of the Hugonots; but it is ſaid that Catherine, hardened to the commiſſion of crimes, and more influenced by motives of ambition than of zeal for religion, had carried her deſigns to a much greater length, and meant to involve the Calviniſts, the Guiſes, and the Montmorencis, in one common carnage. This deſign is imputed to her by the greateſt French hiſtorians; nor is even ſo atrocious a project

the lute with exquiſite ſkill; and in dancing, no lady of the court was her equal, whether in the ſerious, or the lively kind. Her perſon poſſeſſed a thouſand graces, all which Brantome enumerates; but it is her boſom on which he principally dwells, with uncommon pleaſure. "Car jamais," ſays he, " n'en fut veue une ſi belle, ni " ſi blanche, ſi pleine, ni ſi charnue, qu'elle montroit; et " ſi deſcouverte, que la plupart des courtiſans en mou- " roient: voire les dames, que j'ai veues aucunes de ſes " plus confidentes et privées, avec ſa licence, la baiſer par " un grand raviſſement." This paſſage certainly tends to convey no faint idea of the diſſolute and libertine manners of the court of Catherine of Medecis.

incompatible

incompatible with, or contradictory to the genius of the queen-mother, who was capable of forming and executing schemes of vengeance the most unexampled and detestable.

The assassination of the admiral was determined on, as a prelude to the general massacre, and a man named Mourevel, rendered infamous by the murder of the Seigneur de Mouy one of the Calvinist leaders, was selected for that purpose. He posted himself therefore in a little chamber of the cloister of St. Germain de l'Auxerrois, belonging to one of the canons who had been preceptor to the duke of Guise, and near which Coligni usually passed, in his return from the palace of the Louvre to his own house. As the admiral walked slowly on, employed in the perusal of some papers which he held in his hand, Mourevel, from a window which looked into the street, levelled a harquebusse at him loaded with two balls; one of which broke the fore-finger of his right-hand, and the other lodged in his left arm, near the elbow. The assassin fled instantly at another door of the cloister, and mounted a horse provided for him by the duke of Guise, on which he escaped. Coligni, without betraying the least emotion, and turning calmly towards the place from whence came the shot, "Le coup," said he, "vient de là;" pointing with

1572.

22 Aug.

1572. with his finger to the window. His attendants immediately conveyed him home, where his wounds were dressed.*

The

* Davila in his account of this infamous transaction, positively attributes it to Henry duke of Guise, who deemed himself justified in attempting to take away the admiral's life by the same means, which he conceived this latter had formerly used to assassinate Francis his father, at the siege of Orleans. Davila likewise expressly declares that " the " duke of Guise had received the king's commission to take " away Coligni's life, as a blow preparatory to the general " destruction of the Calvinists."

" Mourevel," says Davila, " having shut himself up in " a little lower room of a house near the Louvre, belong- " ing to the duke of Guise's family, and having covered " the window, which had iron bars, with an old tattered " cloak, waited with great secrecy and patience, for a con- " venient opportunity. On the third day he executed his " commission, as the admiral was walking slowly along, " followed by his servants. One of the balls took off the " fore finger of Coligni's right hand; and the second tore " the flesh from his left elbow, and broke the bone. The " doors of the house were immediately burst open, and all " the apartments searched in vain; they found only a little " boy, Mourevel having already escaped by the gate St. " Antoine."

De Thou likewise declares that the duke of Guise acted with the king's consent and privity, in the attempt to cause the admiral to be assassinated by Mourevel. His relation of this whole transaction coincides with that given by Davila in all the leading circumstances. " Coligni, after coming from the council on Friday the 22d of August, says De Thou, accompanied the king who went to play

at

CHARLES THE NINTH.

The king who was playing at tennis in the court of the Louvre, when this news was brought him, feigning the moſt furious indignation, threw down his racket on the ground, and inſtantly left the place. With loud imprecations he denounced vengeance on the miſcreant who had attempted the admiral's life, and named judges immediately for the purpoſe of bringing

at tennis with the duke of Guiſe and Teligni. Having regarded the game as a ſpectator for ſome time, the admiral quitted the place, and returned home on foot, walking ſlowly, and occupied in the peruſal of a memorial which he had juſt received. As he paſſed before the houſe of Pierre de Villemur, who had been preceptor to the duke of Guiſe, Mourevel from a window ſhot him with two balls, of which one broke the fore finger of his right hand, and the other wounded him ſeverely near the left elbow, Guerchy, and Sorbieres des Pruneaux being on each ſide of him. Totally unmoved by the accident, Coligni inſtantly pointed to the place from whence came the ſhot, and diſpatched two of his adherents, Clermont de Piles and Francois de Monins, to inform Charles the ninth of this extraordinary act of perfidy and violence. He then cauſed his arm to be bound up, and continued his return home on foot, ſupported by his ſervants. Only a laquais, a maid ſervant, and a harquebuſſe were found on breaking open the doors of the houſe, Mourevel having already made his eſcape."

Mezerai differs little, if at all, from the two beforementioned hiſtorians; but he ſeems to impute more extended and flagitious ſchemes of deſtruction to the queen-mother, than to Charles, or to the family of Guiſe.

him

1572. him to trial and punishment.* Coligni having signified his wish to communicate some important matters to his Majesty in private, Charles went in person to visit him on the afternoon of the

* At the news of Coligni's accident, says De Thou, Charles the ninth, who was playing at tennis, threw his racket on the ground with all the marks of agitation and distress, exclaiming, "N'aurai-je jamais de repos ? Quoi ! "toujours de nouveaux troubles !" He instantly quitted the place with looks of indignation, and the duke of Guise retired likewise by another door. When the king of Navarre and the prince of Condé came to visit Coligni, he said to them, " Is this, then, that reconciliation of which "the king was guarantee ?"—Meanwhile it became indispensible to amputate the finger which had been broken by the ball, as a mortification had begun to manifest itself in the part. Ambrose Paré the king's surgeon performed the operation without delay; but, unfortunately, owing to the want of proper instruments, he was necessitated to make use of a pair of bad scissars, and could not take off the wounded finger in less than three several attempts. Coligni, notwithstanding, never betrayed any emotion, nor let the slightest complaint escape him, either during the amputation, or when the wound in his left arm was dressed.

Davila mentions the circumstance of the king's having loudly protested that he would revenge so daring an assassination committed at the very gate of his own palace; but, he confesses, that all this resentment and indignation was merely feigned. The precaution which Charles afterwards used, of commanding all the gates of the capital except two to be shut, under pretence of stopping Mourevel's flight, Davila owns, was done only to prevent the escape of the Hugonots.

same

same day, accompanied by the queen-mother, his brother Henry duke of Anjou, and several of the nobility. About the admiral's bed were ranged the king of Navarre, the prince of Condé, and all the Hugonot chiefs or adherents. Charles carried his diffimulation on this occafion, to the greateft pitch of hypocrify; and after a general difcourfe, entertained Coligni near an hour in private converfation. He affected to approve, and promifed to comply with his advice, of attacking the Spaniards in the Low-Countries; he exhaufted every conciliatory art to efface the unfavourable impreffions made upon his mind; and proceeded fo far at this interview, that Catherine herfelf took the alarm, and demanded of her fon with earneftnefs, what advice the admiral had given him; to which the king replied, fwearing as was his cuftom, that Coligni had counfelled him to reign alone, and to be no longer governed by others *.

All

* When Charles the ninth entered the admiral's apartment, he faid, with all the appearances of concern and fympathy, " Mon Pere, la bleffure eft pour vous, et la dou-
" leur pour moi; mais vous ferez vengé d'une maniere
" fi terrible, qu'on s'en fouviendra eternellement."—This is De Thou's account; who, however adds, that it is uncertain whether the king and Coligni had any private converfation, or whether Catherine of Medecis, who feared the effect which the fuggeftions of the admiral might produce upon her fon's mind, did not prevent their converfing together

All this pretended concern could not however diminish the alarm of the Hugonot party, or dissipate their apprehensions. The king of Navarre and the prince of Condé waited on Charles, to request his permission to leave Paris, in which they deemed themselves no longer safe; and could scarcely be restrained by any entreaties from executing their intention, tho' Charles and his mother, with solemn and repeated

gether apart. When Coligni pressed the king to declare war with Philip the second, and to aid the revolted Flemings in the Netherlands, Charles artfully broke off the discourse, by affecting an apprehension lest the admiral's health should suffer from any animated remonstrances, in his present state of body. At his departure, he expressed a desire to see the balls with which the admiral had been wounded, and which were of copper.—The Count de Retz, under pretence of more effectually protecting Coligni against any possible insurrection, or effects of popular violence, proposed to transport him to the palace of the Louvre: Charles approved of this expedient, which would have put the admiral more perfectly and compleatly in his power; but the surgeons declared that it would be dangerous, and probably fatal, to attempt his removal.

Davila says, that the king, accompanied by his mother and the duke of Anjou, after a hasty dinner, went immediately to visit the admiral, who urgently requested his Majesty's permission to retire from Paris, a city hostile and ill-affected to him, and desired leave to cause himself to be transported to his own castle of Chatillon. Charles upbraided and remonstrated with him on his want of confidence, and doubts of his royal protection; opposed such a journey as dangerous

peated denunciations of exemplary vengeance on the aſſaſſin, beſought them not to quit the capital. The Calviniſt nobles called for inſtant puniſhment on Mourevel; and Clermont de Piles, one of them, entered the palace of the Louvre at the head of four hundred gentlemen, threatening to revenge the aſſaſſination of Coligni.

This laſt violent ſtep accelerated the maſſacre, the queen-mother having perſuaded her ſon that he would be himſelf the victim of his own irreſolution, and that his only ſecurity lay in preventing the Calviniſts, by deciſive and ſpeedy meaſures. Many conſultations were held among the Hugonot leaders, reſpecting the conduct neceſſary to be purſued in circumſtances ſo critical and hazardous. John de Ferrieres, Vidame of Chartres ſtrongly urged a retreat, and aſſerted that it was practicable before the people were armed; but Coligni's

dangerous to his health, and reiterated his aſſurances of regard and affection. The phyſicians concurring in opinion that any attempt to move him might be fatal, Coligni, making a virtue of neceſſity, and ſeeing how impoſſible it was to effect his retreat, acquieſced in and ſubmitted to the king's requeſt, recommended himſelf to his majeſty's protection, and demanded juſtice for the late atrocious attempt upon his life.—Charles and Catherine gave him every aſſurance of amity, and having peculiarly recommended the care of his perſonal ſafety to the duke of Anjou as governor of Paris, returned to the palace of the Louvre.

1572. extreme reluctance to rekindle a civil war, made him determine rather to die than to leave the capital; and his son-in-law Teligni strengthened, with all his influence, this sentiment.

Compelled however by the many symptoms which he observed of the approaching and imminent danger, the Vidame renewed his solicitations, and insisted on them with more warmth, as the admiral seemed able to support the fatigue of a removal. A gentleman who had been present at this council, and who betrayed his party, carried immediate intimation of their debates and intentions to the palace of the Tuilleries, where Charles had assembled his secret council in his mother's apartment*.

The

---

* Davila relates the repeated attempts made by the Vidame of Chartres, to induce Coligni to retire to Chatillon, and to quit a city in which his life was not secure for a moment; and he says, that the Vidame's expostulations and arguments *had* prevailed on the Hugonot chiefs to follow his advice. Teligni maintained that he could procure the king's permission for this purpose; while the other leaders offered, in case it was refused, to carry off the admiral by open force. Davila allows that there was treachery in the Hugonot councils, though he does not name the traitors; and adds that the court having received intelligence by the accustomed channel, of their determination to leave Paris, and to renew the civil war, instantly came to a decisive resolution to anticipate such a retreat, and to commence the massacre.

De

CHARLES THE NINTH.

The apprehenſion of Coligni's eſcape, which muſt have involved them in new and deeper embarraſſment, ſtrengthened by the opinion of the Marechal de Tavannes his mortal and inveterate enemy, who loudly adviſed a total extermination of the Hugonots, at length prevailed on the king, and obtained his reluctant conſent. It is ſaid, that he long heſitated on the dreadful meaſure, and ſhuddered at its conſequences: but being overcome by the reiterated and preſsing remonſtrances of thoſe about him, he exclaimed with his uſual imprecations, " Eh

De Thou, who agrees with Davila in his account of the reiterated efforts made by the Vidame of Chartres to prevail on the admiral to remove from Paris, yet maintains that he never could carry his point, as the king of Navarre, the prince of Condé, and Teligni perſiſted to oppoſe an act, which muſt be an outrage to the king, who had given them ſo many marks of affection and regard. He names Bayancourt de Bouchavannes as the perſon who was ſuſpected to have betrayed the Hugonots, and revealed all their intentions to Charles and Catherine of Medecis. —Mezerai coincides with De Thou; and imputes to the repugnance of Coligni, and to the unſuſpecting good faith of Teligni, the rejection of the Vidame of Chartres's advice. He adds, that a gentleman who had been preſent at the deliberations held in the admiral's apartment, carried information of every thing which had been there tranſacted to the palace of the Tuilleries, where Charles had aſſembled his ſecret cabinet; and that upon this gentleman's depoſition it was finally reſolved to commence the maſſacre.

" bien!

"bien! puisque il le faut, je ne veux pas qu'il en reste un seul qui me le puisse reprocher!"

The completion of the design was appointed for the same night; the duke of Guise was constituted chief, as being animated with a peculiar detestation to the admiral, whom he considered as his father's murderer; and the signal was to be made by the striking of the great bell of the palace, on which they should instantly begin the massacre.

As the awful moment approached, Charles's terrors and irresolution encreased. Some principles of remaining honour, some sentiments of humanity, commiseration and virtue, which all Catherine's pernicious maxims and exhortations had not been able totally to destroy, yet maintained a conflict in his bosom. His mind, torn by the agitations of contending passions, affected and disordered his body. Cold sweats bedewed his forehead, and his whole frame trembled, as if under the attack of an ague. He paused upon the threshold of the enterprize, while the slaughter of his innocent people rose before his imagination in all its horror. Catherine exerted every endeavour to support his wavering resolution, and to stifle his nobler feelings. With infinite difficulty she forced from him a precise command to commence the massacre; and having obtained it, still dreading

ing a relapse in her son, she hastened the signal more than an hour, and gave it by the bell of the church of St. Germain de l'Auxerrois*.

When

* "At midnight," says d'Aubigné, "and at the moment when the massacre was to begin, Catherine, who feared some change in the king, entered his apartment, where were assembled the dukes of Guise and Nevers, Birague keeper of the seals, Tavannes, and the Marechal de Retz, whom Henry duke of Anjou had conducted thither. The king was in great emotion and uncertainty; but the queen-mother, among other arguments which she used to encourage him, said, 'Vaut il pas mieux dechirer ces membres pourris, que le sein de l'Eglise, Epouse de notre seigneur?' She finished by a passage taken from the sermons of the bishop of Bitonto, 'Che pieta lor fer crudele; che crudelta lor fer pietosa.'"

The duke of Guise, as De Thou assures us, was not present at the council in which the immediate commission of the massacre was determined, but received his orders and instructions from the king himself, on the evening of that fatal night, to assemble the guards, and to make all the necessary preparations. In consequence of the royal command, the duke disposed every circumstance, and enjoined that the Catholics should wear about their left arm a white scarf, and a cross of the same colour in their hats. Candles, or lights were likewise recommended to be placed in all the windows, to facilitate the projected destruction of the Hugonots, and to enable the Catholics more easily to recognize each other in such a scene of horror and confusion.

De Thou describes the irresolution and fluctuations of mind in the king, previous to the commencement of the

bloody

1572.
24 August.

When Charles heard the dreadful knell, he was seized with new remorse, which was increased by the report of some pistols in the street; and overcome with affright, he sent instantly to command the leaders not to put the design in execution till further orders: but it was too late. The work of death was already begun; and the messengers brought back word that the people become furious, could no longer be restrained or withheld from exercising

bloody tragedy. Catherine, adds he, seeing her son turn pale, and a cold sweat appear on his forehead, reproached him with the want of courage—"Quoi!" said she, "vous "n'osez vous defaire de gens, qui ont si peu menagé votre "autorité, & votre personne?" Charles catching fire at this contemptuous reflection, and piqued at his mother's insinuation of his want of courage, gave orders instantly to begin the massacre; but Catherine, fearful that as his resentment abated, he might retract the declaration, anticipated the signal which was to have been made only an hour before day-break, and caused it to be given immediately.

Mezerai coincides in almost every particular with De Thou; and describes in very affecting colours the agitations and distress of the young king, before his mother with difficulty forced from him a precise order for the commencement of the massacre.

Davila is totally silent on all this part of the history of the night of St. Bartholomew, though minute in his narration of many other circumstances attending that unprecedented act of blood.

cising their vengeance on the Hugonots *. It is not my intention to unveil or describe all the horrors of that fatal night, which are unhappily perpetuated by their atrocity to times the most remote. The picture is best concealed in darkness, and is almost too flagitious and affecting for the pen of history to commemorate. Yet some particulars of it may naturally be expected, and peculiarly those which accompanied Coligni's end, so long the support of the Hugonot religion and party.

---

* After the first signal given by Catherine of Medecis, says De Thou, a tumult having immediately begun, the Hugonots, who were lodged in the vicinity of the Louvre, and who were awakened by the noise in the streets, anxiously enquired what was the occasion of the lights in all the windows, as well as the reason of the people being armed. They were answered, that it was on account of a diversion which was to be exhibited for the queens; and curiosity prompting them to advance towards the Louvre, they were immediately cut to pieces by the guards, who were drawn up before the palace. Catherine of Medecis, anxious to prevent the possibility of her son's retreat, and dreading a change in his resolutions, upon the information which she received of some blood being spilt, went instantly to Charles's apartment; who. terrified at the news of the massacre being begun, had just sent orders to suspend it's further prosecution. The queen-mother having assured him, that " it was too late to revoke his intention, and that " neither the people nor the soldiery could be any longer " restrained," Charles, driven forward, took his decisive resolution, and caused the signal to be made by the bell of St. Germain de l'Auxerrois.

1572. The admiral had been long retired to rest, when the noise of the assassins compelled him to rise; and apprehending immediately their intentions, he prepared as became himself, for death. A German gentleman named Besme, followed by a number of others, burst open the door, and entering his chamber, advanced towards the admiral, holding a long rapier in his hand. Coligni looking at him with an undismayed countenance, and incapable of resistance from the late wounds which he had received, only said, " Young man, respect these " grey hairs, nor stain them with blood!" Besme hesitated a moment, then plunged the weapon into his bosom; and the others immediately threw out his body into the court, where it was impatiently expected by the duke of Guise. He contemplated it in silence, without offering it any injury; but Henry d'Angoulesme, Grand Prior of France, who was with the duke, having wiped the face with a handkerchief, and recognized the admiral's features which were covered with blood, gave the corpse a kick; adding, with a barbarous joy to those about him——" Courage! my friends! " we have begun well: let us finish in the " same manner*."

Teligni,

* Davila has related minutely, though with some little variation, this affecting and tragical story. " At the hour " appointed,"

Teligni, a youth of the moſt beautiful perſon, and the moſt engaging manners, who had married

"appointed," ſays he, "the duke of Guiſe, his uncle the
"duke of Aumale, and Henry d'Angouleſme the king's
"natural brother, attended by about three hundred fol-
"lowers, repaired to the admiral's houſe. They were there
"joined by a company of Catholic ſoldiers, commanded
"by Coſſeins, whom the duke of Anjou had ſtationed for
"that purpoſe, under arms, and with their matches lighted.
"The gate of the court, which was only guarded by a few
"of the king of Navarre's halberdiers, they inſtantly
"forced; putting to death both them, and all the ſervants
"whom they met, without mercy. The nobles waited
"below, while La Beſme, a native of Lorrain, and an im-
"mediate dependant of the duke of Guiſe, went up to
"Coligni's apartment. He was accompanied by Achille
"Petrucci, a Sienneſe gentleman retained by the duke, by
"colonel Sarlebous, and the other ſoldiers.

"The admiral hearing a diſturbance, got up; and
"kneeling down, ſupported himſelf againſt the bed, when
"one of his ſervants, named Cornaſon, burſt into the
"room. Coligni aſked him, 'What occaſion'd the noiſe?'
To which Cornaſon haſtily replied, 'My lord, God calls
'us to him;' and inſtantly ran out at another door. The
"aſſaſſins entered a moment afterwards, and advanced
"towards him: Coligni addreſſing himſelf to La Beſme,
"who had drawn his ſword, ſaid, 'Young man, you
'ought to reverence theſe grey hairs; but do what you
'think proper: my life can only be ſhortened a very little.'
"He had ſcarce ſpoke theſe words, when La Beſme
"plunged the ſword into his breaſt, and the others diſ-
"patched him with their daggers. They then threw his
"body down into the court, from whence it was dragged
"into a ſtable."

De

1572. married Coligni's daughter, was massacred on that night at the same time, having attempted to

De Thou's account differs in no material point whatever from that of Davila, though he mentions some circumstances omitted by the last historian. "Cosseins," says De Thou, " having united himself to the duke of Guise " and his followers on their arrival at the admiral's " house, ordered Labonne, who kept the keys, to open the " door in the king's name. He obeyed without the slight- " est suspicion of treachery, and was instantly stabbed. " The persons who were with him, astonished and ter- " rified at this unexpected assassination, fled; and gain- " ing the staircase, endeavoured to stop the further en- " trance of the ruffians, by barricading the passage with " chairs and tables. Meanwhile Coligni, hearing a noise, " imagined it was caused by some tumult; but persisting " to repose himself on the honour and good faith of the " king, he still conceived his person secure under the " guard which had been assigned for his protection; 'till " hearing a harquebusse fired in the court, he got out of " bed. While he was preparing himself for every event, the " door of the staircase was burst open, and the assassins " mounted to his apartment. Cosseins, d'Attins, Corbe- " ron, Cardillac, Sarlabouz, Petrucci, and a German " named Besme, who had been a servant in the duke of " Guise's house, entered his chamber, all armed with " cuirasses. They forced the door, and Besme advancing " first, with a sword in his hand, said to the admiral. ' Eſt-ce toi qui es Coligni ?' ' C'eſt moi meme,' an- " ſwered he, with a ſerene air ; and ſhewing Beſme his " grey hairs, ' Jeune homme,' added he, ' tu devrois re- ' ſpecter mon age ; mais acheve. Tu ne peux abreger ' ma vie que de fort peu de jours.' Beſme made no re-
" ply,

to save himself on the roof of the house, where he was discovered, and stabbed by the assassins.

"ply, but plunged his sword into the admiral's body, and
"drawing it out, cut him several times across the face.
"It is reported," continues De Thou, "that Coligni ex-
"claimed, on receiving the wound from Besme, ' Au
' moins si je perissois par la main d'un homme de cœur ;
' & non par celle d'un miserable valet !'
"The duke of Guise, who during this unmanly assas-
"sination, had remained in the court below with the
"nobility who attended him, demanded if the busi-
"ness was finished ; and being answered in the affirma-
"tive, ' Monsieur d'Angoulesme,' said he, ' ne le croira
' point, s'il ne voit le traitre a ses pieds.' The body of
"the admiral was immediately thrown down from a win-
"dow ; and the Count d'Angoulesme having with a piece
"of linen wiped off the blood from the face, and recog-
"nized the features, disgraced himself so far as to kick
"the corpse, and to treat it with other indignities."

Brantome, in his "Life of Coligni," relates, with scarce any material variation, all the principal circumstances enumerated by De Thou and Davila. He says, that "Sarla-
"bous, governor of Havre, boasted to have put the
"admiral to death ; but that beyond a doubt Besme
"gave the mortal blow ; as a reward for which act of
"blood, the duke of Guise, whose page he had been,
"married him to the natural daughter of the cardinal of
"Lorrain. Besme, vain of the exploit which he had per-
"formed, and in expectation of receiving from Philip
"the second a reward proportionate to the magnitude and
"importance of it, went into Spain two years afterwards,
"and was treated by Philip with great civility. That
"monarch conferred many favours on him ; but return-
"ing

fins. But the fate of the Count de la Rochefoucault was attended with circumstances which excite peculiar pity and indignation. He had passed the whole evening with the king at play; and Charles, touched with pity for a nobleman so amiable, whom he even personally loved, would willingly have rescued him from the general destruction. With that intention he ordered la Rochefoucault to remain all night in his privy chamber; but the Count, who apprehended that the king only meant to divert himself at his expence by some puerile trick, refused, and retired to his own apartment in the Louvre. "I see," said Charles, " it is the will of God " that he should perish!" When the officer who was sent to destroy him knocked at the door, he opened it himself, apprehending it to have been the king; and seeing several persons enter masqued, he advanced gaily to meet them,

---

" ing into France, God, the just avenger of crimes," says Brantome, " either blinded him, or his malignant destiny " conducted him into the hands of the Hugonots; who " made him prisoner as he passed through Guienne, be- " tween Barbesieux and Chateauneuf. Besme was car- " ried immediately to the castle of Bouteville, where the " Sieur de Bertauville commanded, who detained him a " considerable time, and at length, on pretence of his " having attempted to effect his escape, caused him to be " killed as a victim to the manes of Coligni."

but

but was instantly dispatched with their daggers *.

The Count de Guerchy, who lodged in the same house with Coligni, wrapping his cloak about his arm, died sword-in-hand'; and killed several of his murderers before he fell himself. Soubise, covered with wounds, after a long and gallant defence, was at last put to death under the queen-mother's windows; and the ladies

---

* Even Brantome severely arraigns and condemns the conduct of Charles the ninth, in permitting the Count de la Rochefoucault to be put to death at the massacre of St. Bartholomew. He relates the circumstances attending it, with more minuteness than De Thou: " When Chicot the " king's buffoon, and his brother the captain Raymond," says Brantome, " came in the morning to break open the " door of Rochefoucault's apartment, he immediately rose " and dressed himself, imagining it to be Charles him- " self, who came to play some youthful frolic. The af- " sassins continuing to attempt to force the door, he cried " out, (still conceiving that he addressed his discourse " to the king) ' Ce sont des jeux du feu roy, votre pere ; ' vous ne m'y attraperez pas ; car je suis tout chauffé et ' vestu.' In this fatal and unsuspecting security, he ordered the door to be opened, and was instantly murdered. Charles, in excuse for having permitted a nobleman on whom he had recently bestowed so many marks of personal affection, to be basely assassinated, said, that he had two or three times in vain requested Rochefoucault to remain in his own chamber during that fatal night; — an apology which serves only to heighten the atrocity of the action!

of the court, from a savage and unnatural curiosity, went to view his naked corpse, disfigured and bloody. The bodies of the slaughtered Hugonots were collected and thrown in heaps before the palace of the Louvre, to satiate at once the curiosity and the vengeance of Catherine of Medecis, who fed her eyes with this inhuman spectacle. The Marechal de Tavannes, one of the most violent in the execution of the massacre, ran through the streets, crying, " Let blood! Let blood! Bleeding is " equally wholesome in the month of August, " as in the month of May !" Even the king himself, forgetful of the sacred duties which he owed to his people and to humanity, was personally aiding on that night, in the slaughter of his miserable subjects. It is said that he fired on them with a long harquebusse from the windows of his palace, and endeavoured to kill the fugitives who attempted to escape from the " Fauxbourg St. Germain."

The admiral's body was treated with indignities which dishonour human nature, and underwent all the fury of an enraged and barbarous populace. An Italian first severed his head from the trunk, and carried it to Catherine of Medecis; after which the people cut off the hands, leaving the disfigured remains upon a dunghill. In the afternoon they took the body up again,

CHARLES THE NINTH.

again, dragged it three days in the dirt, then on the banks of the Seine, and laftly, carried it to the village of Montfauçon, where it was hung upon a gibbet by the feet with an iron chain, and a fire lighted under it, by which it was fcorched, without being confumed. In this dreadful fituation, the king went with feveral of his courtiers to furvey it; and as the corpfe fmelt very difagreeably, fome of them turning away their heads, "The body of a dead enemy," faid Charles, "fmells always well!"—The remains of Coligni, after fo many indignities, were at length taken down privately in a very dark night, by order of the Marechal de Montmorenci, and interred with the utmoft privacy in the chapel of the caftle of Chantilli.

Many accidents conduced, notwithftanding the rigorous orders for an univerfal flaughter, to refcue numbers of the Hugonots; and the king himfelf excepted two from the common deftruction. The firft of thefe was his furgeon, the celebrated Ambrofe Paré, whofe fuperior and uncommon profeffional fkill proved the prefervation of his life, Charles having commanded him to remain in his own apartment during that dreadful night. The other perfon was his nurfe, to whom he was warmly attached, and to whom he never refufed any requeft. The duke of Guife himfelf preferved more than

a huna hundred, with intent to attach them to his service, whom he concealed during the violence of the maffacre, in his own palace.

The Montmorencis, all which family had been inrolled in the fatal lift, and devoted by Catherine of Medecis to death, were fecured by the abfence of the Marechal, their eldeft brother, who it was feared might feverely revenge the flaughter of his relations. The tears and entreaties of Mademoifelle de Chateauneuf, prevailed on her lover the duke of Anjou to fpare the Marechal de Coffé, who was allied to her by blood. Biron, grand mafter of the artillery, and afterwards fo renown'd in the wars of Henry the fourth, having pointed feveral culverines over the gate of the arfenal, ftopped in fome meafure the fury of the Catholics, and afforded an afylum to many of his friends and adherents.

The Count de Montgomeri, and the Vidame of Chartres, with near a hundred gentlemen, who were lodged to the fouth of the river Seine, in the " Fauxbourg St. Germain," efcaped on horfeback, half naked; but being purfued by the duke of Guife, and overtaken at break of day, many of them were cut off, only the two chiefs and about ten of their followers arriving fafe on the coaft of Normandy, from whence they paffed over into England.

England. Henry king of Navarre, and the 1572. prince of Condé, were exempted from the general carnage, though not without violent debates in the council. Charles ordered them both to be conducted into his presence, and commanded them, with menaces and imprecations, to abjure their religion, on pain of instant death. The king of Navarre obeyed; but the prince of Condé obstinately refusing to renounce his principles, Charles, at length, frantic with indignation, said to him in three words, "Mort, Messe, ou Bastile!" This threat was effectual, and the young prince, terrified into submission, complied with the necessity of his situation *.

During

* Davila declares, that the duke of Guise strenuously endeavoured to have the two princes of Bourbon included in the massacre; but Charles and the queen-mother thinking it an action so abominable and detestable, to imbrue their hands in the blood of their own relations, that no reasons of state could in any degree justify or authorize it, peremptorily refused their consent. He adds, that the king was peculiarly inclined to this conduct, from personal affection, and regard to the many virtues of Henry king of Navarre.

De Thou says, that the council was unanimous in their opinion that the king of Navarre, so recently allied to Charles by a marriage with his own sister, could not be put to death in the very arms of his bride, and in the palace of his brother-in-law, without reflecting indelible infamy

1572. During a whole week the massacre did not cease, though its extreme fury lasted only for the two

infamy on the perpetrators of such a deed, to the latest posterity. But he adds, that there was more difficulty respecting the prince of Condé, to whom the court bore an hereditary hatred. The entreaties of the duke of Nevers, who had married the princess of Condé's sister, superadded to his own relationship to the blood royal, prevailed however over his enemies, and determined Charles to except him from the general destruction.

Davila and De Thou perfectly coincide in their account of the menaces made use of by Charles the ninth, to compel the two princes of Bourbon to renounce and abjure their religious opinions. The latter of these historians asserts, that about a fortnight after the massacre, on the 9th of September, the king, irritated by the inflexibility of the prince of Condé, called for arms to be brought to him, and determined at the head of his guards to exterminate the surviving Hugonots, of whom the prince himself should be the first victim. The advice and efforts of the young queen his wife, who besought him not to proceed to an act of such vengeance without asking the opinion of his council, induced Charles to dismiss his guards, and to desist from the prosecution of this barbarous purpose. But, on the following day, having sent for the prince, he said to him, with a tone of voice and manner the most indignant, " Messe, mort, ou prison perpetuelle!" " A " Dieu ne plaise," answered Condé, " que je choisisse " la premiere! Pour les deux autres autres, c'est a votre " majesté a decider. Je prie la providence de vouloir la " guider dans la resolution qu'elle prendra." This humble and submissive reply in some degree disarmed the violence of Charles, and induced him to determine on

a milder

two first days; and every enormity which zeal, revenge, and cruelty are capable of influencing mankind to commit, stain the dreadful registers of this unhappy period. More than five thousand persons of all ranks perished by various kinds of death; the Seine was loaded with floating carcases; and Charles saw with satisfaction from the windows of the Louvre, this unnatural and abominable spectacle. A butcher, who entered the palace during the heat of the massacre, is said to have boasted to his sovereign, baring his bloody arm, that he had dispatched himself a hundred and fifty Hugonots *.

1572.

Catherine

a milder treatment. The prince of Condé, yielding soon afterwards to motives of terror more than of conviction, abjured the principles of the reformation, and received absolution in the Pope's name, from his uncle the cardinal of Bourbon, as did his two brothers, the prince of Conti, and the Count de Soissons.

* The account which Margaret queen of Navarre has given us in her Memoirs of the night of St. Bartholomew, is not only of the most incontestible authenticity, but too interesting in its own nature to be omitted. On the evening preceding the massacre, Margaret was at the queen her mother's " Coucher," who ordered her to retire.—" As " I made my courtesy," says she, " my sister of Lorrain" (Claude, princess of France, married to the duke of Lorrain) " took hold of my arm, and stopping me, burst into " tears; ' My God,' said she, ' sister, do not go!' which " frightened me extremely. The queen my mother per-
" ceived

KINGS OF FRANCE.

Catherine of Medecis, who scattered destruction in so many shapes, was not affected
with

"ceived it, and calling my sister to her, reprehended her
"very severely, and forbid her to say any thing to me. I
"saw plainly that they differed, but could not hear their
"words; and the queen commanded me a second time
"rudely to go to bed. My sister, melting into tears, bid
"me good night, without daring to say any thing else;
"and I went out, all trembling and terrified, without
"being able to imagine what I had to fear." The king
of Navarre was already in bed, and Margaret found him
surrounded by thirty or forty of the Hugonot Lords, who
remained the whole night in conversation upon the subject
of the admiral's late wound. At break of day Henry rose,
intending to play at tennis, and fully determined as soon
as Charles the ninth was awake, to demand justice on the
assassins of Coligni. Margaret then yielding to fatigue, ordered the door of her apartment to be shut, and soon fell
asleep; but scarcely had an hour elapsed, when a person
came to the door, and knocking violently at it with his
hands and feet, cried out, "Navarre! Navarre!" The
nurse, who lay in her apartment, rose immediately to open
it, apprehending it to be Henry her husband. A gentleman, named Tersan, covered with wounds, and pursued by
four archers, instantly burst in, threw himself on her bed,
and clasping her in his arms, besought her to save his
life. He had received two wounds; one in the neck
from a sword, and the other in his arm from a halberd.
The archers, notwithstanding, pursued the object of their
fury even into the princess's chamber, and attempted to
tear him from the asylum to which he had fled for refuge; but as Tersan held the young queen closely embraced, it was impossible to separate them, till their cries
brought

with the least remorse or pity at the view of such complicated and extensive misery. She is said to have gazed with a savage satisfaction on Coligni's head which was brought her, and which was sent to Rome, as a present the most acceptable to the sovereign Pontiff. Some weeks after the massacre had ceased, she carried her son to see the execution of Brique-maut, an old Hugonot gentleman of seventy-two years, and of Cavagnes, master of requests, who had escaped in the general slaugh-

1572.

28 Oct.

brought to the spot Nançay, captain of the guards. Margaret says, that in spite of all the horror of the spectacle, Nançay could not help laughing at the situation of Terfan; and then commanding the archers to leave the room, he granted Terfan's life to the princess's entreaties, who caused him to lie in her own cabinet, and ordered his wounds to be dressed, till his cure was complete.

The young queen, frightened into agonies at this horrid sight, put on a night-gown, and ran to her sister the duchess of Lorrain's chamber, where she arrived, more dead than alive. As she entered the antichamber, a gentleman named Bourse was stabbed with a halberd, at two steps from her. Overcome with this second barbarity, she fainted into the arms of Nançay, and she declares that she was sprinkled all over with the blood of these miserable victims. Nançay informed her of the king of Navarre's safety, who was at that time in Charles's closet. She went thither; and throwing herself at her brother's and the queen-mother's feet, implored, and at length procured with difficulty the pardon of Miossans and Armagnac, two Hugonots in her husband's service.

ter, but being afterwards difcovered, were condemned to fuffer capital punifhment. By a refinement in barbarity which impreffes with horror, the king was defirous of enjoying the fight of their laft agonies. As it was night before they were conducted to the gibbet, he commanded torches to be held up to the faces of the criminals, and ftudioufly remarked the effects which the approach of death produced upon their features.

The admiral's effigy was likewife drawn upon a fledge to the fame place, and hung upon a gallows; nor had they forgot to put a toothpick into the mouth of the figure, as Coligni when alive ufually appeared with one. Gafpard de la Chatre, Count de Nançay, had been previoufly difpatched by the court to the caftle of Chatillon, to feize on the admiral's wife and children, as well as on thofe of d'Andelot; but the news of the maffacre having reached them, Coligni's widow and his eldeft fon, together with his daughter who had been married to Teligni, and the Count de Laval fon to d'Andelot, efcaped, and arrived fafe at Geneva. Not thinking themfelves even in that afylum fecure from the vengeance of Catherine de Medecis, they removed into the territories of the Canton of Berne, where they remained concealed. The younger children were all

conducted

CHARLES THE NINTH.

conducted to Paris; and notwithstanding their youth and innocence, fell victims to the barbarous policy of the court of France. The dreadful example of Paris was too faithfully followed through all the provinces, into which similar orders had been dispatched. Some few great and exalted spirits only, whose names the latest posterity will revere, refused to comply with the mandate, though signed by the king's hand, and preserved the Hugonots from outrage in their respective governments *.

Charles's

---

* In the cities of Lyons, Orleans, Rouen, Bourges, Angers, and Thouloufe, the royal orders for maffacring the proteftants were moft implicitly obeyed. In Provence, Claude de Savoye, Count de Tende abfolutely refufed to pay any obedience to fo deteftable a command; " for which," fays Davila, " he was fecretly dif-
" patched foon after at Avignon; and, as it was com-
" monly believed, by a commiffion from the king."—
St. Herem, governor of Auvergne, and De Gordes, who commanded in the province of Dauphiné, declined any compliance with the orders fent to them for the extermination of the Calvinifts. The bifhop of Lizieux protected them from injury in his diocefe, as did the Marechal de Matignon in the city of Alençon; but above all, the glorious anfwer of the Vifcount d'Ortez to Charles the ninth, is never to be forgotten. It was to this effect; " Sire, I
" have read the letter, enjoining a maffacre of the Hu-
" gonots, to the inhabitants of Bayonne. Your majefty
" has many faithfully devoted fubjects in this city, but
" not one executioner." Mezerai eftimates the number

1572.

Sept.

Charles's perplexed and contradictory conduct subsequent to the massacre, plainly evinced his own consciousness of the infamy of that transaction. He first accused Henry duke of Guise as the sole author of it, in his circular letters; and afterwards avowed himself as such. The court, satiated with the sacrifice of so many Hugonots, did not believe it possible that they could rise again in arms, without leaders or any means of support; but in this confidence they were deceived. Though dismayed and oppressed by superior numbers, the zeal for their religion, which this cruel persecution had heightened and confirmed, rendered them invincible. They stood on their defence in several provinces, erected anew the standard of revolt, and resisted with success the efforts of their victorious enemies.

1573.

February.

Rochelle, the grand asylum of Calvinism, having shut its gates upon the royal forces, and prepared to defend itself in case of a siege, the duke of Anjou was sent at the head of a numerous army to invest it, and carried with him almost all the young nobility. The

of Hugonots put to death in the various provinces, at twenty-five thousand; De Thou supposes them to have amounted to thirty thousand; and Davila even carries the computation to more than forty thousand persons, of all ages and conditions.

CHARLES THE NINTH.

duke of Alençon his youngest brother, together with the king of Navarre and the prince of Condé, were in the royal camp, and Catherine had even projected the dissolution of her daughter Margaret's late marriage; but the princess herself opposed this intention, and refused to consent to its execution *.

There

---

* Margaret, in her Memoirs, has given the most minute relation of her mother's measures for procuring a divorce. Catherine demanded of her daughter, whether Henry had consummated the nuptials on the bridal night; and asked her, " Si son mari étoit homme ? parceque si cela n'étoit " pas, ce seroit un moyen de la demarier." The answer which Margaret pretends that she made to this question, is curious; and peculiarly so, if we consider the dissolute character and manners of the princess herself. She assured Catherine, with all the appearance of simplicity and innocence, that " she besought her majesty to believe that she did not " understand what was asked her; but that she would re- " main with the husband whom they had given her; Me " doutant bien," adds she, " que la separation n'avoit " pour but, que la perte de mon mari."—It is hard, and almost ungenerous, to assign any other motive for this conduct in the queen of Navarre, than that of humanity, as she never loved Henry during the whole course of her life; unless we suppose that reluctance to lay down the title of Queen, might have influenced her in the refusal of such a proposition.

That the marriage was consummated, is a point beyond all doubt, since Henry the fourth himself avowed it, tho' the confession was injurious to his interests. Many years after, when his divorce was solicited in the court of Rome,

he

KINGS OF FRANCE.

There are few examples in modern hiftory of a fiege carried on with greater vigour, or fuftained with more determined obftinacy, than that of Rochelle. In vain did the duke of Anjou blockade it on every fide; his reiterated and bloody attacks, in which vaft numbers of his foldiers fell, neither terrified the inhabitants, nor difpofed them to capitulate; while, on the other hand, the intrigues, diffentions, and oppofite factions, with which the royal camp was filled, heightened the obftacles to his fuccefs.

Francis duke of Alençon, the youngeft fon of Henry the fecond, began to difplay his character, and to form a new party in the diftracted ftate. In his perfon, he was little, ungraceful, and deformed. Turbulent and reftlefs, he always beheld with envy and difcontent his brother Henry's fuperior glory; and anxious to raife his own reputation by whatever means, he united himfelf with the Hugonots and the king of Navarre, to revenge the death of Coligni. Irrefolute, capricious, and incapable of firm-

---

he was informed that he had only to imitate the example fet him by Louis the twelfth, of denying the confummation of his nuptials. " No," faid Henry, " it is an affer-
" tion which I cannot make; nor is it credible that a man
" of my conftitution, and a woman of the princefs's com-
" plexion, could poffibly fail to have completed the nup-
" tial rites."

nefs

ness on great occasions, he ever deserted his friends in distress; void of faith and honour, no reliance could be reposed on his promises or engagements. His rank as prince of the blood, and his personal courage, which was undisputed, counterbalanced however all these defects of nature and of character; nor was he altogether destitute of generous and better feelings, which sometimes broke out at intervals *.

His

---

* Francis, duke of Alençon, the fifth and youngest son of Henry the second, was born on the 18th of March, 1554, and at his baptism received the name of Hercules, which his mother Catherine of Medecis afterwards changed, from a superstitious expectation of prolonging his life by that alteration. She never loved him, and frequently called him "Mon fils egaré." Having received in his childhood some impressions favourable to the reformed religion, from the persons who had the charge of his education, he had connected himself very closely with Coligni previous to the massacre, of which he was totally innocent and uninformed. As the duke of Alençon appeared deeply affected by his death, which he bewailed with tears, the queen-mother, desirous of erasing these sentiments from her son's mind, caused a part of the admiral's journal, which had been brought her, to be read to him, in which he had strongly advised Charles the ninth not to give his brothers too much authority, or to assign them a large establishment. "See," said she, "what counsel your good " friend gives the king!" "I know not," replied the duke, "whether he loved me much; but I am con-
" vinced that none except a man most faithful to his ma-
" jesty,

His practices and connection with the king of Navarre were soon divulged, and spread a great alarm at court. Charles sent him a strict prohibition from quitting the camp on any pretence; and ordered the duke of Anjou to hasten by every means the reduction of Rochelle, on account of the urgent necessity which he had of the troops for the protection of his own person.

Already

"jesty, and most zealous for the state, would be the au-
"thor of such advice."

Davila attributes this affected attachment of the duke of Alençon to the memory of Coligni, entirely to the envy and jealousy which he felt at his brother Henry's power and great exploits. That historian has always depictured the duke of Alençon under the most unfavourable colours, as deficient in any talents or qualities worthy of esteem, and as incapable of suffering a comparison with the duke of Anjou. —" La propria capacita, e l'habilita di lui," says Davila, " era stimato molto inferiore, e d'ingegno, & di valore, al " duca d'Angio." In another place, speaking of that prince, he thus delineates his character: " Francesco, " duca d'Alanfone, terzo fratello del ré, il quale non solo " era giovane d'anni, & per difetto dell' eta privo d'espe-" rienza; ma per natura, ancora dotato di poca capacita " d'ingegno, e d'animo cosi volubile, e cosi gonfio, che si " vedeva molto piu inclinato a configli torbidi e precipi-" tosi, che a maniera di vita prudente, e moderata."—De Thou has drawn his portrait in a much more flattering manner, though he admits his defects and weaknesses. " Vif, eloquent, courageux, affable, et magnifique; mais " ambitieux, inquiet, et changeant."—Mezerai, on the

other

Already the miferable king began to awake, 1573. though flowly, from the delirium into which he had been plunged by his mother's fatal advice. The horror of the night of St. Bartholomew remained indelibly impreffed on his imagination; his ufual gaiety and complacency appeared no longer in his countenance; and in its place a fixed and melancholy gloom fat upon his features. He beheld the ignominy and deteftation with which his unparalleled barbarity and perfidy had marked him to the lateft pofterity; nor could he diffemble his refentment of Catherine's pernicious counfels, which had induced him thus to violate the fa-

other hand, fpeaks in terms of difapprobation and contempt, of his qualities both of body and of mind.—
" Prince ambitieux et inquiet," fays he, " meprifé pour
" fa petite taille, et fa mauvaife mine; capable d'em-
" braffer toutes fortes d'entreprifes fans raifon, et de les
" abandonner auffi legerement."

Tho' moft of the French hiftorians defcribe his perfon as mean, and almoft deformed, yet De Thou contradicts that affertion. " Il etoit petit, mais bien fait. Sa phifi-
" onomie etoit agreable, quoiqu'il eut le teint fort brun,
" et le vifage gaté par la petite verole." Thefe are De Thou's words.—Montfaucon, in his " Monumens de
" la Monarchie Françoife," has preferved two portraits of Francis duke of Alençon; one of which is only a buft; the other a whole length, in complete armour. In neither of thefe, does he appear to be either deformed in his figure, or deficient in beauty of features, and perfonal elegance.

cred

cred laws of honour and humanity. The queen-mother having one day reproved him for his furious paſſion with ſome of his ſervants, and told him, that he would do better to exert that anger againſt the rebels who cauſed the deaths of ſo many of his faithful and loyal ſubjects before Rochelle; he replied, " Madame, qui en " eſt cauſe que vous? Par la mort.... vous " êtes cauſe de tout!"

While theſe ſymptoms of animoſity between Charles and his mother began to diſplay themſelves, and while Henry exhauſted his army in ineffectual attempts againſt Rochelle, the news arrived of this latter prince's election to the crown of Poland. It was an event by no means deſired on the part of Catherine and her favourite ſon. The duke of Anjou, who ever conſidered himſelf as immediate heir to the crown of France while his brother had no male iſſue by the queen, and who had from his infancy been accuſtomed to the diſſipations of the moſt magnificent court in Europe, regarded with a ſort of horror the idea of going to reign over a barbarous people, ſo far removed from his native country. He had even, in conjunction with his mother, endeavoured by every ſecret means, to counteract the ſucceſs of the negociation which was to place him on the Poliſh throne; but Montluc biſhop of Valence, who

had

had been sent into Poland to gain the suffrages of the Diet, regarding his sovereign's orders and his own honour, more than Catherine's or Henry's wishes, acted with so much vigour and address at the election, that the duke of Anjou was chosen king. This intelligence formed an honourable pretext for withdrawing his troops, wearied and broken with so unsuccessful a siege. Deputies were appointed on either side; and a general pacification was at length concluded, not only for the city of Rochelle, but for the whole kingdom, on terms less favourable to the Hugonots, than any of the three preceding treaties.

The duke of Anjou having terminated this negociation, embarked on board the royal gallies, together with his brother the duke of Alençon, the king of Navarre, and the prince of Condé. Landing at Nantes, he remounted the Loire to Clery, at which place having performed a vow which he had made, he proceeded to Orleans, where he was received with every mark of solemnity and magnificence. The Polish ambassadors, twelve in number, made their entry into the capital soon after, where Henry had previously arrived. The decree which elected him to the throne, inclosed in a silver box, and sealed with a hundred and ten seals of Prelates, Palatines,

1573.

25 June.

19 Aug.

and

and Castellans, was publicly read; Charles, seated on a scaffold in his royal robes, and accompanied by all the grandees of the court, being present at this ceremony. When Te Deum had been sung, the king rose, and embraced his brother the new sovereign; Henry then kissed the duke of Alençon, and king of Navarre; after which all the noblemen of the court paid him the customary respects and congratulations. Catherine of Medecis displayed all her magnificence and taste on this occasion, in the splendid diversions and entertainments with which she honoured her son's accession to the throne of Poland*.

Charles, who had taken the firm resolution of reigning by himself, and of adopting measures more salutary and beneficent to his people,

---

* Brantome has given us a minute description of Catherine's banquets and amusements on the arrival of the Polish ambassadors. Sixteen ladies of the court, representing the sixteen provinces of France, dressed with the most perfect propriety in habits emblematical of their characters, formed a dance, which was performed in the palace of the Thuilleries. As far as we are able to judge, scarce any of the superb carousals of Louis the fourteenth were superior in elegance, in brilliancy, or in effect, to those of Catherine of Medecis, which were exhibited nearly a century earlier.

Margaret queen of Navarre was the animating soul of these gallant diversions. Her beauty, gaiety, and above all

ple, received with extreme satisfaction the news 1573 of his brother's election to a foreign and distant diadem. He had long perceived the error which his mother's counsels had induced him to commit, of entrusting to Henry so extensive an authority; and he now saw himself on the point of being released from a rival, who became every year more obnoxious. He hastened his brother's departure with a visible anxiety and impatience; but the king of Poland protracted it under a thousand pretences. Not only Catherine's tender and maternal fondness for him; not only the charms of a luxurious court, the possession of a degree of power scarce less than that of the king himself, or the expectation of the crown of France, contributed to detain him: A passion still more violent and tyrannical rendered him deaf to the voice of glory, or the suggestions of reason. He was tenderly attached to the princess of Condé; and his heart naturally soft, and susceptible of the impressions of love, tried in vain to extricate itself from the effect of her charms.

all that air which characterised her, and which breathed and inspired desire, rendered her the most fascinating princess in the world. Lasco one of the noblemen in the Polish embassy, when he was presented to her, was so overcome with the lustre of her attractions, that he broke out into the most passionate exclamations of rapture and astonishment at the sight of so beautiful a woman.

1573. Mary of Cleves, married to Henry prince of Condé, and who was at this time only seventeen years of age, possessed attractions of person the most winning and irresistible. Her mind, improved and elegant, corresponded with her external charms; and her heart, formed to taste the delights of a mutual passion, had not been able to resist so accomplished a lover, as the hero of Jarnac and of Moncontour. A sense of honour, and a regard to the nuptial vow which she had so recently made, long supported her sliding virtue; but Henry, master of all the wiles which such a design inspires and dictates, employed the most effectual methods to obtain the gratification of his wishes. His sister the queen of Navarre lent her assistance in obtaining for him the possession of his beloved mistress: Even the duke of Guise, forgetting his natural haughtiness, and united to the king of Poland by the closest friendship, did not hesitate to aid him with all his eloquence. His uncle the cardinal of Lorrain, was the first to persuade him to undertake this humiliating office, and to procure his own sister-in-law for Henry. Overcome by so importunate a suit, the princess yielded at length; the first decisive interview between herself and the king of Poland took place at the palace of the Louvre; and she was there delivered up

to

CHARLES THE NINTH.

to him as a victim by Margaret of Valois and the duke of Guife*.

Amidft the tranfporting enjoyments to which the two lovers at firft abandoned themfelves, they were equally infenfible to the fuggeftions of ambition and of glory. A diftant crown, which could only be purchafed by a removal from the object of his tendernefs, did not in any degree roufe the enamoured king, or appear to him worthy of the facrifice which he muft make to it, of his beloved miftrefs. But a neceffity more cruel foon compelled him to haften his departure. Charles grew hourly

---

* Neither Davila nor De Thou have defcended to the narration of this interefting ftory; but Mezerai exprefsly affigns the attachment of the king of Poland to the princefs of Condé as the moft infurmountable obftacle to his departure from France. He confirms likewife the part which the duke of Guife acted; and adds, that the duke offered Henry fifty thoufand men to protect him from the refentment of Charles the ninth, if he perfifted to refufe to quit Paris, and to take poffeffion of his new dominions.—Defportes, the celebrated poet, who accompanied the king of Poland to Cracow, has given an account of this amour, and has minutely defcribed the interview of the two lovers, in a poem called " Cleophon." Henry is there named Eurilas; the princefs of Condé, Olympia, and Margaret of Valois, Fleur de Lys. Buffi d'Amboife, the queen of Navarre's lover, is fuppofed to be depictured under the character of Nireus; as are the duke of Guife and his miftrefs Madame de Sauve, under the names of Floridant and Camilla.

1573. more and more impatient at his delays, and at length informed the queen-mother with his usual vehemence, that he would not permit of the king of Poland's longer stay, and that one or the other of them must instantly quit the kingdom.

Henry began his preparations, and ordered all his equipage and attendants to be ready, but still delayed his final departure. The duke of Guise, his intimate friend, flattered him with the hopes of Charles's death, and even offered, if he was determined to stay in France, to protect him against the king's resentment with fifty thousand forces. Three days having elapsed in this state of uncertainty, Charles, irritated at length almost to fury, and persuaded that Catherine chiefly prevented the king of Poland's journey, perhaps from some treasonable and dangerous intentions in his favour, no longer observed any measures with his mother. He ordered the door of his apartment to be shut against her, and began to meditate some more effectual designs against herself and her favourite son.

These open marks of displeasure terrified Catherine, and she implored the king of Poland to delay no longer, if he regarded his own personal safety. Henry consented though with extreme reluctance, and began his journey.

28 Sept.

The

The whole court accompanied him, and Charles himself, more from motives of prudence, than of affection, was among the number. He could not however conduct his brother to the frontier, as he had intended; a slow fever, attended with a violent giddiness in the head, and pains about his heart and stomach, having obliged him to stop at the town of Vitry in Champagne*.

The

---

* De Thou, in his account of the illness of Charles the ninth, and the symptoms attending it, not only attributes it to poison, but he expressly names Charles de Gondi de la Tour, great master of the wardrobe, as the person who, in concert with his two brothers, the Marechal de Retz, and the bishop of Paris, was suspected of having executed this detestable project. The family of Gondi, originally Tuscan, and who had followed the queen-mother from Florence into France, had been elevated by Charles, at Catherine's suggestion, to the highest dignities and employments. The Marechal de Retz had succeeded La Cipierre in the important charge of Governor to the young Monarch, and had enjoyed the greatest degree of his personal favour and affection. But the king, naturally discerning, had begun to manifest some concern at the profusion of honours which he had heaped on this family, and to repent of his own work. To this diminution of his public regard and protection, was added another more wounding, though more private affront on the part of Charles. He had been deeply sensible to the beauty and attractions of Helena Bon, wife to the Count de la Tour, and had removed her husband from court, to facilitate his interviews with the lady. The Count, who suspected their attachment, returned unexpectedly, and was too well satisfied

by

1573.
October.

The queen-mother, the duke of Alençon, with the king and queen of Navarre, and a great train of the nobility continued their rout with

by the evidence of his own senses, that all his apprehensions were founded in truth. Charles, instead of endeavouring to mollify and soften the resentment of the Count, menaced him with the severest effects of his indignation, if he presumed to treat his wife with rigour. The story became public; and it was said, that the duke of Guise, discontented with Charles the ninth, had instigated and inflamed the Count de la Tour to vengeance. The queen-mother herself had not been spared on this occasion, and popular report had asserted that she was not unacquainted with, or adverse to the projects for the king's destruction. Her assurances to the king of Poland at his departure that " he would not be long absent," increased these suspicions, and induced her enemies to pretend that she was privy to the attempts against Charles's life. This is De Thou's account of that prince's disorder, and its cause; the scene of which he lays at the town of Villers Coteretz, between Paris and Vitry in Champagne, to which last place, though severely indisposed, he continued his journey, and where he was absolutely compelled to stop, by more violent attacks of a similar nature.

Davila makes no mention whatever of Charles's illness during the journey of his brother Henry towards the frontiers; but Mezerai speaks of it in very ambiguous and enigmatical terms. " A few days," says he, " after the " menaces which Charles had used towards his mother, " he had been seized with a slow, malignant fever, ac-" companied with a vertigo, and pains about his heart at " every moment." He insinuates that unnatural means were suspected, but leaves the point dark and undetermined.

Henry

Henry to Blamont in Lorrain, where the separation took place between him and Catherine. She held him long in her arms, unable to bid him the laſt adieu, while ſighs and tears interrupted her voice. Among the expreſſions of comfort which ſhe uſed, to diminiſh the exceſs of his grief on this exile from his country; " Allez, mon fils;" ſaid ſhe, " vous n'y de- " meurerez pas long tems!" The ambiguity of this prediction, Charles's illneſs accompanied with extraordinary ſymptoms, the known and recent quarrel which had preceded it, and the queen-mother's partiality to the king of Poland; all theſe circumſtances gave riſe to reports and ſuſpicions, though probably ill-founded and unjuſt, that Charles's ſeizure was the effect of poiſon.

The king's diſorders were more reaſonably attributed to natural cauſes, and all the French hiſtorians agree that ever ſince the maſſacre of Paris, he had betrayed marks of great agitation and diſtreſs. He had beſides much impaired his conſtitution by too violent and laborious exerciſes; and it was ſaid that his lungs were affected by his conſtantly blowing the horn when he went to the chace. He uſed to play at tennis during five or ſix hours without intermiſſion, which extremely agitated and heated his blood: He became incapable of ſleeping except for a

1573. very short time, at intervals; and even then his slumbers were restless and disordered. These causes probably conducted him, though slowly, to his grave, and might fully account for, and justify Catherine's assurances to the king of Poland, that his absence from France would not be of long duration*.

1574. Henry meanwhile, accompanied with several of the first nobility, and a train of five hundred gentlemen, crossed the whole Germanic empire, and arrived at Miezrich, the first

---

* Brantome says, that Charles the ninth never recovered his tranquillity of mind, nor even the exterior appearance of repose, after the massacre of St. Bartholomew. I "saw him," says Brantome, "on my return from the "siege of Rochelle, and found him entirely changed."— "On ne lui voyoit," adds he, "plus au visage cette dou- "ceur qu'on avoit accoutumé de lui voir."—Mezerai enumerates the violent exercises to which the king had accustomed himself; "de courir a la chasse, de piquer de "grands chevaux, de jouër a la paume cinque ou six "heures durant, de forger et battre le fer a tour de bras." All these imprudent excesses had naturally thrown his blood into a state of fermentation, highly injurious to his health; and joined to the uneasy reflexions which continually haunted him, contributed to prevent his recovery. —De Thou equally admits the effect of the massacre on the king's mind, and says, that "after the day of St. Bartho- "lomew he slept little, and his slumbers were interrup- "ted by dreadful dreams; at which times he was accus- "tomed to send for musicians, who by airs and sympho- "nies procured him some repose and sleep."

city

city of his Polish dominions, in the depth of winter. All the princes through whose territories he passed, endeavoured to outvie each other in the honours which they paid to so illustrious a stranger, and he was received at Cracow with every demonstration of joy and public festivity *. His beautiful and majestic person,

1574.
―――
25th Jan.

* The king of Poland, after quitting Blamont, passed through the bishopricks of Spire and Worms, to Heidelberg, the capital of the dominions of the Elector Palatine. That prince, walking with his royal guest in a gallery of the palace, which was ornamented with the portraits of illustrious persons, undrew a curtain from before a picture of Coligni, and pointing to it, said to Henry, "Of all the French nobility whom I have seen, that is the man whom I have found most zealous for the glory of his country; and I am not afraid to assert, that the king of France has sustained a loss in him, which he never can repair." The king of Poland felt the severity of the censure, and made no reply.—Continuing his route through Mentz, he stopped during the festival of Christmas at the abbey of Fulda, and on leaving it was received by the Landgrave of Hesse with extraordinary honours. Having passed the river Elbe at Torgau, the Elector of Saxony, who was himself indisposed by sickness, dispatched his son-in-law to conduct the young monarch through the Saxon dominions, at the head of two thousand cavalry; and on his passing the frontiers, he found an escort of fifteen hundred horse waiting for him, sent by the emperor Maximilian the second. The prince of Prussia attended him to Francfort on the Oder; and Henry arrived in the territories of Poland upon

the

person, his condescending and courteous manners, and his unbounded liberality to all ranks of people, rendered him in the beginning the idol of his new subjects; but these external endowments, calculated to charm at first view, soon lost their effect, and he became splenetic, melancholy, and reserved.

Disgusted with the barbarous customs and character of the Poles, he was no longer easy of access, or affable towards them, as he had been on his arrival. He remained whole days shut up in his apartment, abandoned to chagrin, and under the greatest uneasiness at not receiving the letters which he expected from France. He passed his whole time in perusing the billets of the princess of Condé, which he kissed and bathed with his tears; she was ever present to his imagination, and maintained her empire over his affections. He wrote letters to her

---

the 25th of January, 1574, where the bishop of Cujavia harangued him in the name of the Polish senate and the nobility. The king proceeded immediately to Cracow, the capital of his new dominions, where the Count de Retz had previously assisted as his representative, at the obsequies of the late sovereign, Sigismund Augustus. The senate and nobles advanced to meet him half a league from Cracow, into which city he was received with all the testimonies of public festivity. The anecdote respecting the Elector Palatine and the portrait of Coligni, is confirmed by Mezerai and by Brantome in the strongest manner, as well as by De Thou.

of the fondeſt attachment entirely in his own 1574.
blood, and filled with proteſtations of inviolable fidelity; while Deſportes the poet, who attended him to Cracow, continually fed his paſſion by ſonnets in praiſe of his beloved miſtreſs. His dejection of ſpirits was ſtill more encreaſed by the propoſition which the Poliſh ſenate made him of marrying Anne Jagellon, ſiſter to the deceaſed monarch Sigiſmund Auguſtus, a princeſs of a diſagreeable perſon, and already advanced in years.

It was natural to ſuppoſe, that the departure January. of the king of Poland would have tended to diffuſe a tranquillity over the court and kingdom of France; but Charles's reign ſeem'd deſtined to every ſpecies of civil commotion. The duke of Alençon, ever forming ſchemes of ambition which he afterwards abandoned from fickleneſs and irreſolution, rekindled the flame of expiring ſedition. The genius of Calviniſm, ſpringing from its own aſhes, re-appeared in every quarter of France; and undiſmayed by the late dreadful maſſacre of its votaries, animated them to new efforts againſt the government.

The king's ſtrength began to fail juſt as he entered the prime of life, and appeared to promiſe happier times. His capacity, naturally clear and diſcerning, enabled him at length to ſee the train of errors and crimes,

into

into which his youth had been betrayed; and all his actions indicated the resolution which he had taken, to govern by other principles than those which had actuated his past conduct. He applied himself in person to the affairs of state, and expressed the most anxious desire to relieve his people from the many calamities which they had experienced since his accession to the crown. In opposition to the advice of several of his ministers, he discharged them from a third part of the taxes, and would only retain three companies of the regiment of guards about his person; the rest were disbanded.

Though he detested Calvinism and the Hugonots, he had yet determined to disgrace and banish for ever from his presence and councils, the advisers of massacre and bloodshed. He intended to restore to his parliaments the administration of justice; to repress the dangerous power of the two houses of Guise and Montmorenci; to renounce his prosecution of the chace and other dissipations, and to dedicate his whole attention to the more important and glorious labours of a great monarch. But it was in vain that he formed these salutary plans; enfeebled by the progress of his disorders, and unable to resist their violence, he rapidly approached the end of his days before he had yet expiated his past offences.

Meanwhile

Meanwhile the Hugonots, whose courage was revived by the duke of Anjou's removal, and the king's languid state of health, which rendered him unfit for any exertion of vigour, rose again in arms. La Noue and Montgomeri, in whom survived the genius of Condé and Coligni, re-assembled their dismayed and scattered party. The duke of Alençon, to whom Charles, at the solicitation and advice of his mother Catherine, had refused the post of lieutenant-general of the kingdom, was privy to their enterprize; Henry king of Navarre, and the prince of Condé, had promised to declare openly in their favour; and many noblemen of the court were secretly disposed to join the insurgents. The duke of Alençon even engaged to quit the court, and to put himself at their head; but de Chaumont, who, with a body of cavalry had approached the palace of St. Germain to facilitate his escape, as had been preconcerted, having mistaken the day, and arrived near a week before the time, the duke, naturally fickle, and incapable of a bold and decisive resolution, had not the courage to perform his agreement.

La Mole, his principal favourite, conscious that the design could not long remain concealed, went immediately and revealed the whole conspiracy to the queen-mother. The court was instantly filled with confusion; and Catherine affecting a degree of terror which she

1574. she did not really feel, with an intent to render the conspirators greater objects of public hatred, fled to Paris at midnight in the utmost disorder, and was followed by most of the ladies and courtiers. Charles himself did not remove before the ensuing day, when he went to lodge at the castle of the "Bois de Vincennes," where his brother Francis and the king of Navarre were likewise conducted, not as close prisoners, but accompanied by a guard who carefully watched their motions. On their subsequent examination in presence of the king and queen-mother, the duke of Alençon behaved with the meanest pusillanimity, trembling, and as a criminal; but Henry answered the interrogatories put to him with intrepidity, rather as an injured than as a guilty person, and refused to make any confession injurious to his friends and followers*.

Charles's

* De Thou has given several very curious and interesting particulars of the defence of Henry king of Navarre, when interrogated before Charles and Catherine, which may serve to throw some light upon the conclusion of this disastrous reign, and to evince that there were at least intentions of hastening Charles's death by unnatural means. Henry asserted positively, that he could adduce proofs of designs having been meditated against his own life; and that though he might have despised the danger which menaced himself, he could not be insensible to that which threatened the king. He declared that after the departure

CHARLES THE NINTH.

Charles's diforders, which had given him fome refpite during the winter, revived with double violence on the approach of fpring. The late practices of his brother the duke of Alençon, and of the king of Navarre, added to the renewal of the civil war with the Hugonots, affected him deeply, and irritated the other difeafes which preyed on his enfeebled conftitution. " At leaft," faid he, " they " might have waited for my death. It is too

1574.
April.

ture of the king of Poland, a fecret council was held for the purpofe of deliberating on the methods of difpatching Charles the ninth; and added that the Catholics wifhed his death, in the hope and expectation that his brother Henry afcending the throne of France, would finifh the extermination of the Proteftants. He then complained of the ill ufage which he had himfelf fuftained from Catherine of Medecis; and particularly of her having excluded him from the council, and prevented his accefs to the perfon of the king. " I have frequently," added he, " fpoken to the king of Poland refpecting the bad defigns " of fome turbulent fpirits in the court; but I am well " perfuaded that my franknefs difpleafed him, fince " at his departure from Blamont, he did not deign " to mention me to the queen-mother, though he re- " commended to her all thofe who were prefent, and even " many perfons who were abfent at that time." Five days afterwards the king of Navarre repeated the fame affertions in the queen-mother's prefence, in that of the Cardinal of Bourbon, and of other commiffaries appointed to enquire into the confpiracy: he even fpoke with more force and warmth than on his firft examination.

" much

1574. "much to diſtreſs me now, that I am debili‑
"tated by illneſs*!"

Catherine, ever attentive to her own inte‑
reſts, and foreſeeing that the king's end could
not be very diſtant, with her uſual ſagacity be‑
gan to concert meaſures for ſecuring to her‑
ſelf the future regency. Her ſon's declining
health, and incapacity of perſonal application
to affairs of ſtate, having in a degree reſtored
to her the authority of which he had pre‑
viouſly began to deprive her, ſhe exerted it to
render herſelf miſtreſs of thoſe perſons, who
might otherwiſe oppoſe her taking poſſeſſion
of the ſupreme power, in caſe of Charles's
death.

11 April. La Mole, and the Count de Coconas, an
Italian nobleman, both favourites of the duke
of Alençon, were arreſted. The former de-

* It was not poſſible, ſays Brantome, to aſcertain of what
nature was the king's diſorder; ſo various and uncommon
were the ſymptoms. Theſe are his own words which follow:
"Car il lui ſurvint une fiévre catartique, qui tantôt etoit
"quarte, tantôt continue: et penſoit Monſieur Mafille,
"ſon premier médecin, qu'il ſe porteroit de bien en
"mieux, ainſi que la fiévre diminueroit." He adds, that
the duke of Alençon and king of Navarre's colluſion with
the rebels aggravated all the ſymptoms of his complaint;
and that from that time his majeſty grew much worſe.—
"Dont on en ſoupçonna," adds he, "quelque poiſon,
"enchantment, et enforcellement."

nied

nied every thing imputed to his charge, and 1574. perſiſted invariably in that aſſertion; but the Count, flattered with the hopes of life and of a large reward, being examined in the royal preſence, confeſſed all he knew, and even accuſed the Marechals de Montmorenci and de Coſſé, as accomplices in the conſpiracy. This depoſition, though probably extorted only by the expectation of eſcaping an ignominious puniſhment, furniſhed Catherine with the pretext which ſhe wanted for arreſting the two Marechals, who might, ſhe feared, in caſe of Charles's death, form an impediment to the ſucceſſion of the king of Poland.

A circumſtance which very ſtrongly marks the ſuperſtition of that age, in which the effects of charms and ſorcery were objects of general belief, ſerved to haſten the execution of La Mole and Coconas. A little image compoſed of wax, was found in the houſe of the former, the heart of which was pierced through with a needle in many places; and it was pretended that this waxen figure repreſented the king, whom La Mole had devoted to death by the force of enchantments. He denied the charge, and aſſerted that he had procured it from Coſmo Ruggieri, a Florentine who had followed the queen-mother into France, and who profeſſed the art of magic. Ruggieri being interrogated, confirmed

1574. La Mole's assurances; and added, that the intention of the charm was to gain the affections of a lady, to whom that gentleman had been fondly attached *.

Notwith-

* All the French historians relate this story, and it is mentioned in nearly similar terms by De Thou, by Mezerai, and by Davila. This last writer speaks of La Mole and of the Count de Coconas in terms of equal detestation and contempt. "Bonifacio, Signore della Mola," says he, " huomo di poca levatura, ma ripieno di pensieri " misurati e vasti; et Annibale Conte di Coconas, Bandito " Piemontese." With respect to the figure of wax, found in the possession of La Mole, it was a characteristic of the age, which was infected to the greatest degree with a belief in magic; a species of madness which did not terminate 'till towards the close of the reign of Louis the fourteenth. A priest, named Des Eschèles, who was executed about this time in the " Place de Greve" at Paris, for having had a communication with evil spirits, accused near twelve hundred persons of the same crime. Catherine of Medecis was peculiarly credulous on that point, and always carried about her person cabalistical characters, written on the skin of an infant born dead. Several talismans and amulets were found in her cabinet after her death, and she consulted an astrologer on the fortunes of all her children. Favin, in his history of Navarre, relates a curious anecdote upon this subject. "The queen," says he, " having early applied to a magician to know the " destiny of her sons, he made her see in a magic mirror " the number of years that each would reign, by the " number of turns which they made. Francis the second, " Charles the ninth, and Henry the third, passed succes- " sively in review before her: she even saw Henry duke

" of

CHARLES THE NINTH. 275

1574.

Notwithstanding this defence, La Mole was executed some days after, with the Count de Coconas, in the "Place de Greve" at Paris. Their bodies being quartered, were placed on wheels, and their heads fixed on two poles. La Mole was peculiarly acceptable to, and beloved by the queen of Navarre, as his accomplice was equally by the duchess of Nevers; and it is confidently asserted by many of the cotemporary historians, that these two princesses caused the heads of their lovers to be taken down, on the night after their execution, and interred them with their own hands in the chapel of St. Martin, near Paris *.

The

" of Guise, who disappeared on a sudden; and Henry
" the fourth, who made twenty-four turns. This pre-
" diction and apparition encreased her original aversion
" to the king of Navarre."—Cosmo Ruggieri, of whom
mention has been made, was sent to the gallies; but
Catherine soon after liberated him from that state of servitude and punishment, to make use of the secrets which
she supposed him to possess, and he died in high repute at
Paris, under Louis the thirteenth's reign, in 1615.

* Mezerai mentions this extraordinary fact, and Henry the fourth, in his memorial relative to the dissolution of his marriage, presented to the Pope, expressly asserts and confirms it, as well as the intrigue by which it was preceded. "The Duchess of Nevers," says he, " being attached to the Count de Coconas, persuaded " her friend the queen of Navarre to commence an amour " with La Mole, their common confident," " pour lui " épargner le chagrin de garder les manteaux, pendant

T 2 " qu'ils

1574.   The two accused noblemen, Montmorenci and Coſſé, either from a reliance on their own innocence, or from a confidence in their rank and authority, came immediately to court, to juſtify themſelves from the ſuppoſed treaſon attributed to them; but they were committed by Catherine to the Baſtile, and the Pariſians furniſhed with alacrity eight hundred men to prevent their eſcape. Orders were likewiſe iſſued for the arreſt of Henry prince of Condé, who, as governor of Picardy, reſided at A-miens; but he had the good fortune to make his eſcape, and quitting that city in diſguiſe, arrived ſafe at Straſbourg, where he ſolemnly abjured the Catholic religion, and made a public profeſſion of Calviniſm.

In Normandy, the Hugonots being preſſed by the Marechal de Matignon, were almoſt every where reduced to lay down their arms; and the Count de Montgomeri, ſo long inured to war, and one of their greateſt commanders, was obli-

25 May. ged to ſurrender himſelf to Matignon, who inveſted him in the town of Domfront. The ſtipulation of his life was one of the conditions; but the queen-mother, who had determined to ſacri-

"qu'ils étoient enſemble."—"The connection was of
"ſhort duration. The two lovers left their heads upon a
"ſcaffold; and their miſtreſſes, having cauſed them to
"be taken down, put them in a coach, and buried
"them in St. Martin's chapel, below Montmartre."

fice

fice this victim to the memory of her husband, caused him to be executed after the death of Charles the ninth, in defiance of the convention.

The king began to sink apace under the weight of his disorders, which increased every day; and though he long endeavoured to resist their attacks, yet his strength diminishing continually, at length compelled him to take to his bed, at the palace in the " Bois de Vincennes." Catherine improving the opportunity afforded by the decay of her son's strength of mind, used every exertion to induce him to invest her with the regency. As long as Charles retained in any degree his usual faculties, he persisted invariably to deny her this proof of his confidence; and could only be persuaded to grant her letters to the governors of the different provinces, which enjoined them, that " during " his illness, and in case that it should please " God to take him, they should obey his mo- " ther till the return of the king of Poland."

One of the most awful and affecting pictures which can be held up to human survey, is that of Charles the ninth, cut off in the flower of his age by a disorder very unusual, if not unprecedented, and accompanied with many circumstances strongly calculated to excite horror and compassion. During the two last weeks of his life, nature seemed to make ex-

traordinary

traordinary efforts for his relief. He trembled, and all his limbs were contracted by sudden fits; while his acute pains did not suffer him to enjoy any repose, or to remain scarce a moment in one posture. He was even bathed in his own blood, which oozed out of the pores of his skin, and at all the passages of his body, in great quantity. His constitution, naturally sound and robust, supported him however for some time, against the progress of this cruel and unsurmountable disease.

Only three days before he died, the queen-mother having informed his majesty, that the Count de Montgomeri was taken prisoner by the Marechal de Matignon, he received the news without any mark of joy, or change of countenance. " Quoi! mon fils," said she, " ne vous rejouissez vous point de la prise de " celui qui a tué votre pere?"—" I am no " longer interested," answered the expiring prince, " about that, or any other affair." Catherine regarded this indifference as the infallible prognostic of his speedy and approaching dissolution.

On the morning of the day when Charles the ninth breathed his last, she availed herself of the condition in which he then lay, to reiterate to him her entreaties to nominate her to the regency. He complied with her request, though rather

rather by compulsion and through weakness, than from choice; and she immediately dispatched other letters into the different parts of the kingdom, announcing the king's pleasure. Yet only a few hours before he expired, Charles openly gave marks of his alienation from his mother. Henry king of Navarre coming near his bed, Charles embraced him many times; and after other demonstrations of confidence and attachment, said to him, "Je me fie en vous de ma "femme, et de ma fille; Je vous les recom- "mende, et Dieu vous gardera! Mais ne vous "fiez pas à—" Catherine, fearing he was about to name herself, interrupted him with—"Mon- "sieur, ne dites pas cela."—" Je le dois "dire," answered the dying monarch, "car "c'est la verité."

When he found his end approaching, he prepared himself for it with perfect composure and dignity of mind. He ordered the duke of Alençon and the king of Navarre to be brought into his presence; Birague the chancellor, Monsieur de Sauve secretary of state, and the Cardinal of Bourbon, with several others of the nobility, being likewise admitted. He addressed himself to them with the earnestness of a person about to quit the world, and declared his brother Henry king of Poland, successor to the crown of France, the Salic law excluding

1574. his own child, a daughter, from the throne. He implored the duke of Alençon not to molest, or attempt to impede his elder brother's entry into the kingdom; and obliged all present to take the oath of allegiance to the absent sovereign, and of obedience to Catherine, 'till his arrival.

He commanded the Viscount d'Auchy, captain of the guards, to look well to his charge, and to preserve unshaken his loyalty to the king of Poland. He requested Poquenot, lieutenant of the Swifs guards, to make his dying recommendations to his allies the thirteen Cantons; and he particularly charged the Count de la Tour, master of his wardrobe, to carry his tender and constant remembrances to his mistress, the beautiful Mary Touchet, whom he had long loved. These acts performed, he fell into an extreme weakness, and yielded his last breath about three o'clock in the afternoon; wanting only twenty-one days to have accomplished his twenty-fourth year[*].

30 May.

The

---

[*] Brantome, who was in the court at the time of Charles's death, is very minute in his relation of all the circumstances which attended the last illness of that prince. These are his own words:—" Il mourut le propre jour de " la Pentecoste, l'an 1574, trois heures après midi, sur le " point que les médecins et chirurgiens, et tous ceux de " la cour le pensoient se mieux porter : car le jour avant
" il

The reports of poifon were again renewed with fome appearances of reafon, and Catherine of Medecis was even accufed of having haftened her fon's death; but from this deteftable and unnatural crime, fhe muft be acquitted on an impartial examination *.

1574.

Charles

" il fe portoit bien ; et nous croyions qu'il s'en alloit
" guery ; mais nous donnames de garde que fur le matin
" il commenca à fentir la mort, laquelle il fit très belle
" et digne d'un grand Roi."

* It may be curious, however, to enter a little into this difquifition, almoft all the writers of that period having made mention of the fufpicion, though they in general exculpate the queen-mother, and pronounce her guiltlefs. So abominable an action, if true, would probably have been authenticated, and handed down to us by inconteftible evidence and authority. Davila never once hints at poifon; but exprefsly attributes Charles's death to " an illnefs oc-
" cafioned by too violent exercife in running, hunting,
" wreftling, and riding the great horfe; to all which re-
" creations he was immoderately attach'd."——In another place he fays, " The king's life was now haftening faft to
" its period; he had begun to fpit blood fome months
" before, and being exhaufted with a flow, continued,
" internal fever, he had entirely loft his ftrength."—
Davila recounts the particulars of his calling into his chamber the princes and great officers of ftate previous to his death ; and adds, that " Charles having difmiffed all
" prefent with weighty and affecting admonitions, ftill
" continued to hold his mother's hand faft in his own,
" and in that pofture ended the courfe of his troublefome
" reign."—The very act in which he expired, feems to indicate filial piety and affection. Even Henry Etienne, a

violent

KINGS OF FRANCE.

1574. Charles left by his queen only one daughter, named Mary-Elizabeth, who survived him about

violent declaimer against Catherine of Medecis, and who accuses her of many murders, makes no mention of, nor imputes to her that of Charles the ninth.

Monsieur De Thou hesitates, and leaves the point undecided; yet he rather seems to insinuate poison as the cause of the king's death, and charges indirectly the queen his mother. "Charles," says he, "embraced Catherine "of Medecis tenderly before his decease, and thanked "her for the obligations which he owed her; having "thus continued his dissimulation to the last moments of "his life; for it is certain that his affection for, and con- "fidence in the queen-mother were considerably dimi- "nished. It is even pretended, that he had it in con- "templation to send her into Poland to her beloved "son Henry." De Thou asserts likewise, that the Count de Coconas, previous to his execution, had warned the king of attempts which were meditated against his life from more than one quarter; and La Popeliniere confirms this fact. Henry king of Navarre, in repeated declarations, accused Catherine either by name, or by implication, of practising against the life of Charles the ninth, with intent to place the crown on the head of the king of Poland. De Thou likewise relates, that on opening the body of Charles, very suspicious appearances were discovered, and that poison was commonly believed to have been the cause; "cujus rei, suspicio ut purgaretur, "mortui corpus a chirurgiis et medecis apertum est; in "quo livores, ex causa incognita reperti, conceptam opi- "nionem auxerunt, potius quam minuerunt." These are the words of that great historian.

Brantome on the other hand, denies this assertion, and positively

bout four years. His widow, Elizabeth of Auſtria, retired ſoon after into the dominions

poſitively declares, that no marks of violence or poiſon were diſcoverable on the king's body.—" Le jour enſuivant " ſon corps fut ouvert en preſence du magiſtrat, et n'y " ayant été trouvé au dedans aucune meurtriſſeure ny " tache, cela oſta publiquement l'opinion que l'on avoit de " la poiſon." He adds that Monſieur de Strozzi and himſelf demanded of Ambroſe Paré, the king's ſurgeon, to what cauſe he imputed that monarch's death ? who replied, " that he had deſtroyed his lungs and vitals by conſtantly " and immoderately blowing the horn." A moment afterwards, however, he talks of poiſon.—" Si eſt ce qu'on ne " ſcauroit oſter aucuns d'opinion qu'il ne fut empoiſſonné, " des que ſon frere partit pour Pologne, et diſoit on que " c'étoit de la poudre de corne d'un lievre marin, qui fait " languir long tems la perſonne, et puis après peu à peu " s'en va, et s'eteint comme une chandelle. Ceux qu'on " en a ſoupçonné autheurs, n'ont pas fait meilleure fin." Theſe are Brantome's own expreſſions.—Mezerai, though he mentions the ſuſpicions of poiſon, yet never formally accuſes the queen-mother by name.

The Marechal de Baſſompiere ſays, that having one day told Louis the thirteenth, that Charles the ninth had burſt a vein in his lungs by blowing the horn, which cauſed his death; the king replied, that he would not have died ſo ſoon, if he had not drawn on himſelf his mother Catherine's reſentment, and afterwards been ſo imprudent as to truſt himſelf near her, at the Marechal de Retz's perſuaſion.—Catherine of Medecis was ſo conſcious of her ſon's death being imputed to her by the people, that ſhe thought it neceſſary to inform the governors of the provinces of all the circumſtances of his diſorder, with intent to vindicate herſelf from the ſuſpicions univerſally received againſt her, and too generally credited

of

1574. of her father the emperor Maximilian, and died in retreat, at Vienna*. By his miſtreſs Mary Touchet, he had one ſon, Charles, Grand Prior of France, Duke of Angouleſme, and Count de Ponthieu; well known in hiſtory by his treaſonable connections with the duke of Biron, under the reign of Henry the fourth.

There is perhaps no character upon which we ſhould decide with ſo much candour and

* Elizabeth of Auſtria, queen dowager of France, after having made a viſit to the caſtle of Amboiſe to bid adieu to her infant daughter, left Paris on her return into the Imperial dominions, upon the 5th of December, 1575. Rodolphus the ſecond, her brother, who had then ſucceeded to the emperor Maximilian the ſecond, received her; and under his protection ſhe remained till her death in January, 1592. She was generous, beneficent, and humane in the higheſt degree, though tinctured with all the devotion characteriſtic of the age, and of the houſe of Auſtria. Margaret queen of Navarre, her ſiſter-in-law, found in her more than a ſiſter's affection; Elizabeth having during the impriſonment and diſtreſs of that princeſs, when confined in the caſtle of Uſſon in Auvergne, divided with her the dowry aſſigned her as a queen of France. She always preſerved an attachment to the memory of Charles the ninth, and refuſed to yield to the importunities of Philip the ſecond king of Spain, who requeſted her hand in marriage. When Henry the third paſſed through Vienna, on his return from Poland into France, Maximilian the ſecond propoſed to him an alliance with his daughter, the young queen dowager; but the offer was declined by Henry. Elizabeth founded the convent of St. Claire at Vienna, in which ſhe reſided, and where ſhe ended her life.

caution,

caution, as on that of Charles the ninth. Educated in a corrupt and vicious court, under the pernicious counsels of Catherine of Medecis, all the sentiments of virtue and grandeur of mind, with which nature had liberally endow'd him, were extinguished, or perverted into destructive and furious passions. In the powers of genius, discernment and capacity, he was hardly, if in any respect inferior to Francis the first, his grandfather. He possessed a comprehensive and retentive memory, an energy of expression the most happy, and uncommon personal and intellectual activity. Master of keen penetration, he knew the human heart, and piqued himself on his skill in discovering its feelings through the closest disguise.

No prince of the house of Valois excelled him in intrepidity and courage: His munificence was truly royal, because it was unlimited and impartial; not confined to favourites and parasites, like that of his brother Henry the third. With an intent to prevent him from application to affairs of state, those who were about his person endeavoured to seduce him into debauches of wine and women; but to the latter he was little addicted; and having once perceived that wine had so far disturbed his reason, as to induce him to commit some acts of violence, he never could be persuaded to engage a second time in such excesses, and
carefully

1574.

1574. carefully abstained from them during the remainder of his life. "Princeps præclara in- "dole, et magnis virtutibus," says De Thou, "nisi quatenus eas prava educatione et matris "indulgentia corrupit."

In the midst of all the civil dissentions with which the sad annals of his reign abound, he yet cultivated assiduously the politer studies of a liberal mind; he even took a peculiar pleasure in the company of learned and ingenious men, in a select company of whom he often amused himself, and held a sort of academy. He possessed an easy vein of poetry, and some of his compositions in verse yet remain, which do honour to his genius. With talents so comprehensive and various, he would doubtless under other instructors, and in happier times, have been ranked amongst the greatest monarchs whom France has seen reign. His vices and crimes were evidently the result of his misguided youth, and of passions naturally impetuous. Even for the massacre of Paris, a mind tinctured with compassion for human error and weakness, will make some apology; since to his mother alone, and to his pernicious counsellors, that deed of sanguinary and abominable revenge may justly be attributed*.

In

* Brantome, who freely and fully enumerates Charles's defects, and who speaks in terms of detestation of the massacre

In his perſon he was tall, and well ſhaped, though he ſtooped in his walk, and his head uſually leaned a little on one ſide. His complexion was pale, his hair of a deep black, his noſe aquiline, and the air of his countenance keen and penetrating. His neck was long and ſlender, his cheſt raiſed, and all his limbs juſtly proportioned, except that his legs were rather too large. He excelled in every martial exerciſe, and rode the horſe with diſtinguiſhed grace and addreſs: of the diverſion of hunting he was immoderately fond, and purſued it to the injury of his health and conſtitution. The Marechal de Retz, and thoſe perſons to whom the charge of his education was committed, had ſo accuſtomed him to the habit of ſwearing, that he uſed oaths and imprecations in his common diſcourſe †.

1574.

Cut-
ſacre of Paris, yet exculpates him on account of his youth, his unprincipled preceptors, and the general corruption of the whole court. I much admire the paſſage, which breathes a generoſity and candour of ſentiment. "J'ai veu plu-
"ſieurs s'etonner," ſays Brantome, "que veu la corrup-
"tion de ſon regne, et depuis la perte qu'il fit de Monſieur
"de Sipierre, qui le nouriſſoit ſi bien, comme il fut ſi
"magnanime, ſi genereux, valeureux, et liberal, comme
"il a eté. Car il a autant etendu ſa liberalité que fit ja-
"mais roi, à toutes ſortes de gens."

† Brantome, who reſided in the court of Charles the ninth, and who perſonally knew all the firſt nobility of his time,

1574. Cut off by an immature and miserable death, just as he began to emerge from the abyss of time, paints the Marechal de Retz in the most frightful colours, and accuses him of having corrupted the noble nature of his royal pupil, by every pernicious precept and example. " Albert de Gondi," says he, " Marechal " de Retz, etoit un Florentin, fin, caut, corrumpu, men- " teur, et grand diffimulateur." Then continuing his account of the family of Gondi; " to speak of him in two " words," adds Brantome, " his grand-father was a miller, " only two leagues from Florence; his father was a bank- " rupt at Lyons; and his mother, grande Revendereffe de " Putaines, on account of which talent Henry the second " conceived a friendship for her, and made her governess " of his children, particularly of Charles the ninth. The " Marechal de Retz himself was for a long time a com- " miffary of provisions in the royal army, 'till Charles ad- " vanced him; and he in return taught the king to swear " and to diffemble." Brantome proceeds to draw a comparison, or rather a contrast, between him and the Seigneur de la Cipierre, who had been Charles's preceding governor, and who possessed all the endowments of mind and character, requisite for the due discharge of so important a trust. After his death, the Marechal de Retz perverted all the great qualities of the young king, and accustomed him to deceit and to imprecations; ." si bien que le roi," adds Brantome, " apprit de lui ce vice; car de son natu- " rel, il ne l'etoit nullement en sa jeuneffe, etant fort " ouvert, prompt, actif, vigilant, et eveille."

This description of Brantome is confirmed by almost all the best historians, who impute many of the calamities of this reign, and many of the vices of Charles's character, to the pernicious precepts of the Marechal de Retz.

guilt

guilt and infamy, into which a deference to his mother's fatal advice had plunged him; and fcarce known in hiftory, except as the author of the maffacre of St. Bartholomew, pofterity have regarded his reign with deteftation rather than pity, and condemned him too feverely for errors and crimes which can fcarcely be deemed his own. Commiferation for a prince, whofe youth and inexperience rendered him but too eafily the victim of a pernicious fyftem of politics; the fatisfaction which we feel in attempting to refcue from ignominy, a character not originally or naturally debafed; and the impartiality which every writer fhould cultivate and encourage;—thefe fentiments alone have induced me to regard Charles the ninth in a far more favourable light, than that in which he has generally been reprefented by all the Englifh hiftorians.

The fame indecent neglect which had been exhibited at the funeral of Francis the fecond, attended that of Charles; and, fome difputes relative to precedence having arifen among the nobility who followed in the proceffion, his body was quitted by them between Paris and St. Denis, and conducted, without any pomp or royal ftate, to the tomb of his anceftors [*].

---

[*] Brantome was himfelf, as a gentleman of the bed-chamber, one of the very few who accompanied his royal mafter's

master's body, and saw it deposited at St. Denis.—" Le
" corps du Roi fut quitté," says he, " estant à l'eglise
" de St. Lazare, de tout le grand convoy, tant des prin-
" ces, seigneurs, cour de parlement, et ceux de l'eglise
" et de la ville; et ne fut suivy et accompagné que du
" pauvre Monsieur de Arozze, de Funcel, et moi, et de
" deux autres gentilhommes de la chambre, qui ne vou-
" lusmes jamais abandonner notre maître, tant qu'il seroit
" sur terre. Il y avoit aussi quelques archers de la garde.
" Chose, qui faisoit grand pitié à voir!"—A singular fatality seems to have accompanied this unhappy prince; and the continual dissentions which marked his reign, pursued him even after death.—Elizabeth, queen of England, though of a different religion from Charles the ninth, yet celebrated his funeral with extraordinary solemnity and magnificence, in the church of St. Paul, at London.

F I N I S.

BOOKS

Printed for, and Sold by,

C. DILLY.

1. A Tour through the Western, Southern, and Interior Provinces of France; written by Mr. Wraxall, and now first published separate. Price 2s. 6d. in boards.

2. Liberal Education; or, a Practical Treatise on the Methods of acquiring useful and polite Learning, 2 vols. 6s. By Mr. Knox.

3. Essays Moral and Literary, by the same Author, 2 vols. 7s.

4. Bath Society Papers on Agriculture, Planting, &c. 2 vols. 8vo. 12s.

5. Cavallo on General Electricity, 8vo. 7s.

6. ——— on Medical Electricity, 8vo. 3s. 6d.

7. ——— on Air, with an Introduction to Chemistry, 4to. 1l. 8s.

8. Carver's Travels through North America, large 8vo. 9s.

9. Chesterfield's Miscellaneous Works, 2 vols. 4to. 2l. 8s.

10. The same, 4 vols. 8vo. 1l. 4s.

11. Chapone's Letters on the Improvement of the Mind, 2 vols. 6s.—Another edition, in 1 vol. 3s.

12. ———'s Miscellanies, in Prose and Verse, 3s.

13. Justamond's Private Life of Lewis XV. 4 vols. 8vo. 1l. 4s.

14. Falconer on Climate, &c. 4to. 1l. 1l.

15. Ives's Voyage from England to India, in the Year 1754, 4to. 1l. 5s.

16. Parker's

BOOKS *printed for* C. DILLY.

16. Parker's Evidence of our Tranſactions in the Eaſt Indies, 4to. 10s. 6d. in boards.

17. Cronſtedt's Syſtem of Mineralogy, tranſlated from the Swediſh Original; enlarged and improved, according to the lateſt Diſcoveries made ſince the Death of the Author, 2 vols. 12s.

18. Clark's conciſe Hiſtory of Knighthood, 2 vols. 12s.

19. Hanbury's complete Body of Planting and Gardening, 2 vols. fol. 4l. 4s.

20. Hiſtory of the Revolution of Ali Bey againſt the Ottoman Porte, with a Map of Lower Egypt, the ſecond edition, 8vo. 6s.

21. Letters from Italy to a Friend reſiding in France, written by Lady Miller, of Bath-Eaſton Villa, 2 vols. 8vo. 12s.

22. Playfair's (Dr.) Syſtem of Chronology, elegantly printed on a new Great Primer Type, and a fine Royal Paper, in one large volume, fol. 2l. 12s. 6d.

23. Townſend's Free Thoughts on Deſpotic and Free Governments, 4s.

24. Cooke's Voyage to Ruſſia, 2 vols. 12s.

25. Johnſon's Dictionary, 2 vols. fol. 4l. 10s.

26. ――――――――――― Abridged.—In 2 vols. 8vo. 10s.

27. Kitchin's Traveller's Guide thro' England and Wales, 3s. 6d.

28. Jacob's Law Dictionary, fol. 2l. 2s.

29. Fothergill's (Dr.) Works, with the Life of the Author, by Dr. Lettſom, 3 vols. 8vo. 1l. 1s.

30. Gerard's Sermons, 2 vols. 8vo. 12s.

31. Hederici Lexicon, new edition, corrected and enlarged, 4to. 1l. 1s.

32. Parry's (of Cirenceſter) Sermons on Practical Subjects, 8vo. 6s.

33. Tillotſon's Sermons, 12 vols. 8vo. 3l.

34. Walker's (Robert of Edinb.) Sermons, 3 vols. 8vo. 18s.

www.ingramcontent.com/pod-product-compliance
Lightning Source LLC
Chambersburg PA
CBHW032047230426

43672CB00009B/1508